Joseph H. Maiden

A Manual of the Grasses of New South Wales

Vol. 1

Joseph H. Maiden

A Manual of the Grasses of New South Wales
Vol. 1

ISBN/EAN: 9783337325756

Printed in Europe, USA, Canada, Australia, Japan

Cover: Foto ©Andreas Hilbeck / pixelio.de

More available books at **www.hansebooks.com**

NEW SOUTH WALES.

A

MANUAL OF THE GRASSES

OF

NEW SOUTH WALES

BY

J. H. MAIDEN,

GOVERNMENT BOTANIST AND DIRECTOR OF THE BOTANIC GARDENS, SYDNEY.

(WITH ILLUSTRATIONS.)

By Authority of the Minister for Mines and Agriculture.

SYDNEY: WILLIAM APPLEGATE GULLICK, GOVERNMENT PRINTER.

1898.

[4s. 6d.]

CONTENTS.

-

INTRODUCTORY.

I TRUST this little Manual will supply a two-fold demand—that of the farmer and pastoralist, and that of the botanist. The former, whom it is primarily intended to help, may lay aside the botanical descriptions and find, perhaps, that the other notes and the references to plates will not only assist them in identifying the various kinds of grasses, but also in appraising their value, and guide them in taking steps to cultivate and improve them.

As far as our knowledge extends at present, there are about 3,200 species of grasses, of which 196, comprised in 56 genera, are indigenous to this Colony. When it is pointed out that the short turf of the tops of our mountain ranges, and some of the tall reedy plants of our lagoons, are alike grasses, it will be at once understood how different in appearance and pro-perties are the plants we call by this name.

Grasses have flowers and seeds as well as gum-trees or lilies, but owing to the enormous number of herbivorous animals—domestic, such as sheep, cattle, and horses—and wild native animals, such as wallabies and kangaroos, (to say nothing of the ubiquitous rabbit), the flowering and seeding parts of the plant are usually eaten down, so that the diversity that grasses would naturally present is frequently not apparent; consequently, in many cases, in looking at grasses in the field we have only the leaves to look at, and as there is much similarity between the leaves of many grasses, the difficulty of the pastoralist in learning about them is much increased. If, however, he exercises care, he will see in paddocks from which stock are excluded, or under the shelter of shrubs, fences, stones, &c., grasses which have been allowed to flower, and by examination of these he can usually be able to discriminate most of the grasses on his holding. Nevertheless, however it may be sim-plified, there is no golden road to a knowledge of the grasses any more than to any other branch of knowledge, and those interested in the subject may be reminded that the Department will always be willing to name and give information in regard to any specimen that may be sent. But the grass must be sent in flower or grain; it will not suffice simply to send blades.

What we know as grass consists of a number of plants growing closely together—for grasses will grow together far more closely than is the case with most plants. If a piece of turf be pulled apart it will be seen to be composed of little plants with complete roots and leaves, and if not kept

b

iv

cropped close each of these little plants may flower; so that it will be at once seen how countless is the number of grass-plants in even one small paddock. As the value of the paddock for grazing depends on the kinds these little grass-plants are, it will be seen how desirable it is to set about improving the various kinds, for when we change a grass we do it as regards millions of plants.

Just as florists' flowers and vegetables have been vastly improved by selection of seed and improved methods of cultivation on the part of the gardener, so as regards grasses (though not to the same extent perhaps, but who can tell?), we look forward to improvements of paddocks not only by substituting good for inferior species, but we hope to be able to vastly increase the value (from the point of view of the farmer and pastoralist), of existing species. Many of us are apt to look upon grasses as the very embodiment of a stationary thing, as containing a fixed and definite quantity of nutriment for stock, incapable of improvement, an idea which, if persistently held, will be a bar to all improvement.

I desire to thank Messrs. Ernst Betche and William Forsyth for the patient care with which they have assisted me to revise the proofs.

CULTIVATION OF NATIVE GRASSES.

ATTENTION has often been drawn in this Colony to the desirability of encouraging the growth of our native grasses, but the recommendations have frequently been in advance of the time. In this connection the words of P. Cunningham, written over seventy years ago, will be read with interest :— "We want much to have a course of experimental trials with our native grasses, in order to ascertain how far they are capable of improvement from cultivation, and of being associated with the most suitable of the English grasses in ameliorating our swards. It is in this point of view that Government farms are calculated to be of use ; and certainly the Government of a young country like ours could not devote a thousand or two yearly to a better purpose than experimentalising upon systems and substances likely to be conducive to the awakening of its slumbering energies and the progressive advancement of its wealth."—*Two Years in New South Wales ;* by P. Cunningham, R.N. 2nd edition, vol. i, p. 197 (1827).

Now that we have a Department of Agriculture the work is being taken up in earnest. Our grasses are experimented with more or less at all the experimental farms. Under my own immediate supervision I have a number of Australian and American grasses under cultivation, in good soil near the coast, viz., in the Botanic Gardens ; in poor, sandy soil in the Centennial Park ; and in clay soil at the State Nursery at Campbelltown. The past year has been the most discouraging year for many years to planters, because of the drought, and of what I may term the " awkward" periods at which the small amount of rain we had fell ; but such bad seasons teach some lessons which good seasons fail to do.

Most of the reports on our native grasses refer to them strictly in the wild state, but cultivation frequently changes the nature of grasses in the direction of making them tender. In other words, our knowledge of native species is not as favourable to many of them as we may reasonably expect it to be on further acquaintance.

There is another matter for consideration. Much depends upon the soil and situation in which a grass has been grown. Mr. T. R. Kidston, a man of wide experience of the western country, puts the case in this way :—

" With regard to the nutritive qualities of grasses, I hold that they depend mainly on the soil on which they grow. If the ' blue,' ' umbrella,' or ' kangaroo ' grasses are found on the rich plains, where the salsolaceous plants abound, they are very fattening ; but the same grasses growing in a stringy-bark gully or on a ridge are very deficient in fattening properties. In the first case the stock are always in high condition, in the second, however green and abundant the grass, the stock never thrive."

This should be borne in mind, not only in assessing the normal value of any particular grass, but also in our experiments with the view to their improvement. Because certain grasses have shown their adaptability to the conditions of certain soils and situations, it does not follow that they would not produce more valuable results elsewhere. This is the very basis of all acclimatisation work. If plants are all at the present time in their best and

A

most congenial situations, let well alone, and not waste either time, money,
or energy in endeavouring to modify their surroundings. But we know that
the contrary is the case, and the intelligent grazier should ever be on the
alert to seize opportunities of improving his pastures, by cultivating well-
known grasses, and by the introduction and cultivation of new ones.

CONSERVATION OF NATIVE GRASSES.

EACH holding should have a few acres of its best grasses fenced off for
one or two seasons for seeding purposes. As land is usually stocked,
grasses are frequently not permited to seed, and consequently are only able
to propagate themselves by root-division. Who has not noticed how grasses
flower and seed when they get a chance, e.g., along the railway lines within
the fences? In many places these situations are the only ones where one
can get a little grass-seed.

In addition, it would be very desirable for every selector and squatter to
have a small grass-nursery, in order that he might test for himself the
various native and imported grasses. Then he could ascertain their behaviour
and habit in the climate and soils of his own district. The nursery should
be in a place handy to the homestead, and if it would be a source of expense
I would not advocate it. The principal cost would be that of a rabbit-proof
fence, while the return to the grazier in the improved knowledge he would
secure of the grasses suited to his district would be great.

It would be, of course, very desirable to extend the idea of fencing off
small paddocks. The very human mistake is made here, and in all parts of
the world, of overstocking, with the result that the grasses most palatable
to stock are temporarily (or perhaps permanently) eaten out, while their
place is taken by weeds and inferior grasses,—grasses which have spread,
because they have been comparatively uninterfered with by stock. The
remedy, and there is only one remedy for this, is to periodically give
paddocks a rest. In most parts of the Colony it is rarely that more can be
done than this, but in the United States it has been abundantly shown how
advantageous may be the breaking-up of the surface, and even the application
of some kinds of manure. I will give one instance:—

" An experiment made at the Kansas Station in 1892 shows what a thorough
stirring up of soil will do for an upland prairie pasture. The experiment
was made on a pasture in which the grasses had been dying out for some
time, and the weeds were beginning to appear in abundance. It had been
reduced to this condition by drought and over-pasturing. The surface was
thoroughly loosened up by driving a weighted disc-harrow over the field in
several directions. The pasture was sown to a mixture of orchard grass,
meadow fescue, blue grass, timothy, red top, clover, and alfalfa, which was
harrowed in, and a roller was driven over the field to level the surface and
firm the ground. The seed germinated quickly, and the tame grasses made
an excellent start, but by September the wild grasses had crowded them out
and held complete possession of the field. In this case the stirring of the
soil and the season's rest not only enabled the prairie grasses to recover and
to overcome the weeds, but to crowd out a good stand of tame grasses as
well." (Thomas A. Williams.)

Professor Lamson-Scribner, the well-known American authority, thus
speaks on the question of conserving the native grasses:—

" It is very important that every possible effort should be made to preserve the native grasses. They are naturally adapted to the conditions

3

which prevail in the region, and it is quite improbable that introduced forms can be had to take their places satisfactorily, at least for years to come. That some of the native forms flourish under conditions that would kill the common cultivated ones is seen by the situation in Stark County, North Dakota. At Dickinson, the Weather Bureau reports for 1895 show a rainfall of 11·75 inches. Of this amount, 5·75 inches fell in June and July. The small precipitation of 0·64 inch in the three months of August, September, and October favours the important process of curing on the ground. This enables thousands of cattle to live during the winter on the nutritious forage furnished by this method of curing the grasses which grow at this point." (Brannon.) "Such a climatic condition would soon destroy the ordinary cultivated grasses, but the native species have flourished under it for centuries, and there is no reason why they should not continue to do so and still yield plenty of forage, if properly handled." (*Grasses and Forage Plants*, United States Department of Agriculture, Bulletin No. 6, pp. 6 and 7.)

The above might have been written with much of our western country in view, so similar are the conditions, at least as regards rainfall.

And again: "Experience has shown that many of the most valuable of the native grasses are very much benefited by a judicious application of even a small amount of water. As a rule there is sufficient rainfall to give the grasses a good start in the spring, and if enough water could be had to keep up a strong growth when the dry, hot summer weather comes on, an abundant forage crop would be assured." (*Op. cit.* p. 7.)

It may be that the water from our artesian bores, and other water available for irrigation, may be utilised to an even greater extent than it has been in the past, in directly irrigating pasture land for part of the year.

Mr. Thomas A. Williams gives the following summary of his recommendations for the renewing of worn-out pastures of native grasses:—

" (I.) Avoid overstocking.

(II.) When the soil begins to get baked and packed stir it up with a harrow.

(III.) Give an occasional light top-dressing of well-rotted stable manure

(IV.) Fill in thin with hardy tame or wild grasses before the weeds get a start.

(V.) Keep the weeds mowed off so that the grasses may get the benefit of all the plant-food there is in the soil."

ANALYSES OF GRASSES.

VERY few analyses have been made of our indigenous grasses, but it is very desirable that a comprehensive investigation of them should be carried out. To do the work properly we require specimens of the same species collected in different parts of Australia, in different seasons, and in different stages of growth. In order to secure strictly comparable results, it would be desirable to set apart one chemist whose attention should not be distracted with any other kind of work. He could do the work with reasonable thoroughness in three years, and his researches would settle the comparative value of many of our esteemed indigenous grasses, and also give us specific information in regard to the value of some grasses in respect to which we only possess vague information. If, in addition, we could only obtain analyses of introduced grasses grown in the colonies, the results would be of enhanced value.

PLAN OF THE WORK.

IN the Manual each grass has been dealt with in a uniform manner, and in the following order :—

1. Botanical name.	6. Botanical notes.
2. Synonyms.	7. Value as a fodder.
3. Vernacular names.	8. Other uses.
4. Where figured.	9. Fungi found on the grass.
5. Botanical description.	10. Habitat and range.

These appear to me the most important points on which information is likely to be required in a work of this kind.

1. *Botanical name.*—The nomenclature followed has been that of Bentham's *Flora Australiensis*. I hold the opinion that, except in the very rare instances in which Bentham is actually wrong, this work should be loyally respected as a standard of nomenclature of Australian plants. Until the time comes for a second edition of the *Flora*, in which any necessary corrections can be made, Bentham's work should be followed as closely as possible. The numbering of the genera and species is that of the *Flora Australiensis*, so that the present publication may be conveniently referred to while studying the classic. The order of sequence of course indicates botanical affinity, and an advantage will be that as additional species are discovered in the Colony, notes in regard to them can readily be inserted in the text.

2. *Synonyms.*—I have, under this head, noted where the name in Mueller's *Census* differs from that of the *Flora*. I have, in a few cases, given, in addition, well-known names whether in the *Census* or not. In a few cases obsolete names have been noted, only because under such names good plates of grasses have been figured.

3. *Vernacular names.*—Many of our grasses, not being specifically recognised by Australians, have no common names. In a few cases names, clumsy perhaps, have been coined for them. In regard to others, where species are not endemic in Australia, the names under which they are known in Europe, the United States, India, &c., are given as a matter of convenience.

4. *Where figured.*—I have given the names of works where grasses have been figured. Where names have been given, the title of the illustrated work referred to will be found under "Works consulted.," see page 5. It will be found that the references are to works which are for the most part readily accessible to the people of this Colony.

Some excellent figures of dissections of grass-flowers will be found at plate 4 of Vasey's work; also *Report of Secretary for Agriculture* (U.S.A.), for 1879, 1880. Admirable figures, illustrating the genera of grasses (American), will be found on plates vii to xv of Gray's *Manual of the Botany of the Northern United States.*

5. *Botanical description.*—This is taken, both as regards genus and species, from the *Flora Australiensis*, and, as a very general rule, word for word.

6. *Botanical notes.*—Under this head will be found a few general notes, which may perhaps be useful to the student,—notes which are not of an economic character, and which do not form part of the plant description.

7. *Value as a fodder.*—This is by far the most important value of a grass, at all events in Australia. It will be observed that we have but imperfect knowledge of the fodder-value of many of our grasses, and correspondence is invited on subject.

8. *Other uses.*—As a general rule these are more interesting than useful, and some are inserted for completeness sake.

9. *Fungi found on grass.*—As a general rule these will be found to be microfungi, such as what are known as "smuts," "rusts," black spots," &c. Very few fungi have been recorded on Australian grasses, and now that attention has been drawn to the subject, I feel sure that collectors will speedily increase the number very largely. I shall be glad to receive specimens of grasses, blighted or with various small stains, patches, or spots thereon.

The following fungi have been recorded on Australian grasses, genera not stated. Where the genus or species has been recorded, the information has been given when dealing with the grass in question :—

Grass—
Hypocrea (Hypocrella) axillaris, Cooke.
Isaria graminiperda, var. *fuciformis,* Berk.
Leocarpus fragilis, Dicks.
Phoma nitida, Rob.
Spunaria alba, Bull.

Grass, culms—
Phoma graminis, West.

Grass, decaying—
Choetonium elatum, Kzl.

Grass, leaves of—
Phyllachora graminis, Pers.
Sphærella graminicola, Fckl.

Grass, roots of—
Agaricus (Naucoria) frusticola, Berk.
Agaricus (Tubaria) inquilinus, Fr. ; var. *ecbolus,* Fr.

Grasses, undefined—
Epichloë cinerea, Berk. et Br.

10. *Habitat and range.*—We have much to learn in this direction yet. I have given the localities with some precision as regards our own Colony, making brief notes suffice in regard to the range in the other colonies. We want additional information in regard to the occurrence of many species within our own Colony, and collections of grasses are cordially asked for, it being understood that the fullest particulars will be returned to senders concerning their consignments.

LIST OF WORKS CONSULTED.

FOLLOWING is the list of works consulted by me, and to which I am more or less indebted :—

1. Sinclair, G.
Hortus Woburnensis gramineus.—Account of the result of experiments on the produce and nutritive qualities of different grasses and other plants. London, J. Ridgway, 2nd edition, 1825.
2. Bentham, G.
Notes on Gramineæ.—*Proc. Linn. Soc.* (Botany), xix, 14.
3. Hackel, Edward.
The True Grasses.—Translated from *Die natürlichen Pflanzenfamilien,* by F. Lamson-Scribner and Effie A. Southworth. Westminster, Archibald Constable and Co., 1896.
4. Labillardière, J. J.
Novæ Hollandiæ Plantarum Specimen. Paris, 1804. (2 vols., 4to., with numerous plates.)
5. Bentham, G., and Mueller, F.
Flora Australiensis.—A description of the plants of the Australian territory, in 7 vols. 1863-78. (B. Fl. is the usual contraction for this work.)

6. **Mueller, F.**
    Fragmenta Phytographiæ Australiæ, in 11 vols. and 1 part. Melbourne, 1858–82.
7. —— Second Systematic Census of Australian Plants. Melbourne, 1889.
8. —— Select Extra-tropical Plants.
9. **Cunningham, P.**
    Two Years in New South Wales.—Chapter on " Our Native Grasses." Vol. i, p. 194. 1824. •
10. **Bacchus, W. H.**
    A Description of some Victorian and other Australian Grasses.—Second Annual Report of the Secretary for Agriculture. Melbourne, 1874.
11. **O'Shanesy, P. A.**
    Contributions to the Flora of Queensland. *Daily Northern Argus* Office, Rockhampton, 1880.
12. **Bailey, F. M.**
    Inquiry for Seeds of Grasses and other Fodder-plants. Brisbane, Thorne and Greenwell, 1877. 12mo., p. 21.
13. —— An Illustrated Monograph of the Grasses of Queensland (plates by K. T. Staiger). Vol. i, 1878. Published in 1879 by Warwick and Sapsford, Brisbane. Large 4to. (This is the work in which the figures referred to as " Bailey" are to be found.)
14. —— A Few Queensland Grasses : A publication prepared for the Queensland Commission, Melbourne Exhibition, 1888.
15. Dairying in Queensland : A pamphlet issued by the Department of Agriculture, Brisbane, for circulation in England. The greater portion is taken up by a chapter on Queensland grasses by Mr. F. M. Bailey.
16. **Vasey, G.**
    The Agricultural Grasses and Fodder-plants of the United States. United States Department of Agriculture. Government Printing Office, Washington, 1889.
17. **Lamson-Scribner, F.**
    Grass Gardens. Year-book United States Department of Agriculture for 1895.
18. —— Grasses of Salt Marshes. *Ib.*
19. **Kearney, Thos. T., jun.**
    Notes on Grasses and Forage-plants of the South-eastern States. Bulletin No. 1, Division of Agrostology, United States Department of Agriculture, 1895.
20. **Smith, Jared G.**
    Forage Conditions of the Prairie Regions. Year-book of United States Department of Agriculture for 1895.
21. **Williams, Thomas A.**
    Grasses and Forage-plants of the Dakotas. Bulletin No. 6, United States Department of Agriculture, Division of Agrostology, 1897.
22. **Rydberg, P. A., and Shear, C. L.**
    A Report upon the Grasses and Forage-plants of the Rocky Mountain Region. United States Department of Agriculture, Division of Agrostology, Bulletin No. 5, 1897.
23. **Buchanan, John.**
    The Indigenous Grasses of New Zealand. Government Printer, Wellington, N.Z., 1880.

24. **Church, A. H.**
Food-grains of India. London, Chapman and Hall, 1886. Includes illustrations and particulars as to the alimentary value of several grasses.
25. **Duthie, J. F.**
The Fodder-grasses of Northern India. Roorkee, India, 1888. Printed at the Thomason Civil Engineering College Press.
26. Dictionary of the Economic Products of India. Article "Fodder-grasses," vol. iii, p. 420.
27. Kew Bulletin of Miscellaneous Information.
28. **Trinius, C. B.**
Species Graminum Iconibus et Descriptionibus. Petropoli, 1828-1836. (3 vols.)

GRASSES FOR SPECIAL PURPOSES OR SITUATIONS.

FOLLOWING is a small and imperfect selection. Further particulars are, of course, given under each species :—

For planting under shade of Trees.

Panicum foliosum.
,, *pygmæum.*
Oplismenus.

For arid Situations.

Panicum flavidum.
,, *helopus.*
,, *distachyum.*
,, *adspersum.*
,, *effusum.*
,, *decompositum.*
,, *prolutum.*
Neurachne.
Pollinia fulva.
Andropogon.
Anthistiria membranacea.
Astrebla.
Chloris truncata.
,, *ventricosa.*
Eleusine ægyptiaca.
Bromus arenarius.

For wet Lands.

Paspalum scrobiculatum.
,, *distichum.*
Panicum melananthum.
,, *crus-galli.*
,, *indicum.*
,, *decompositum.*
Chamæraphis.
Hemarthria compressa.
Isachne australis.
Glyceria.

Soil-binders, *e.g.*, on River-banks.

Paspalum scrobiculatum.
,, *distichum.*
Panicum distachyum.
,, *foliosum.*
Andropogon intermedius.
Heteropogon contortus.
Imperata arundinacea.
Cynodon dactylon.
Phragmites communis.

Sand-binders (interior).

Spinifex paradoxus.
Cynodon dactylon.

Coast Sand-binders.

Paspalum distichum.
Panicum repens.
Spinifex hirsutus.
Zoysia pungens.
Imperata arundinacea.
Cynodon dactylon.
Sporobolus virginicus.
Distichlis maritima.
Schedonorus litoralis.
Lepturus.

A few of the most valuable Grasses.

Eriochloa.
Panicum, various species.
Andropogon, various species.
Sorghum halepense.
Anthistiria ciliata.
Microlæna stipoides
Agrostis, various species.
Danthonia ,,
Astrebla ,,
Cynodon dactylon.
Chloris truncata.
,, *ventricosa.*
Eragrostis Brownii.

KEY TO THE GENERA.

Primary Series **A. PANICACEÆ.**—Spikelets articulate on the pedicels below the glumes. Spikelet with one fertile flower, the male or barren flower, if any, below it.

Tribe I.—PANICEÆ.—Fertile spikelets with one terminal bisexual or female flower, with or without a male one below it. Glumes four or three, the upper flowering one of a firmer texture, the outer one usually smaller, sometimes wanting. A palea to each flower. Stamens three, rarely fewer. Grain enclosed in the hardened (rarely thin, but stiffened) upper glume and palea. Awns rare, and when present neither twisted nor bent back.

Series i. Spikelets bisexual.

Infloresence not bracteate. No bristle-like involucre.

Fruiting glume hardened.

Spikelets with three glumes.

Pedicels not callous at the summit. Flowering glume not awned ... ... 1. Paspalum.

Pedicels with a callous annulus or cup at the summit. Flowering glume with a point or short awn ... ... 2. Eriochloa.

Spikelets with four glumes.

Outer glume shorter than the others, often minute, not awned ... . 3. Panicum.

Outer glume with a long awn ... ... 4. Oplismenus.

Spikelets surrounded by or intermixed with abortive branches of the panicle, forming a lobed or bristly involucre. Fruiting glume hardened.

Spikelets intermixed with long persistent bristle-like branches, and falling off from them ... 5. Setaria.

Involucres crowded or distant along a simple rhachis, each enclosing one to three spikelets, and falling off with them.

Involucres of numerous simple or plumose bristles completely surrounding the spikelet ... ... 7. Pennisetum.

Involucre of several outer bristles and inner flat lobes completely surrounding one to three spikelets and at length hardened 8. Cenchrus.

Branches of the particle produced beyond the base of the last spikelet. Fruiting glume stiff, but scarious and rather thin.

Spikelets solitary, or few along the slender in-articulate branches of the panicle ... 9. Chamæraphis.

Series ii. Spikelets unisexual.

Stems prostrate. Spikelets diœcious, in dense heads 13. Spinifex.

Tribe II.—ANDROPOGONEÆ.—Fertile spikelets with one terminal bisexual or female flower, with or without a male one below it. Glumes four or rarely fewer, one of the outer ones the largest enclosing the fruit, the third smaller, thin and hyaline, sometimes wanting, the upper or flowering one very thin and hyaline, often bearing a twisted and bent awn. A palea to each flower, sometimes very small or deficient in the fertile flower. Stamens three, rarely fewer.

(The awn when present is terminal or between the notches of the flowering glume in all except Arthraxon.)

Subtribe I.—**Zoysieæ.**—Spikelets solitary or rarely in clusters of two or three, inserted all round the articulate rhachis of a simple spike or raceme. Awns none on the flowering glume, none or straight on the outer ones.

Spikelets sessile in notches of the rhachis and closely appressed.
Glumes two, smooth...   ...   . 14. Zoysia.

Spikelets two, rarely three or four together on very short pedicels.
Glumes usually three, the larger one echinate, a minute outer one sometimes wanting and a small hyaline flowering one   ...   . 15. Lappago.

Spikelets in a dense spike, not awned. Glumes four, the outer one the largest   ...   . 16. Neurachne.

Spikelets in a loose spike or raceme, very narrow.
Glumes three, the two outer ones with straight awns   ...   . 17. Perotis.

Subtribe II.—**Rottboelliæ.**—Spikelets awnless, in pairs or rarely solitary, in alternate notches of the articulate rhachis of a simple spike, one sessile fertile and more or less embedded in a cavity of the rhachis, the other pedicellate.

Spike one-sided, the rhachis scarcely articulate.
Pedicel-like spikelet barren   ...   ... 19. Hemarthria.

Subtribe IV.—**Euandropogoneæ.**—Spikelets in pairs or threes, rarely solitary, one sessile and fertile and one or two pedicellate and male neuter or rudimentary, rarely fertile or deficient. Flowering glume of the fertile spikelet usually awned or reduced to the awn.

(The awn is deficient in Imperata, in Ischæmum pectinatum, and sometimes minute or deficient in some varieties of other species.)

Spikelets in pairs along one side of a simple spike or of the spike-like branches of a simple panicle.
Spike single. Spikelets unisexual, the awned females turned to one side, the awnless males imbricate behind them ...   ... 24. Heteropogon.

Spikes single or digitate. Sessile spikelet with a male flower below the fertile one   ... 25. Ischæmum.

Spikes digitate. Spikelets one-flowered with a barren pedicel in the same notch. Awn dorsal near the apex   ...   . 27. Arthraxon.

Spikes digitate. Spikelets in pairs, both one-flowered and usually fertile   ...   ... 28. Pollinia.

Spikes solitary digitate or several nearly sessile on a simple rhachis. Sessile spikelet one-flowered and fertile, pedicellate one male or neuter ...   . 29. Andropogon.

Spikelets in single or few pairs or triplets on the
slender branches of a more or less compound
panicle.

Panicle long and dense, usually cylindrical, the
spikelets awnless, concealed under long
silky hairs ... ... 30. Imperata.

Panicle loose. Fertile spikelets awned.

Outer glume either membranous or narrow
and rigid with two prominent often
muricate lateral nerves... ... ... 31. Chrysopogon.

Outer glume when in fruit hard, smooth
and shining, ovate or lanceolate ... 32. Sorghum.

Spikelets in triplets (one sessile and fertile between
two pedicellate and male neuter or rudimentary) within sheathing bracts.

Triplets surrounded by an involucre of four male
or neuter spikelets at the base of the
peduncle... ... ... 33. Anthistiria.

Triplets sessile or pedunculate within the bract
without any involucre ... ... 34. Apluda.

Subtribe V.—**Tristegineæ.**—Spikelets paniculate, all similar, the terminal
flowering glume more or less stiffened or enlarged when in fruit almost as in
Paniceæ, but the awn twisted and bent as in Andropogoneæ.

Glumes four, two empty, the third with a male
flower or empty. Panicle loose ... 35. Arundinella.

Primary Series **B. POACEÆ.**—Spikelets not articulate below the outer
glumes. Rhachis of the spikelet articulate above the two or three lowest
glumes, or wholly continuous. Spikelets with one or more fertile flowers, the
males or imperfect ones, if any, above or very rarely below them.

(In a few Phalarideæ the lower glumes are deficient.)

Tribe IV.—PHALARIDEÆ.—Spikelets with one terminal bisexual flower
and rarely two male flowers lower down. Glumes two to six, all keeled or
with a central nerve, two below the articulation of the rhachis persistent or
in several genera deficient, four or fewer above the articulation, of which two
enclose the grain without any distinctly two-nerved palea.

Stamens six, rarely three. No glumes below the
articulation.

Spikelets very flat. Glumes two, without any
small ones ... ... 38. Leersia.

Spikelets not flattened. Glumes four, membranous, the two outer very small ... 40. Potamophila.

Stamens six or four, very rarely three or two. Two
persistent glumes below the articulation.

Stamens four, rarely two. Spikelets paniculate,
more or less awned ... . 42. Microlæna.

Stamens four. Spikelets not awned ... ... 43. Tetrarrhena.

Stamens three, rarely two. Glumes three, none below
the articulation.

Flowering glume awned. Panicle dense, cylindrical, spike-like ... ... 44. Alopecurus.

Stamens three, rarely two; two persistent glumes
below the articulation, two inner ones enclosing the grain, two intermediate ones small
or enclosing male flowers.
Panicle loose. Intermediate glumes enclosing
  male flowers with two-nerved paleæ ... 47. Hierochloe.

Tribe V.—STREPTATHERÆ.—Spikelets with one, two, or rarely several
bisexual flowers, and rarely a male flower above or below. Flowering glume
usually bearing an awn twisted in the lower part, bent or divided about the
middle. Palea two-nerved, usually thin or small, in a few Avenaceæ as large
as in Festucaceæ.

(The awn is very small and straight or deficient in a few species of Agrostis
and Deyeuxia, the twisted portion below the branches very short or obsolete
in one section of Aristida.)

Subtribe I.—Stipaceæ.—Spikelets one-flowered. Awn terminal, simple or
three-branched. Lodicules three. Fruiting glume usually narrow, hardened,
enclosing the grain.

Awn three-branched ...   . 48. Aristida.
Awn simple, at length articulate on the glume   ... 49. Stipa.

Subtribe II.—Agrostideæ.—Spikelets one-flowered. Awn either terminal
between the lobes of the glume or dorsal, in a few species very small or
deficient. Lodicules two. Fruiting glume enclosing the grain, usually thin.

Awn terminal between the lobes of the glume (two
  on each side), rhachis of the spikelet not
  continued beyond the flower   ...   ... 51. Pentapogon.
Awn more or less dorsal, sometimes minute or deficient.
No bristle continuing the rhachis beyond the
  flowering glume.
Awn fine and near the tip of the glume.
  Palea more than half as long as the glume. 53. Dichelachne.
Awn dorsal or none. Palea not more than
  half the length of the glume or minute
  or none ...   . 54. Agrostis.
Rhachis of the spikelet usually produced into a
  point or bristle beyond the flower or
  bearing an empty glume. Awn various.
  Palea more than half as long as the
  glume   ...   . 55. Deyeuxia.

Subtribe III.—Avenaceæ.—Spikelets with two or in a few genera more
than two perfect flowers (only one in Anisopogon), the rhachis produced
above them (except in Aira). Awn either dorsal or terminal between the
lobes of the glume. Grain enclosed in the glume and palea, and sometimes
adnate.

Awn dorsal.
Flowers both bisexual, the rhachis not at all or
  scarcely produced. Grain adnate   ... 56. Aira.
Flowering glumes keeled. Two or three perfect
  flowers.
  Awns attached below the middle. Grain free 59. Deschampsia.
  Awns attached above the middle, grain free,
    glabrous ...   . 60. Trisetum.

Flowering glumes rounded on the back. Five or
more perfect flowers. Grain glabrous.
Seed deeply furrowed ... ... 62. Amphibromus.
Awn terminal between the rigid lobes or lateral awns
of the glume
Spikelets one-flowered (large with long awns)... 63. Anisopogon.
Spikelets several-flowered ... ... 64. Danthonia.

Tribe VI.—ASTREPTÆ.—Spikelets with several or in a few genera only one
or two bisexual flowers, the rhachis usually produced and often bearing one or
more empty glumes above them. Flowering glume unawned or with one or
more terminal untwisted awns. Palea prominently two-nerved or two-keeled,
usually as long or nearly as long as the glume.

(The rhachis is not produced above the perfect flowers in Milieæ, and in a
few species of other subtribes.)

Subtribe I.—**Pappophoreæ.**—Spikelets one or several flowered, in a dense
compound head, or in a spikelet or looser panicle. Flowering glumes rounded
on the back, with three or more nerves leading to three or more terminal
lobes or teeth, all unawned, or the central one or all tapering into untwisted
awns.

(See also Chloris, which has often a small awn or narrow lobe on each
side of the awn, and a few Festucaceæ have the hyaline tip two-lobed in
front of or on the side of the awn.)

Spikelets with one perfect flower (one or more additional male flowers or empty glumes in
Pappophorum).
Lobes of the flowering glumes three. Spikelets
capitate.
Lobes of the flowering glume all with long
points or fine awns. Rhachis not produced above the flower... ... ... 65. Amphipogon.
Central lobe only of the flowering glume
awned. Rhachis continued in a small
bristle ... ... 66. Echinopogon.
Lobes of the flowering glume nine (in the N.S.W.
species). Spikelets in a short dense or
loose panicle ... ... 67. Pappophorum.
Spikelets with several perfect flowers.
Spikelets sessile in two rows on one side of one
or two simple spikes, flowering glume
three-lobed, the central lobe alone
awned ... ... 68. Astrebla.
Spikelets paniculate.
Flowering glume with three narrow awned
lobes ... ... 69. Triraphis.
Flowering glume with three unawned lobes
or teeth ... ... 70 Triodia.

Subtribe II.—**Chlorideæ.**—Spikelets one or several flowered, sessile in
simple secund or unilateral spikes, which are either solitary or digitate, or
scattered on a common rhachis. Flowering glumes usually keeled, entire and
unawned, or with one, rarely three untwisted awns.

13

(Astrebla has the inflorescence, but not the glumes of Chlorideæ.)

Spikelets one-flowered.

Spikelets awnless, in digitates pikes, the rhachis
of the spikelet not at all or minutely
produced above the flower ... ... 72. Cynodon.

Spikelets awned, in a simple or in digitate spikes,
with one or more empty glumes above
the flowering one ... ... 73. Chloris.

Spikelets several flowered (rarely one flowered in
Leptochloa).

Flowering glumes entire.

Grain or seed within the pericarp loose and
rugose. Spikelets in digitate or scattered spikes, awnless or with long
pointed glumes ... . 74. Eleusine.

Grain smooth, the pericarp adnate. Spikelets
awnless, in scattered spikes ... ... 75. Leptochloa.

Flowering glumes with a minute point between two
small hyaline lobes. Spikelets in a single
or in scattered spikes, awnless ... ... 76. Diplachne.

Subtribe III.—Milieæ.—Spikelets one or two flowered, in a loose or
narrow and dense panicle, the rhachis of the spikelet not produced above the
upper flower. Outer glumes usually convex, several-nerved or almost
nerveless, unawned. Flowering glumes nearly similar, unawned or with one
straight awn. Grain free.

Rhachis of the spikelet glabrous or nearly so. Outer
glumes faintly-nerved. Flowering glumes
unawned.

Spikelets one-flowered ... ... 77. Sporobolus.

Spikelets two-flowered, the flowering glumes
close together or little distant, hardened
as well as the palea round the grain as
in Panicum ... ... 79. Isachne.

Rhachis of the spikelet hairy round the flowering
glumes.

Spikelets two-flowered. Outer glumes many-
nerved. Flowering glumes awned or
unawned ... ... 81. Eriachne.

Subtribe IV.—Festucaceæ.—Spikelets several—often many-flowered in
a loose or narrow and dense panicle or capitate, the rhachis of the spikelet
usually produced beyond the last flower or ending in an empty glume.
Outer glumes usually narrow, acute or rarely obtuse, unawned. Flowering
glumes entire or slightly notched, obtuse, acute or the keel or midrib
produced into a point or straight awn.

Group i. Several empty awned glumes above one or two flowering ones.

Spikelets in a narrow and dense or loose and spreading
panicle ... ... 82. Ectrosia.

Group ii. Only one empty glume above the flowering ones, sometimes
rudimentary or deficient.

Rhachis of the spikelet with long hairs enveloping the
flowering glumes. Lowest flower male.
Panicle large and loose ... ... 85. Phragmites.

Rhachis of the spikelet glabrous. Spikelets diœcious,
few with closely imbricate glumes. Pericarp
thick and spongy ... ... 86. Distichlis.

Rhachis of the spikelet glabrous or shortly or loosely
hairy. Spikelets bisexual.

Grain free from the palea (except in a few Poæ).

Spikelets usually flat; the flowering glumes
keeled, entire.

Flowering glume and palea thinly
scarious or hyaline, the glume
acute or shortly awned, the palea
keels broadly winged.

Spikelets in globular clusters in a
long interrupted spike ... 87. Elytrophorus.

Flowering glume membranous or
herbaceous, three or five nerved.
Spikelets usually many-flowered.

Flowering glumes three-nerved. 91. Eragrostis.

Spikelets few flowered. Flower-
glumes five-nerved ... ... 92. Poa.

Spikelets flattened, flowering glume with
hyaline tips, notched or two-lobed, the
keel forming a small point between the
lobes or just below them ... ... 93. Schedonorus.

Spikelets narrow. Flowering glumes rounded
on the back with three or more nerves
not reaching to the obtuse hyaline apex 94. Glyceria.

Grain adnate to the palea when ripe.

Ovary pubescent, obtuse. Flowering glumes
with a dorsal point or awn below the
entire or notched hyaline tip ... ... 96. Bromus.

Ovary glabrous. Spikelets usually narrow.
Flowering glumes entire, acute or
awned ... ... 98. Festuca.

Subtribe V.—**Hordeaceæ.**—Spikelets one or several flowered, sessile on
the opposite sides or alternate notches of the rhachis of a simple spike.
Glumes entire, awned or unawned.

Spikelets several-flowered, flat, one side or face of the
spikelet next to the continuous scarcely
notched rhachis ... ... 99. Agropyrum.

Spikelets one or two flowered, with the rhachis produced above the flower, half embedded in
the notches of the more or less articulate
rhachis ... ... 102. Lepturus.

15

LIST OF GRASSES.

SPECIES confined to Australia are marked with an *; those confined to this Colony with †; the rarer species, of which specimens are particularly desired, are marked with the letter R.

A. PANICACEÆ.

Tribe I.—PANICEÆ.

1. *Paspalum scrobiculatum.*
   „ *distichum.*
   „ *brevifolium.*
   R „ *minutiflorum.*
2. *Eriochloa punctata.*
   „ *annulata.*
3. *Panicum.*

Series i.—Digitarieæ.
   Panicum cænicolum.
   * „ *divaricatissimum.*
   * „ *macractinium.*
   „ *sanguinale.*
   * „ *tenuissimum.*
   * „ *parviflorum.*
   * „ *Baileyi.*

Series ii.—Trichachneæ.
   Panicum leucophæum.
   „ *semialatum.*

Series iii.—Paspaloideæ.
   Panicum flavidum.
   * „ *gracile.*
   „ *helopus.*
   „ *distachyum.*
   * „ *reversum.*

Series iv.—Echinocbloæ.
   Panicum crus-galli.

Series v.—Myuroideæ.
   Panicum indicum.

Series vi.—Paniculatæ.
   Panicum foliosum.
   „ *adspersum.*
   * „ *uncinulatum.*
   „ *repens.*
   * „ *pygmæum.*
   * „ *marginatum.*
   * „ *obseptum.*
   * „ *bicolor.*
   * „ *melananthum.*
   * „ *effusum.*
   * „ *Mitchelli.*
   „ *decompositum.*
   * „ *trachyrhachis.*
   * „ *prolutum.*
4. *Oplismenus compositus.*
   „ *setarius.*
5. *Setaria glauca.*
   „ *macrostachya.*
7. *Pennisetum compressum.*
8. *Cenchrus australis.*
9. *Chamæraphis spinescens.*
   * „ *paradoxa.*
13. *Spinifex hirsutus.*
   * „ *paradoxus.*

Tribe II.—ANDROPOGONEÆ.

Sub-tribe I.—Zoysieæ.
14. *Zoysia pungens.*
15. *Lappago racemosa.*
16. *Neurachne alopecuroides.*
   * „ *Mitchelliana.*
   * „ *Munroi.*
17. *Perotis rara.*

Sub-tribe II.—Rottboellieæ.
19. *Hemarthria compressa.*

Sub-tribe IV.—Euandropogoneæ.
24. *Heteropogon contortus.*
25. *Ischaemum triticeum.*
   * „ *australe.*
   „ *ciliare.*
   „ *pectinatum.*
   „ *laxum.*
27. R *Arthraxon ciliare.*
28. *Pollinia fulva.*

29. *Andropogon*—
    Section i.—Gymnandropogon.
    Andropogon erianthoides.
        ,,   *sericeus.*
    *   ,,   *affinis.*
        ,,   *pertusus.*
        ,,   *intermedius.*
    Section ii.—Cymbopogon.
    Andropogon bombycinus.
        ,,   *refractus.*
        ,,   *lachnatherus.*

30. *Imperata arundinacea.*
31. *Chrysopogon Gryllus.*
        ,,   *parviflorus.*
32. *Sorghum halepense.*
    *   ,,   *plumosum.*
33. *Anthistiria ciliata.*
    *   ,,   *avenacea.*
    *   ,,   *membranacea.*
34. R *Apluda mutica.*

Sub-tribe V.—Tristegineæ.

35. *Arundinella nepalensis.*

B. POACEÆ.

Tribe IV.—PHALARIDEÆ.

38. *Leersia hexandra.*
40. R† *Potamophila parviflora.*
42. *Microlæna stipoides.*
43. *Tetrarrhena juncea.*

44. *Alopecurus geniculatus.*
47. *Hierochloe redolens.*
    *   ,,   *rariflora.*

Tribe V.—STREPTATHERÆ.

Sub-tribe I.—Stipaceæ.
48. *Aristida*—
    Section i.—Arthatherum.
    Aristida stipoides.
    *   ,,   *arenaria.*
    Section ii.—Chætaria.
    Aristida Behriana.
    *   ,,   *leptopoda.*
    *   ,,   *vagans.*
    *   ,,   *ramosa.*
    *   ,,   *calycina.*
    *   ,,   *depressa.*
49. *Stipa elegantissima.*
    R   ,,   *Tuckeri.*
        ,,   *micrantha.*
    *   ,,   *flavescens.*
    *   ,,   *setacea.*
    *   ,,   *semibarbata.*
    *   ,,   *pubescens.*
    *   ,,   *aristiglumis.*
    *   ,,   *scabra.*

Sub-tribe II.—Agrostideæ.
51. *Pentapogon Billardieri.*
53. *Dichelachne crinita.*
        ,,   *sciurea.*
54. *Agrostis Muelleri.*
        ,,   *scabra.*
    *   ,,   *venusta.*

55. *Deyeuxia Forsteri.*
    *   ,,   *Billardieri.*
    *   ,,   *plebeja.*
    *   ,,   *montana.*
        ,,   *quadriseta.*
    *   ,,   *frigida.*
    *   ,,   *scabra.*
    *   ,,   *nivalis.*
    R† ,,   *breviglumis.*
    Sub-tribe III.—Avenaceæ.
56. *Aira caryophyllea.*
59. *Deschampsia cæspitosa.*
60. *Trisetum subspicatum.*
62. *Amphibromus Neesii.*
63. *Anisopogon avenaceus.*
64. *Danthonia*—
    Section i.—Micrathera.
    Danthonia paradoxa.
    Section ii.—Monachathera.
    Danthonia bipartita.
    *   ,,   *carphoides.*
    Section iii.—Eudanthonia.
    Danthonia pallida.
    *   ,,   *longifolia.*
    *   ,,   *robusta.*
        ,,   *racemosa.*
        ,,   *pilosa.*
        ,,   *semiannularis.*
        ,,   *pauciflora.*

17

Tribe VI.—Astreptæ.

Sub-tribe I.—Pappophoreæ.

65. *Amphipogon strictus.*
66. *Echinopogon ovatus.*
67. *Pappophorum nigricans.*
    *   ,,   *avenaceum.*
68. *Astrebla pectinata.*
    *   ,,   *triticoides.*
    R*   ,,   var. *elymoides.*
69. *Triraphis mollis.*
    R†   ,,   *microdon.*
70. *Triodia Mitchelli.*
    *   ,,   *irritans.*

Sub-tribe II.—Chlorideæ.

72. *Cynodon dactylon.*
73. *Chloris acicularis.*
    *   ,,   *truncata.*
    *   ,,   *ventricosa.*
    R*   ,,   *scariosa.*
74. *Eleusine ægyptiaca.*
      ,,   *indica.*
75. *Leptochloa subdigitata.*
      ,,   *chinensis.*
76. *Diplachne loliiformis.*
      ,,   *fusca.*

Sub-tribe III.—Milieæ.

77. *Sporobolus virginicus.*
      ,,   *indicus.*
      ,,   *diander.*
    *   ,,   *pulchellus.*
    *   ,,   *Lindleyi.*
    *   ,,   *actinocladus.*
79. *Isachne australis.*
81. *Eriachne aristidea.*
    *   ,,   *pallida.*
    *   ,,   *mucronata.*
    *   ,,   *obtusa.*

Sub-tribe IV.—Festucaceæ.

82. *Ectrosia leporina.*
85. *Phragmites communis.*
86. *Distichlis maritima.*
87. R *Elytrophorus articulatus.*
91. *Eragrostis—*
    Section i.—Chaunostachya.
    Eragrostis tenella.
      ,,   *nigra.*
    *   ,,   *megalosperma.*
      ,,   *pilosa.*
    *   ,,   *leptostachya.*
    Section ii.—Megastachya.
    Eragrostis diandra.
      ,,   *Brownii.*
    *   ,,   *laniflora.*
    *   ,,   *eriopoda.*
    *   ,,   *chætophylla.*
    Section iii.—Cylindrostachya.
    Eragrostis lacunaria.
    *   ,,   *falcata.*
92. *Poa cæspitosa.*
    *   ,,   *nodosa.*
    *   ,,   *lepida.*
93. *Schedonorus littoralis.*
94. *Glyceria Fordeana.*
      ,,   *fluitans.*
    *   ,,   *latispicea.*
    *   ,,   *ramigera.*
96. *Bromus arenarius.*
98. *Festuca duriuscula.*

Sub-tribe V.—Hordeaceæ.

99. *Agropyrum scabrum.*
    *   ,,   *velutinum.*
    *   ,,   *pectinatum.*
101. *Lepturus incurvatus.*
      ,,   *cylindricus.*

B

18

A.—Panicaceæ.

Tribe i.—Paniceæ.

Series i.—1. Paspalum.   5. Setaria.

2. Eriochloa.   7. Pennisetum.

3. Panicum.   8. Cenchrus.

4. Oplismenus.   9. Chamæraphis.

1. PASPALUM.

Spikelets one-flowered, not awned, not callous at the base, in one or two rows along one side of slender spikes, either forming the branches of a simple panicle or rarely solitary.

Glumes three, two outer ones empty, usually membranous and equal, or nearly so, the third flowering, of a firmer texture.

Palea within the flowering glume smaller and more involute.

Styles distinct, rather long.

Grain enclosed in a hardened palea and flowering glume, and free from them.

Spikes two to five, usually distant. Spikelets orbicular or broadly
 ovate, obtuse, about 1 line long ... ... 1. *P. scrobiculatum.*
Spikes two, close together, or scarcely distant. Spikelets ovate-
 oblong, acute, or acuminate, 1½ to 2 lines long ...   ... 2. *P. distichum.*
Spikes two or three, digitate or nearly so. Spikelets ovate,
 about ¾ line long   ...   . 3. *P. brevifolium.*
Spikes rather numerous, filiform. Spikelets narrow ovate, about
 ¾ line long   ...   . 4. *P. minutiflorum.*

1. Paspalum scrobiculatum, Linn.

Botanical name.—*Paspalum,* Greek *paspalos,* one of the millets, (*paspale* is a Greek word signifying "finest meal"); *scrobiculatum,* Latin *scrobiculus,* a little ditch or furrow, referring to the outer glumes, which are scrobiculate or furrowed.

Synonym.—*P. orbiculare,* Forst. (referring to the orbicular spikelets).

Vernacular names.—Sometimes called "Ditch Millet," from the situation in which it grows. Called "Cow Grass" in Queensland, according to O'Shanesy. The "Koda Millet" and "Hureek" of India are varieties of this grass.

Where figured.—Buchanan, Duthie, Church, *Agricultural Gazette* (N.S.W.)

Botanical description (B. Fl., vii., 460).—Erect or ascending, attaining 1 to 2 feet, the Australian specimens glabrous, or rarely with a few long hairs at the base of the leaf-blades.

Spikes varying from two to five, alternate, spreading, usually distant, 1 to 2, or rarely nearly 3 in. long, the rhachis usually flat, and about 1 line broad, and sometimes minutely pubescent at the base.

Spikelets sessile or shortly pedicellate in two close rows, or rarely in part, at least, of the spike, crowded into three or four rows, ovoid-orbicular, obtuse, flat, about 1 line long when in fruit.

Outer empty glumes thinly membranous, with a prominent midrib, sometimes minutely pubescent.

Fruiting glume similar in shape but soon hardened, very finely striate, the central nerve visible only in the young state.

Palea hardened like the flowering glume, the inflected margins dilated at the base into broad hyaline auricles enveloping the flower.

Botanical notes.—" All or nearly all the Australian specimens belong to the variety still distinguished by some as a species under Forster's name *orbiculare*, usually a more slender plant, with smaller spikelets, the rhachis often pubescent at the base, and the outer glumes scarcely or not at all scrobiculate. The marginal indentures and the intermediate nerves between the midrib and the marginal ones of the typical *P. scrobiculatum* are chiefly prominent in cultivated varieties." (B. Fl.)

Value as a fodder.—A long, rather coarse grass, which not only grows on poor land, but also on swampy ground. In warm, moist situations it forms a great bulk of nutritious fodder, but it is coarse and fibrous when old. In tropical climates it sometimes becomes a weed in cultivated land, but it is less noxious in this respect in our climate. It will stand close feeding. Duthie states that it is cultivated as a rainy-season crop throughout the plains of India and at low elevations on the Himalaya. It is there usually sown on the poorer kinds of soil, and the straw is used as fodder.

This grass sometimes deleterious.—Cases of poisoning are occasionally met with in India through the use of this grain as an article of food. The symptoms are the same as those caused by the European Darnel (*Lolium temulentum*). According to popular belief there are two kinds, the sweet or non-poisonous, and the poisonous (Dymock).

In the same country this grass, called " Hureek," and perhaps identical with Ghohona grass, is said to render the milk of cows that graze upon it narcotic and injurious. Rosenthal pronounces it pernicious perhaps only when long and exclusive use is made of it. A probable cause of the deleterious properties is the liability of the grain to ergotism.

Fungi recorded on this grass.—*Cerebella paspali*, Cke. and Mass., and *Ustilago Cesatii*, Waldh.

Other uses.—A good variety of this grass ("Koda Millet") is used in India as a food-grain by the poorer classes. The composition of "Koda Millet" (husked), is as follows:—

	In 100 parts.	In 1 lb.
		oz. gr.
Water	11·7 ...	1 382
Albuminoids ...	7·0 ...	1 52
Starch	77·2 ...	12 154
Oil	2·1 ...	0 147
Fibre	0·7 ...	0 49
Ash	1·3 ...	0 91
		(Church.)

This grass is much used by the Fijians for strewing the floors of their houses and public buildings. (Seemann.)

Habitat and range.—Port Jackson to the Tweed, and westward as far as the Blue Mountains; also in New England and the other table-lands. Frequents damp places. Found also in Queensland and Northern Australia. Common in tropical and sub-tropical Asia and Africa ; also in the Pacific Islands and New Zealand.

2. Paspalum distichum, Linn.

Botanical name.—*Distichum*, Latin, consisting of two rows, applied (amongst other things), to the arrangement of grains in an ear of barley, having the spikelets in two rows.

Synonym.—*P. littorale*, R. Br.

Vernacular names.—"Silt Grass" is the name adopted by Baron von Mueller. "Water Couch" is another name. "Sea-side Millet" is the name for the coast form. Knot-grass and Joint-grass of the United States.

Where figured.—Buchanan, Flint, Illust. North American Grasses, *Agricultural Gazette.*

Botanical description (B. Fl., vii, 460).—Stems often creeping and rooting in the sand to a great extent, the ascending extremities varying from short and entirely covered with the leaf-sheaths, to slender, 1 foot long or more, with the leaves distant.

Leaves either linear-lanceolate and flat or involute and almost subulate, glabrous, or with a few long hairs at the orifice of the sheath and base of the lamina.

Spikes two, close together, or the lowest at a distance of 1 or 2 lines, quite glabrous, the rhachis not above ½ line broad.

Spikelets sessile in two rows, oval-oblong, acute or acuminate, flat, 1½ to nearly 2 lines long.

Outer empty glumes equal and distinctly three-nerved.

Fruiting glume hardened and very faintly three-nerved, or the central nerve alone perceptible.

Botanical notes.—Bailey separates *P. littorale* from *P. distichum*, as a variety. Both are united in the *Flora Australiensis*. It is doubtful whether the normal species is truly indigenous in New South Wales. In any case it thrives remarkably well in the Colony. Bailey observes that the two forms preserve their characters when grown side by side. The normal form ("Silt Grass") will not, he observes, stand the least salt-water. The variety *littorale* ("Sea-side Millet") "has the same running underground stems as the normal species, but it differs in its narrower leaves, erect stems, and in being only met with in coast swamps. It thrives best in brackish swamps."

Value as a fodder.—Although not a forage-plant of the highest class, it is valuable because it supplies nutritious food for stock in damp, muddy localities, where valuable grasses are not usually found. Its creeping, joint-rooting habit enables it to stand close feeding. O'Shanesy says the kangaroo is particularly fond of it.

That it will endure such a cold situation as Walcha (New England) shows that it need by no means be confined to the warmer coast districts.

Mr. A. R. Crawford writes : " It is becoming quite a common grass on the table-land. I noticed it five years ago in the town of Walcha (3,500 feet). It is now all over the town. Twenty years ago I introduced it on our station (Cunderang, on the eastern slopes). It is now to be found in many places along the river. It makes a rough-looking but valuable hay, much esteemed on the Macleay River. I have seen a horse leave corn and chaff in his manger to eat hay made of this grass. For pasture it is one of the most fattening kinds."

This grass has been so carefully studied in the United States that the experience of American observers in regard to it is especially valuable.

For example, " Several species of *Paspalum* have received attention in the South as being useful pasture grasses, and very durable from their creeping and rooting habit. *P. distichum* is one of these species. It grows principally in low, moist ground. Its stems and culms are mostly prostrate and running, sending up here and there a few flower-bearing culms."

Mr. W. A. Sanders, of California, writes : " Are you aware of the value of *P. distichum* for seeding pond-holes that dry up, or nearly so, in autumn ? Such ponds are usually spots of bare, stinking mud, but when well set to this grass will yield all the way up to 80 tons (in the green state) of autumn feed for stock, especially valuable for cows first, then follow with sheep till every vestige is devoured. Surely it has an immense food value in such places." (Vasey.)

" Joint grass is adapted to warm, moist, alkaline soils, and in New Mexico is most abundant in low lands that are flooded occasionally, and upon the ditch-banks late in the season. In this latter place it is more or less of a nuisance, though possibly of some little value as a soil-binder. So far as I am able to state, it is not used as a pasture grass or as a hay crop. It is cut by the Mexicans much as Barnyard grass (*Panicum crus-galli*), and other grasses, to be fed green to stock before corn has matured. Its nutritive ratio of 1 to 16·7 indicates that it is not a very valuable feed, and its manner and place of growth are not such as to make it a desirable grass to cultivate." (*Some New Mexican Forage Plants,* Bulletin No. 18, p. 63.)

Having enumerated some of its good qualities, we must not forget that it is not without drawbacks. It mats together, and to such an extent does this sometimes occur on land prepared for crops, that farmers have the greatest difficulty in ploughing through it. It often fills the gutters, as Sydney suburban, and other municipalities know to their cost. It turns blackish on drying, which is a drawback to its use for hay. Mr. Seccombe, who made many experiments with native grasses on the Richmond River, does not look with favour on this grass; in fact, he advises discontinuance of its cultivation. He remarks that its growth starts late in the spring and ceases early in the autumn.

Other uses.—The rhizome is used in India as a medicine for inflammation of the gums and against conjunctivis, and in the Argentine Republic for liver complaint (Hackel); also for kidney troubles and gonorrhœa (*Some New Mexican Forage Plants*).

It has considerable value as a soil or river-bank binder, and, as regards the coast form, as a sand-binder in addition. Some references to its merits for binding soil have already been made. Kearney says that on the beach (U.S.A.) he found sterile shoots 6 feet or more in length, making excellent sand-binders. Lamson-Scribner says it often does good service in binding soils subject to wash, and that it can well be recommended for this use. Mueller recommends it for fern-tree tubs to produce a green sward and some over-dropping foliage.

Habitat and range.—Port Jackson to the Tweed, extending west to the table-land. The var. *littorale* is found on littoral swamp-land and wet bottoms among sandhills on the coast-line, and the species generally in damp or swampy land. It also occurs in Queensland and Western Australia. It is also widely distributed over the tropical regions of both the New and Old World.

3. Paspalum brevifolium, Flügge.

Botanical name.—*Brevifolium*, from two Latin words signifying "short-leaved" (*brevis, folium*).

Synonym.—*Panicum tenuiflorum*, R.Br.

Vernacular names.—" The short-leaved Paspalum " is a name that may be coined.

Botanical description (B. Fl., vii., 461).—Stems from a creeping or much-branched base, erect, slender, 1 foot high, or rather more.

Leaves short, narrow, flat, the sheaths usually villous or pubescent, the ligula scarious, jagged.

Spikes or panicle branches two or rarely three, digitate at the end of the peduncle, filiform, 1 to 2 inches long.

Spikelets scattered along one side of the rhachis, on short curved pedicels, ovate, rather obtuse, or almost acute, about ¾ line long, sprinkled with short, fine, appressed, silky hairs.

Empty glumes two, rather obtuse, nearly equal, thin, finely five-nerved.

Value as a fodder.—A small grass, having a creeping underground stem, from which leafy tufts are sent up, the broad, tender foliage affording good but short early summer feed, the flowering stems very slender, and from 1 to 2 feet high. (Bailey.)

Habitat and range.—It extends from Port Jackson to Queensland and Northern Australia, mostly in the coast districts. It is widely spread over tropical Asia.

4. Paspalum minutiflorum, Steud.

Botanical name.—Minutiflorum, from two Latin words signifying small-flowered (*minutus, flos floris*).

*Vernacular names.—*The small-flowered *Paspalum.*

Botanical description (B.Fl., vii, 461).—A rather tall, glabrous grass closely resembling at first sight the *Panicum parviflorum*, R. Br., but with the characters of *Paspalum* and nearly allied to *P. brevifolium.*

Leaves flat, rather long and narrow, the ligula short, not ciliate.

Spikes or panicle branches rather numerous, filiform, alternate or the upper ones clustered, 3 to 5 inches long.

Spikelets numerous, very shortly but unequally pedicellate, narrow ovate, rather acute, about ¾ line long.

Empty glumes two, nearly equal, prominently three-nerved, glabrous or the margins minutely ciliate.

Fruiting glume acute, smooth, and shining.

*Botanical notes.—*Bailey remarks, "it might be called the autumnal form of *P. brevifolium.*"

*Value as a fodder.—*Gives good pasture and plenty of seed. (Bailey.)

*Habitat and range.—*It occurs in damp land on our Northern rivers, and along the Queensland coast districts. Widely spread over tropical Asia.

2. ERIOCHLOA.

Spikelets 1-flowered, without protruding awns, with a callous annular or almost cuplike base, articulate on a short pedicel, in one or two rows along one side of the slender branches of a simple panicle.

Glumes three, two outer ones empty, usually membranous, equal or nearly so, the third or flowering glume shorter, of a firm coriaceous texture, obtuse, but tipped with a point or short awn not exceeding the other glumes.

Palea within the flowering glume coriaceous and involute.

Styles distinct, rather long.

Grain enclosed in a hardened palea and flowering glume, and free from them.

Spikelets usually above 1½ lines long, the rhachis of the spikes and main axis of the panicle pubescent or hirsute	1. *E. punctata.*
Spikelets usually under 1½ lines long, the rhachis and main axis glabrous	2. *E. annulata.*

1. Eriochloa punctata, Hamilt.

Botanical name.—Eriochloa, from two Greek words signifying wool and grass, or rather, the blade of young grass (*erion, chloe*); *punctata*, Latin for dotted, apparently from the annular disc at the base of the flowering glume, which gives the inflorescence a dotted appearance, accentuated when the annulus is (as it often is), of a dark colour.

*Synonym.—*Both *E. punctata* and *E. annulata* are included under *E. polystachya*, Humb. et Kth., in Mueller's *Census.*

Vernacular names.—" Early Spring Grass." "Everlasting Grass" is an American name.
Where figured.—Duthie (as *E. polystachya*) ; *Agricultural Gazette.*
Botanical description (B.Fl., vii, 462).—An erect grass, attaining 2 or 3 feet ; glabrous, except the inflorescence, and sometimes a slight pubescence in the upper part.

Leaves rather long, flat or convolute when dry.

Spikes or panicle branches about five to eight, distant, erect, secund, the lowest often above 2 inches long, the others gradually shorter.

Rhachis, as well as the main axis, pubescent or hairy.

Spikelets all pedicellate, but often rather close.

Pedicels 1 to 2 lines long, usually bearing a few hairs.

Spikelet ovoid, acute or shortly acuminate, rather above 1½ lines long, seated on a thick annular or almost cupular disk, articulate on the pedicel.

Empty glumes membranous, broad, and usually five-nerved, or the inner one rather narrower and sometimes only three-nerved, both more or less hairy outside, and sometimes rather densely covered with long hairs.

Flowering glume much shorter, coriaceous, faintly three or five nerved ; obtuse, but the midrib produced into a point or awn as long as the outer glumes, as in *Panicum helopus.*

Value as a fodder.—One of the best pasture grasses of the Colony, particularly of the coast districts, though it will endure considerable drought. It grows freely, is succulent, and much esteemed by stock.

A good account of New South Wales experience with this grass is by Mr. Seccombe, who experimented with it on the Richmond River. He reported : " This perennial grass is fairly plentiful, and in sheltered situations in this district it maintains some growth all the winter. It grows rapidly from very early spring to late summer, and, if undisturbed, reaches a length of 2 or 3 feet. It grows on various kinds of soil. Under cultivation its growth is wonderful, as well as its power of seed-producing. I took as much as six cuttings for seed off my plot during the season 1894 to 1895. This grass has been introduced to our district, no doubt through the agency of travelling stock, for it can be found more or less on the old, much-used highways. It is seldom seen to any satisfaction in open situations, as stock and padamelons keep it cropped very close. This close clipping has given rise to frequently-expressed ideas that *Eriochloa punctata* banishes Mullumbimby Couch [*Kyllingia monocephala*, a great pest.—J.H.M.]. It is a grass, I feel confident, our dairy-farmers should introduce to their holdings ; it has great vitality, unquestionable milk and butter qualities, as well as the invaluable property of rapid reproduction."

I also quote a valuable report on it from the United States, of which country it is also a native :—

" Irrigated but uncultivated fields usually produce an abundant crop of the above grass each season. After the corn is 'laid by,' or during what little rainy weather we have in the summer, this grass appears in the cornfields, along the ditch-banks and in the fence-rows, and makes a very rapid growth during the hot days of August and September. It occasionally does considerable damage as a weed in the Alfalfa (Lucerne) fields.

" It produces many culms from each stool, many broad green leaves, and abundance of seed, and will reseed the ground each year. Land once seeded with it would produce a crop of fair hay after a crop of wheat has been taken off, provided the wheat stubble be turned under and the land irrigated. It is generally associated with *Panicum crus-galli* and *P. colonum.*

" No grass, however good it may be, is grown for hay or pasture in this section, since Alfalfa supplies these demands; so it is not customary to cut this one for hay except when it appears as a weed in the Alfalfa fields. But the occasional lack of water would seem to be the only good reason why a crop of hay might not be cut from the fields that lie idle during the latter half of the season. Quite a good deal of it is cut by the Mexicans, and fed green to stock while waiting for corn to mature.

" The grass is a native of this south-western arid section, being reported from Kansas, Colorado, Texas, and New Mexico, notably from the creek bottoms of this territory. The nutritive ratio of 1 to 9·3 is narrower than in the case of Timothy hay of the eastern States, and so far as can be judged from the analysis, it should be a valuable forage plant." (*Some New Mexican Forage Plants*, Bulletin No. 18, March, 1896, p. 64.)

Habitit and range.—Found on every kind of soil and widely spread as *E. annulata,* being common in the tropics of both the New and Old World and New Guinea. It occurs in all the colonies except Tasmania.

2. Eriochloa annulata, Kunth.

Botanical name.—*Annulata,* Latin *annulus,* a ring; in allusion to the annular callus or ring-like base of the spikelet.

Synonyms.—See *E. punctata.*

Vernacular name.—Early Spring grass (Bailey).

Where figured.—*Agric. Gaz.* See *E. punctata.*

Botanical description (B. Fl., vii, 463).—A smaller and more slender grass than *E. punctata,* the leaves usually narrower, glabrous.

Spikes slender, 1 to 1½ inches long, the main axis of the infloresence as well as the rhachis usually glabrous, the pedicels sometimes bearing a few short hairs.

Spikelets narrow, tapering at the end, scarcely 1⅓ lines long, including the point, which is rather longer than in *E. punctata.*

Empty glumes much less hairy than in that species, three or rarely five nerved.

Flowering glume the same.

Variety *acrotricha,* spikelets rather longer, with long points and rather more hairy, and the hairs of the pedicels more numerous, with a few sometimes also on the rhachis (*B.Fl.*) Found from the coast and table-land to the interior.

Value as a fodder.—This is a valuable grass, one of the best, and, as already pointed out, closely related to *E. punctata.* In any case the remarks on these two grasses may, from the point of view of the farmer and pastoralist, be considered to be interchangeable. Mr. Seccombe has experimented on the grasses, side by side on the Richmond River, and following is his statement :—" It is said that this grass makes excellent hay. Like *E. punctata*, it has been introduced by travelling stock, either from Queensland or our own open country at the back. It is more plentiful probably than *E. punctata*, particularly around Lismore, so that any settler could secure a few plants by seeking some near the stone quarry. The grass is highly recommended to dairy farmers for systematic cultivation, either for permanent pasture or to cut for hay. Both the *Eriochloas* referred to in this paper are sufficiently vigorous to force a footing in old pastures, the seed springing into life from August to March."

Habitat and range.—Same as the preceding species.

3. PANICUM.

Spikelets with one terminal hermaphrodite and occasionally a male or rudimentary flower below it, rarely awned, variously arranged along the branches of a simple or compound panicle rarely reduced to a simple spike, the partial rhachis very rarely produced beyond the last spikelet; barren awnlike branches none, or very rarely a single one.

Glumes usually four, the outer one smaller than the others, not awned, often very small, deficient only in *P. gibbosum*, the second and third very variable in relative proportions, the third occasionally with a palea with or without three stamens in its axil; fourth or fruiting glume smaller, or as long as the third, of a firmer consistence, enclosing a *palea* and hermaphrodite flower.

Styles distinct or very shortly united at the base.

Grain enclosed in the hardened fruiting glume and palea, but free from them.

SERIES I.—DIGITARIEÆ.

Spikelets mostly in pairs along the outer and lower side of the simple slender branches of the panicle, one of each pair always pedicellate, the other sessile or on a shorter pedicel, the upper ones of each branch occasionally solitary, the lower ones very rarely clustered. *Outer glume* usually very small.

Branches of the panicle often numerous, the lower ones long and verticillate, the upper ones scattered.
Lowest spikelet of each pair sessile. Spikelets 1½ to 2 lines long, more or less silky-hairy ... ... 1. *P. cænicolum.*
Spikelets 1 to 1½ lines long, more or less silky-hairy ... 2. *P. divaricatissimum.*
Spikelets 1 to 1½ lines long, not silky, but the lateral nerves on the third glume ciliate with rigid hairs seated on tubercles 3. *P. macractinium.*
Branches of the panicle few, three to eight, digitate or clustered at the end of the peduncle.
Spikelets of each pair similar, both fertile, glabrous, or softly ciliate ... ... 5. *P. sanguinale.*
Branches of the panicle scattered or the upper ones approximate, the lower ones rarely clustered, and not verticillate.
Branches, usually three, distant, 1 to 1½ inches long. Spikelets ovoid, about ½ line long... ... ... 8. *P. tenuissimum.*
Branches often numerous, 2 to 6 inches long. Spikelets glabrous, ½ to ¾ line long, the lower ones often clustered ... ... 9. *P. parviflorum.*
Branches often numerous, 2 to 6 inches long. Spikelets narrow, nearly 1 line long, silky-hairy ... ... 10. *P. Baileyi.*

1. Panicum cœnicolum, F.v.M.

Botanical name.—Panicum, Latin for a millet-like grain (indirectly from *panis,* bread), some of the species yielding food-grains; *cœnicolum,* from the Latin cœnum, dirt, filth, manure; *colonum,* inhabitant, the grass being commonly found near the droppings of cattle.

*Vernacular name.—*Mr. Koch informs me that, in common with *Pappophorum commune* and some other grasses and small herbage, this grass is called "Kanta" by the aborigines of the Mount Lynd-hurst district, South Australia.

Where figured.—Agricultural Gazette.

Botanical description (B. Fl., vii, 467).—Stems from a knotty branching base, ascending to 1 foot or more.

Leaves flat, usually softly pubescent or villous.

Panicle of rather numerous slender simple branches, 3 to 4 inches long, at first erect, at length spreading, the lower ones verticillate, the upper ones alternate and distant, or rarely in pairs.

Spikelets in pairs, one sessile, the other pedicellate, oblong, 1½ to 2 lines long.

Outer glume not exceeding ¼ line in our specimens, *the second* rather shorter than the spikelet, five or seven nerved, *the third* seven to eleven nerved, both more or less silky-hairy and empty.

Fruiting glume, smooth, acute.

*Value as a fodder.—*Valuable as a lasting grass for moist meadows. (Mueller.)

Produces a fine bottom, although the panicles are large, dry, and spreading, and give it anything but an inviting appearance; it is a kind well worth growing.—(Bailey.)

*Other uses.—*The grain, known as "Power-tandra," is eaten by the aborigines of Mount Lyndhurst, South Australia.—(Koch).

*Habitat and range.—*In the more arid districts of this Colony, and also of Victoria, South and Western Australia.

2. Panicum divaricatissimum, R.Br.

Botanical name.—Divaricatissimum, superlative of *divaricatus,* a Latin word signifying straddling or spread out, in allusion to the spreading branches of the panicle.

Vernacular name.—" Spider Grass."

Where figured.—Agricultural Gazette.

Botanical description (B. Fl., vii, 467).—Stems from a branching base, sometimes under, sometimes much above 1 foot high.

Leaves glabrous or more or less pubescent or softly villous, the ligula not prominent and not ciliate.

Panicle of rather numerous rigidly filiform simple branches, 3 to 8 inches long, at first erect, at length spreading, the lower ones in a dense verticil, the upper ones alternate and distant.

Spikelets in pairs, or rarely solitary along the branches, one sessile, the other pedicellate, 1 to 1½ lines long, glabrous, or covered with long silky hairs, spreading when in fruit.

Outer glume very small, ovate, obtuse, the second and third nearly equal and both empty, or the third rarely with a minute rudimentary palea, the second usually three-nerved, the third five-nerved.

Fruiting glume ovoid, not gibbous, glabrous, smooth, acute.

Botanical notes.—There are four varieties of this species :—

1. *Glaberrimum.*—Stems tall ; branches of the panicle sometimes more than 8 inches long, the whole plant glabrous, spikes 1½ lines long, glabrous. Hitherto only recorded from Queensland.

2. *Normale.*—Foliage glabrous, or nearly so, panicle branches 4 to 8 inches long, spikelets 1½ lines long, silky-villous, rarely nearly glabrous. Coast districts of New South Wales ; also Queensland.

3. *Ammophilum.*—Foliage softly villous, spikelets small, covered with long silky hairs, spreading when in fruit. Syn. : *P. ammophilum,* F.v.M. Interior of South Australia and of New South Wales.

4. *Radiatum.*—Foliage softly villous, spikelets small, glabrous, or nearly so. Syn. : *P. radiatum,* R.Br. Coast districts of New South Wales ; also Queensland.

Value as a fodder.—This variable grass is more widely diffused in the drier regions, and it is not only a drought-resisting species, but it yields palatable and nutritious fodder. It also seeds freely.

Habitat and range.—In all the colonies except Tasmania and Western Australia. Adapts itself to a great variety of soils and climatic conditions, from the coast to the dry country.

3. Panicum macractinium, Benth.

Botanical name.—*Macractinium,* from two Greek words, *macros,* long, and *actis, actinos* a ray ; referring to the long rays of the panicle.

Vernacular name.—".Roly-poly Grass." So called because its panicles, when ripe, break off and are blown and roll about by the wind. Hence it has got into bad repute, because of useless plants which behave in a similar manner.

Where figured.—Bailey.

Botanical description (B. Fl., vii, 468).—Allied to *P. divaricatissimum,* but taller and quite glabrous.

Panicle similar, the slender branches rigid, often 6 to 8 inches long, the lower ones in a dense verticil, the upper ones alternate and distant.

Spikelets distant in pairs, one almost sessile, the other on a longer pedicel, both fertile and similar, narrow, acute, about 1½ lines long.

Outer glume ⅓ to ¾ line long, ovate, oblong, obtuse, the second nearly as long as the third, three or five nerved, the margins ciliate, the third rather longer, very prominently three-nerved, ciliate, with rigid hairs proceeding from a row of prominent tubercles.

Flowering glume narrow, acute.

Value as a fodder.—One of the dry-country grasses ; grows in tufts, and is nutritious. It is especially valuable in producing a quantity of palatable feed when young and green ; later on the natural hay is still sought after by stock.

Habitat and range.—In New South Wales and Queensland, from the coast to the interior.

" Although it is often found on rich downs country, it is often met with on the poorest sandy ridges." (Bailey.)

4. Panicum sanguinale, Linn.

Botanical name.—Sanguinale, Latin, " belonging to blood "; hence blood-coloured, referring to the red or purple colour this grass frequently assumes, especially on the approach of cold weather.

Vernacular names.—" Summer Grass " ; " Crab Grass" of the United States. Other names are "Finger Grass," "Hairy-finger Grass," and " Manna Grass."

Where figured.—Duthie, Vasey, Hackel, Trinius, *Agricultural Gazette.*

Botanical description (B. Fl., vii, 469).—Decumbent and often shortly creeping and rooting at the base, ascending to 1 foot, or rather more.

Leaves flaccid, flat, usually pubescent, and sprinkled with long hairs, especially on the sheaths, but sometimes nearly glabrous.

Spikes, or panicle branches, three to eight, crowded at the end of a long peduncle, all from nearly the same point, or shortly distant, 1½ inches to 3 inches, or in some varieties above 4 inches long ; the rhachis slender but angular, flexuose, scabrous-ciliate.

Spikelets in pairs, one nearly sessile, the other pedicellate, oblong, rather acute, about 1½ lines long.

Outer glume minute, rarely above ¼ line long ; *second glume* lanceolate, three-nerved, from half to three-quarters the length of the spikelet ; *third glume* usually five-nerved, glabrous, or slightly ciliate in the Australian specimens, empty.

Fruiting glume shorter, smooth.

Botanical notes.—Most of the Australian specimens have the glumes glabrous, or nearly so. Some, however, have them more or less ciliate with soft hairs on the lateral nerves or margins, which constitutes the *P. ciliare*, Retz. (B. Fl.)

Value as a fodder.—The " Summer Grass" is looked upon with mingled feelings. In the early summer it springs up with surprising rapidity, forming smothering tufts, which speedily cover gardens, orchards, or any soil which is not repeatedly hoed over. It is a very light grass ; that is to say, it possesses but little substance, a load of the fresh grass shrivelling to very little. O'Shanesy says he has seen it give 1½ to 2 tons per acre, but does not state the weight of hay. In this Colony it is not a favourite with stock, as they do not eat it unless they are somewhat pressed with hunger. I have, however, seen horses eat it often enough. It will be noted from what follows that it appears to produce more valuable fodder in the Southern United States than with us. Duthie states that the grass is much used for fodder in India.

" Crab Grass is generally considered the best hay-grass of the Southern States. It is never cultivated in the ordinary sense, but comes up spontaneously on arable land after the cultivated crop is taken off. Sometimes the ground is lightly rolled, but that is the only preparation made for it. After a crop of corn or cotton, one, or sometimes two, good catches of crab-hay are made on the land. On account of its rapid growth, crab-grass is peculiarly adapted for its functions as an after crop. In good soil, when favoured by sufficient rain, it attains considerable size. At Mobile it was seen nearly 4 feet high. It is a tender grass, and makes a sweet hay, but is slow to give up its moisture, and, therefore, rather difficult to cure. When allowed to get the better of the cultivator it becomes a troublesome weed, but with ordinary care it is easily subdued. At Aiken I saw a large lawn, quite a good-looking one, composed almost exclusively of this grass." (Kearney.)

"This is an annual grass, which occurs in cultivated and waste grounds, and grows very rapidly during the hot summer months. The culms usually rise to the height of 2 or 3 feet, and are bent at the lower joints, where they frequently take root. At the New Orleans Exposition there were specimens of this grass 5 ft. 10 in. long.

"Professor Killebrew, of Tennessee, says: It is a fine pasture grass; although it has but few base leaves and forms no sward, yet it sends out numerous stems or branches at the base. It serves a most useful purpose in stock husbandry. It fills all our cornfields, and many persons pull it out, which is a tedious process. It makes a sweet hay, and horses are exceedingly fond of it, leaving the best hay to eat it.

"Professor Phares, of Mississippi, says that the corn and cotton fields are often so overrun with it that the hay which might be secured would be more valuable than the original crop. It is sometimes mowed from between the rows, sometimes cut across the ridges, and with the corn.

"Although so much esteemed in the South, it is considered a pest in the Northern States." (Vasey.)

"The spontaneous growth affords excellent pasturage, as well as hay of the first quality, if properly cured. It contains but little fibre, and dries quickly when cut, but if after cutting it is wet by rains or heavy dews its value for hay is almost entirely destroyed." (Lamson-Scribner.)

Other uses.—"It produces much seed, of which birds are fond. The common method of collecting and preparing it in Germany is as follows :—At sunrise the grass is gathered or beaten into a hair-sieve from the dewy grass, spread on a sheet, and dried for a fortnight in the sun. It is then gently beaten with a wooden pestle in a wooden trough or mortar, with straw laid between the seeds and the pestle, till the chaff comes off ; they are then winnowed. After this they are again put into the trough or mortar in rows, with dried marigold flowers, apple, and hazel-leaves, and pounded till they appear bright ; they are then winnowed again, and being made perfectly clean by this last process are fit for use. The marigold leaves are added to give the seed a finer colour. A bushel of seed with the chaff yields only about 2 quarts of clean seed. When boiled with milk and wine it forms an extremely palatable food, and is in general made use of whole, in the manner of sago, to which it is in most instances preferred." (Hortus Gramineus Woburnensis).

Habitat and range.—All over the colonies, except Tasmania and South Australia, in all soils and situations. Occurs also in Europe, Asia, Africa, America, and the Pacific Islands.

8. Panicum tenuissimum, Benth.

Botanical name.—Tenuissimum, superlative of the Latin *tenuis,* thin or slender. The grass is a very slender one.

Botanical description (B.Fl., vii, 470).—Erect, very slender, much branched at the base, often above 1 foot high.

Leaves short and narrow, quite glabrous, the ligula short, scarious and jagged.

Spikes or panicle-branches few, usually three, filiform, spreading, distant, 1 to 1½ inches long.

Spikelets in pairs, ovoid, quite glabrous, but little more than ½ line long, both pedicellate, but one pedicel twice as long as the other.

Outer glume minute, almost microscopic, orbicular.

Second and third nearly equal, both empty, obtuse, membranous, three to five nerved.

Fruiting glume rather acute, usually slightly exceeding the empty ones.

*Value as a fodder.—*A palatable grass, which is probably nutritious.

*Habitat and range.—*Along the Northern rivers; also in Queensland.

9. Panicum parviflorum, R.Br.

Botanical name.—Parviflorum, Latin *parvus,* small, and *flos, floris* a flower; small-flowered.

*Vernacular name.—*Small-flowered Finger-grass.

*Where figured.—*Bailey, *Agricultural Gazette.*

Botanical description (B.Fl., vii, 470).—A tall but slender usually glabrous grass.

Leaves long and narrow, the *ligula* scarious, often long, jagged at the end.

Panicle-branches often numerous, spreading, simple, filiform, 2 to 4 inches or in some specimens 5 to 6 inches long, the lower ones distant, the upper ones often crowded.

Spikelets ovoid, glabrous, ½ to ¾ line long, mostly in pairs along the flexuose rhachis, one on a longer pedicel than the other; but in the lower part of the branch often clustered, the longer pedicel bearing two or three spikelets.

Outer glume very small, ovate usually one-nerved.

Second and third glumes nearly equal, both empty, membranous, obtuse, the second usually three-nerved, the third five-nerved.

Fruiting glume as long, more acute, smooth.

*Value as a fodder.—*A rather tall, slender grass, which is so eagerly sought after by cattle that it does not usually mature seed, except in sheltered situations. There is no doubt it is a valuable grass, and attention has been drawn to it chiefly by Bailey and O'Shanesy. Mr. Bailey (speaking of Queensland) observes that there are several forms of it. "That on the dry ridges is somewhat wiry when in flower, but makes a good tufty bottom. The tall form is usually met with near watercourses and in rich scrub-land."

*Botanical notes.—*Var. *pilosa,* more or less hairy. Common in Southern Queensland, and very probably to be met with in Northern New South Wales.

*Habitat and range.—*Coast district to the table-land, from North Illawarra to Queensland.

10. Panicum Baileyi, Benth.

Botanical name.—Baileyi, in honor of Frederick Manson Bailey, the well-known colonial botanist of Queensland.

Botanical description (B.Fl., vii, 471).—A glabrous rather slender grass of 1½ to 2 feet, with the inflorescence of *P. parviflorum,* but the spikelets rather of *P. divaricatissimum.*

> *Leaves* flat, narrow, the *ligula* shortly prominent, scarious, not ciliate.
> *Panicle* of several simple filiform branches of 3 or 4 inches, all distant or the upper ones rather crowded, or the lower ones sometimes clustered, not verticillate.
>
> *Spikelets* narrow-ovoid, rather acute, nearly 1 line long, mostly in pairs, one on a much longer pedicel than the other, or in the lower part of the branch, the longer pedicel with two or three spikelets.
>
> *Outer glume* very small, ovate, one-nerved.
>
> *Second and third glumes* nearly equal, fringed with rather long hairs spreading when in fruit, the second usually five-nerved, the third rather broader and seven-nerved.
>
> *Fruiting glume* acute, smooth, and shining.

Value as a fodder.—"Very near *P. parviflorum* in general appearance, and, like that species, a good pasture or hay grass ; it attains the height of from 2 to 4 feet, and is plentifully supplied with leaves. It is usually met with on good soil." (Bailey.) Doubtless a nutritious grass, but we require information in regard to New South Wales experience of it.

*Habitat and range.—*Northern New South Wales and Queensland.

SERIES II.—TRICHACHNEÆ.

Spikelets silky-hairy, or fringed with long hairs, sessile, or shortly pedicellate, clustered, or rarely in pairs along the rhachis of the simple spike-like panicle, or of the two or few long erect branches.

Spike-like branches, few or spike single. Spikelets mostly clustered,
    1 to 1½ lines long, the outer glume present, but small and often
    concealed by the long silky hairs   ...   .   12. *P. leucophæum*
Spike-like branches few. Spikelets 2 to 2½ lines long, fringed with
    long hairs connected by a prominent nerve or membrane.
    Glumes with fine points   ...   .13. *P. semialatum*

12. Panicum leucophæum, Humb. et Bonpl.

Botanical name.—Leucophæum, a Latinised form of two Greek words (*leucos,* white, and *phaios,* brown), denoting a grey, or russet, or brown dusky colour, in allusion to the appearance of the inflorescence.

Vernacular name.—" Cotton Grass " of the United States. This name is sometimes adopted for this grass in Australia.

Where figured.—Agricultural Gazette.

Panicum semialatum, R. Br.

"The Half-winged Panic Grass."

Botanical description (B. Fl., vii, 472).

Stems from a branching base, 1 to 2 feet high.

Leaves narrow, long or short, usually glabrous.

Panicle of few long slender and erect spike-like branches, very unequal, and sometimes reduced to two nearly equal ones, or to a single one, the longest 3 to 4 inches, or in some very lax Queensland specimens, 5 inches long; secondary branches short, slender, erect, the lower ones with four or five sessile or pedicellate spikelets, the upper ones with only one or two.

Spikelets scarcely 1½ lines long, rather acute, densely covered with long silky, silvery, or purple hairs, often spreading when in fruit.

Outer glume scarcely ¼ line long, obtuse.

Second and third glumes nearly equal and empty, both densely hairy, the second usually three-nerved ; the third, five-nerved.

Fruiting glume shorter, smooth, rather acute, and often slightly gibbous at the base.

Botanical notes.—Var. *monostachyon*, Benth. Spike simple as in *P. gibbosum*, but the outer glume present. (Western New South Wales.)

As observed by Bentham, the Australian forms of this species vary much, especially in the degree of development of the inflorescence and the size of the spikelets.

Value as a fodder.—A grass more particularly valuable for the drier districts of the Colony as it is an·excellent resister of drought, and it produces a fair quantity of palatable feed. Like most other grasses, it produces more favourable results with better soil and increased moisture.

Other uses.—The fibrous under part of the leaf is peeled off when young, and twisted with the fingers, as it is drawn off into a thread, and used by Queensland aborigines to make twine. (E. Palmer.)

Habitat and range.—In all the colonies, except Tasmania, most usually in the drier districts, but by no means exclusively so ; it is not uncommon in the Queensland coast districts. It occurs also in tropical Africa and America.

13. Panicum semialatum, R.Br.

Botanical name.—*Semialatum*, half-winged, from the Latin, *semi* half ; *alatum* winged, perhaps in allusion to the membranous outer glume, which is about half the length of the spikelet.

Vernacular name.—" Cockatoo Grass " of parts of Queensland.

Where figured.—*Agricultural Gazette.*

Botanical description (B. Fl., vii, 472).—

Stems erect, 2 to 3 feet high, silky-pubescent about the nodes, otherwise glabrous, or nearly so.

Leaves narrow, with involute margins or subulate, usually pubescent, the lower ones sometimes densely clothed with long silky hairs.

Panicle 3 to 6 inches long, consisting of two to five long erect or slightly diverging branches, clustered at the end of a long peduncle.

Spikelets 2 to 2½ lines long, few together, in erect clusters or short branches along the rhachis.

Glumes all ending in a short subulate point, the outer one membranous, three nerved, about half the length of the spikelet.

C

Second glume the largest, membranous, five-nerved, fringed on each side with long pale or dark-coloured hairs, spreading in fruit, and connected at the base on the intramarginal nerve.

Third glume more rigid, though thin, with a small palea, and sometimes three stamens in the axil.

Fruiting glume more rigid, with a rather longer point, the palea also rigid, but the inflexed margins thin, with a distinct lobe at the base on each side.

Value as a fodder.—A strong-growing useful grass, much relished by stock, particularly when young and tender.

Other uses.—Lumholtz found this grass, in Northern Queensland, to form the principal food of white cockatoos. (Bailey.)

Habitat and range.—Extends from this Colony to Queensland and Northern Australia, from the Liverpool Plains northerly and westerly to the dry country. O'Shanesy says that (in Queensland) it indicates a poor clay soil. It is also found in Africa, and in tropical Asia from Ceylon and the Indian Peninsula to the Malayan Archipelago and South China.

Reference to Plate.—A, Portion of a panicle; B, Spikelet, showing relative size of outer glume; C, Spikelet dissected, showing outer glume, second and third glume, and fruiting glume with its palea; D, Part of fruiting glume, tipped with a minute point, and minutely transversely rugose.

SERIES III.—PASPALOIDEÆ.

Spikelets sessile or very shortly pedicellate, in one or two rows, very rarely in pairs, along the short simple alternate, often distant, spikes or spike-like branches of the panicle, rarely reduced to a single terminal spike.

Spikes erect, several, distant. Spikelets usually sessile, glabrous in two close rows.
　Spikelets oblique, 1 to 1½ lines long, in close regular rows; second
　　glume broad, gibbous; third glume flatter, with a palea in its
　　axil ... ... 17. *P. flavidum.*
　Spikelets nearly straight, 1 to 1½ lines long, the rows not always
　　regular, and sometimes very few in the spike; second and
　　third glumes nearly equal, both empty ... ... 18. *P. gracile.*
Spikes usually approximate, erect, or at length spreading. Spikelets
　　not so closely sessile, nearly 2 lines long, in two rows, and
　　frequently subtended by hairs or bristles. A broad palea in the
　　third glume. Fruiting glumes obtuse, with an awn-like point 20. *P. helopus.*
Spikes distant, at length spreading or reflexed. Spikelets alternate
　　along the rhachis, but not close, and appearing almost uni-
　　seriate.
　Spikelets near together on a flattened rhachis ... ...24. *P. distachyum.*
　Spikes reflexed, the rhachis flattened, ending in an awn-like point,
　　and a rigid awn-like bristle under the lowest spikelet... ... 25. *P. reversum.*

17. Panicum flavidum, Retz.

Botanical name.—*Flavidum*, a Latin word signifying yellow, or inclining to yellow, the " ear " being usually of that colour.

Vernacular names.—" Vandyke Grass." I recommend this local name on account of having seen the large variety in great luxuriance at Vandyke, beyond Springsure, Queensland. (Bailey.) " Warrego Summer Grass."

Where figured.—Duthie, Trinius, *Agricultural Gazette.*

Botanical description (B. Fl., vii, 474).—

Stems erect, branching at the base, rather rigid, attaining 1 to 2 feet, or rather more.
Leaves acute, sometimes rather broad, but the margins involute when dry, glabrous,
  except a few short hairs at the orifice of the sheath.
Panicle of several often numerous, erect distant branches or sessile spikes, the
  lowest sometimes above ½ inch long, the upper one shorter.
Rhachis flexuose, slightly dilated.
Spikelets sessile in about two rows, in the typical form very oblique, ovoid, about
  1½ lines long, or rather more in several Australian specimens.
Outer glume very short, broad, and obtuse.
Second glume the largest, broad, several-nerved, very concave and incurved.
Third smaller, flat on the back, enclosing a palea large and broad in the typical
  form, but no stamens.
Flowering glumes usually shortly acuminate.

Var. *tenuior*, Benth. Spikelets rather small, not quite so oblique, the palea within the third glume usually very small, the fruiting glume very rugose. (Widely distributed over New South Wales; also in Queensland.)

Value as a fodder.—This is undubitably a good grass, producing a large quantity of nutritious, palatable feed, and yielding far more seed than most species. It is not particular as to soil or situation. It is especially valuable for the drier parts of the Colony. Bailey records that it was stated to be the best fattening grass of the Warrego District of Queensland. Duthie states that it affords excellent fodder for both bullocks and horses in India. Bailey speaks of the variety *tenuior* as a small grass, the stems often prostrate from the weight of seed. "It forms a good pasture, as besides the seed it gives a large quantity of leaves." (F.M.B.)

Other uses.—Said to be the cheapest grain grown, and will keep many years without being eaten by insects. For this reason it is stored up as a provision against years of scarcity and famine. (Duthie.)

Habitat and range.—From the Illawarra and Camden Districts and Port Jackson to the table-lands and interior; also in Queensland. It extends over tropical Asia.

18. Panicum gracile, R.Br.

Botanical name.—*Gracile*, a Latin adjective denoting slender or weak, in allusion to the habit of the plant.
Where figured.—*Agricultural Gazette.*
Botanical description (B. Fl., vii, 475).—Erect, much branched towards the base, quite glabrous, usually slender, from under 1 foot to above 1½ feet high, but exceedingly variable in stature and aspect.

Leaves from very narrow to rather broad.
Panicle usually long and slender, the branches or sessile spikes or clusters erect, distant, the lower ones 3 to 4 lines or rarely ½ to 1 inch long, the upper ones smaller,
  often reduced to short clusters or to single spikelets towards the end of the
  panicle.
Rhachis of the branches often but not always produced beyond the last spikelet into
  a point sometimes as long as the spikelet.
Spikelets singly sessile or in pairs, one pedicellate, the other sessile along the rhachis,
  rarely more or less distinctly in two rows almost as in *P. flavidum*, ovoid, 1 to
  1¼ lines long, nearly straight.
Outer glume ovate acute, rather less or more than half as long as the spikelet.
Second and third nearly equal, both empty, membranous, and about five-nerved.
Fruiting glume as long or rather longer, minutely transversely rugose.

Value as a fodder.—A tufty, often rather wiry grass, but nevertheless palatable to stock. It grows in the poorest soils—almost pure sand—as well as in good soils. In favourable situations it forms very large spreading tufts, and forms really superior herbage. It is extensively distributed in the Colony, and is worthy of every encouragement. O'Shanesy testifies that it makes excellent hay.

Habitat and range.—Found in all the colonies except Tasmania. It extends all over this Colony.

20. Panicum helopus, Trin.

Botanical name.—*Helopus,* Greek *helos* a swamp, and *pous* a foot, the grass growing in swamps.

Vernacular name.—The " Kuri," of India.

Where figured.—Duthie, Trinius.

Botanical description (B. Fl., vii, 476).—

Stems usually rather tall.

Leaves lanceolate, often rather broad and cordate at the base, with loose sheaths, usually more or less hirsute, especially the sheath, but sometimes nearly glabrous.

Panicle of few simple branches, sometimes three to five, almost sessile above the last leaf, sometimes six or seven on a rather long peduncle.

Spikelets irregularly alternate in two rows along the rhachis, or the lower ones clustered and the upper ones more distant, ovoid, acute, nearly 2 lines long, pubescent, villous, or glabrous.

Outer glume very short and broad, three-nerved, the second about seven-nerved, the third about the same length, but narrower, five-nerved, with a palea in its axil but no stamens.

Fruiting glume minutely rugose, obtuse, but the central nerve produced into a short, awn-like point, not exceeding the empty glumes.

Botanical notes.—The short, awn-like point to the fruiting glume is its best distinguishing character (Duthie) ; and Bentham points out that not only does it resemble *Eriochloa annulata* in this respect, but the two grasses are somewhat similar in aspect. The spikelet has, however, the outer glume developed, and is not seated on the peculiar disc-like base of *Eriochloa.*

Value as a fodder.—This is a valuable, drought-resisting grass, found in the drier parts of the Colony. It is a useful, nutritious grass, and Duthie observes that it is an excellent fodder-grass for both horses and cattle in India.

Habitat and range.—In the interior of this Colony, and also in South Australia, Queensland, and Northern Australia. Common in tropical Asia and Africa.

24. Panicum distachyum, Linn.

Botanical name.—*Distachyum,* a Latinised form of two Greek words— *dis* (twice) and *stachys* (an ear of corn). The spikelets are sometimes approximate in two distinct rows.

Vernacular names.—" Two-finger Grass" ; the " Rockhampton Hay Grass" of Bailey.

Where figured.—Duthie, Trinius, *Agricultural Gazette.*

Panicum reversum, F. v. M.

"Reflexed Panic Grass."

Botanical description (B. Fl., vii, 478).—

Stems decumbent or creeping, and rooting at the lower nodes ; slender, and ascending to 1 foot, or rather more.
Leaves flat, glabrous, or with a few hairs, especially at the orifice of the sheaths.
Panicle, a few (usually two to four, but occasionally six or seven) distant simple
secund branches, 1 to 2 inches long, at first erect, at length spreading or reflexed,
the *rhachis* slender or slightly dilated, often sprinkled with a few hairs.
Spikelets sometimes loosely alternate along the rhachis almost in a single row ; sometimes more numerous and approximate in two distinct rows, sessile or shortly
stipitate, ovoid, rather acute, 1½ lines long, quite glabrous.
Outer glume scarcely half the length of the spikelets, thin, very broad, the margins
overlapping each other.
Second and third glumes nearly equal, prominently three-nerved ; a narrow palea in
the third.
Fruiting glume nearly as long, very obtuse, hardened, but the three nerves very
visible.

Value as a fodder.—A valuable grass, yielding abundance of nutritious feed. A correspondent from the Wilcannia district refers to it
as a " sweet and hardy grass." It is undoubtedly of great value for
the western as well as the northern districts. It is one of several
indigenous grasses tested at Gracemere, near Rockhampton (Queensland), and considered to be the best for hay-making. Bailey recommends it to be sown with Landsborough grass (*Anthistiria membranacea*) for the purpose of hay. O'Shanesy, also referring to
Queensland, remarks that it is of considerable value as fodder, but
that it must be sown thickly, as otherwise it grows too rank. Duthie
states that as a fodder-grass it is probably as nutritious as any of the
other Indian *Panicums*, but less plentiful.

Other uses.—It has been recommended for consolidating river banks.

Habitat and range.—In the drier parts of the Colony, principally;
also in South Australia, Queensland, and Northern Australia. Widely
distributed over Eastern India and the Malayan Archipelago.

25. Panicum reversum, F.v.M.

Botanical name.—*Reversum*, Latin " turned back," the branches
and the panicle being reflexed (bent or turned back) as shown in the
drawing.
Where figured.—*Agricultural Gazette.*
Botanical description (B. Fl., vii, 478).—A weak, glabrous, rather
glaucous, much-branched grass.

Leaves long and narrow.
Panicle usually of three or four simple distant branches, at first erect, but soon
spreading, and at length reflexed like those of *P. distachyum.*
Rhachis generally, though not always, dilated, produced into a rigid point beyond
the last spikelet, and bearing under the lowest spikelet a rigid linear bristle (an
abortive branch ?) as long as the spikelet.
Spikelets not numerous, alternate and distant along the rhachis so as to appear in
one row ; ovoid, oblong, fully 2 lines long in some specimens, rather under 2
lines in Drummond's.
Outer glume three-nerved, obtuse, at least three-quarters the length of the spikelet.
Second and third glumes equal, many nerved, both empty in the spikelets I examined,
but F. Mueller found a palea in the third.
Fruiting glume hardened, as in the genus.

Value as a fodder.—We know very little about the value of this
grass for fodder ; but, as it is very easily recognised, perhaps friends

in the interior will keep it under observation. It certainly belongs to a group which contains a number of fodder-plants known to be very valuable to the pastoralist, and the appearance of this grass leads one to the belief that it yields a fair quantity of tender herbage. Baron von Mueller records that at the Murchison River, in Western Australia, it attains a height of 3 feet.

Habitat and range.—An interior species; found in all the colonies except Tasmania and Victoria.

Reference to Plate.—A, Portion of a spike, enlarged, showing the flattened rhachis, which ends in an awn-like point, and the rigid awn-like bristle under the lowest spikelet; B, C, Spikelet dissected, showing the outer and second and third glumes; also the fruiting glume and palea; D, Spikelet, showing relative size of outer glume; E, Grain. Note the characteristic way in which the spikes are bent back or reflexed.

SERIES IV.—ECHINOCHLOÆ.

Spikelets sessile and crowded in three or four rows, or irregularly along the simple alternate, usually secund spikes or spikelike branches of the panicle. Glumes sometimes awned.

27. Panicum crus-galli, Linn.

Botanical name.—*Crus-galli* (Latin)—*crus*, the shank, or that part of the leg between the knee and what corresponds to the ankle; *galli* "of a cock." Name given from a fancied resemblance of the crowded spikelets to the foot rather than the leg of a cock.

Vernacular names.—" Barn-yard Grass" of U.S.A. Other American names are " Cock's-foot" (not to be confused with *Dactylis*), " Large Crow-foot Grass," " Water Grass."

Where figured.—Duthie, Vasey, Trinius, *Agricultural Gazette.*

Botanical description (B. Fl., vii, 479).—A coarse, decumbent annual, ascending to 1 or 2 feet, the leaves rather broad, without any ligula.

Panicle dense, and usually secund, of simple branches or sessile spikes, the lowest 1 or 2 inches long, the upper ones gradually shorter; the whole panicle in some varieties densely hispid with the long purplish or green awns.

Spikelets about 1½ lines long, more or less pubescent, acuminate or awned, crowded and clustered along the branches.

Rhachis usually bearing numerous cilia or capillary bristles amongst or below the spikelets.

Outer glume very short and broad.

Second and third glumes nearly equal, and three-nerved, usually ciliate on the margins. *Second* produced into a rather short awn.

Third in the common Australian form, with an awn varying from ½ to 1 inch, and a thin palea, and very rarely a male flower in its axil.

Fruiting glume smooth and shining, without any or only a very short point.

Botanical notes.—The species with which this grass is most likely to be confused is *P. colonum*, a tropical grass, which has been introduced also into this Colony. The two grasses can usually be most readily distinguished by the larger size and the longer awns of *P. crus-galli*. The latter species is, however, exceedingly variable in the matter of awns (" bristles "); sometimes they are quite short and scarcely observable; sometimes great variation exists in the same panicle. Some authorities unite them, but it is better to keep them apart. Perhaps the two species hybridise, which adds to the difficulty of the situation. *P. crus-galli* prefers moister situations than does *P. colonum.*

Value as a fodder.—It is a large, coarse, succulent grass, which may be cut like *Sorghum*, as it produces great bulk of feed. It has shown great adaptability to climate and soil, flourishing in most places which are not too dry. It grows luxuriantly along river-banks, and will not object to moderate alkalinity in the soil.

It is scarcely an exaggeration to say that, during the last few years it has been sent to the Department of Agriculture for inquiry almost as frequently as all other grasses put together. It has been sent from the Coast districts, from the Dividing Range and table-land, and from the Lachlan district. It may also be found in almost every suburb of Sydney, usually at the edges of roads which have not been kerbed and guttered, generally in damp places, and sometimes actually growing in water. It often appears in freshly broken-up land, rubbish-heaps, &c.

Although a recent introduction into many of the localities in which it is now found, it is a real Australian native, although it is also found in many parts of the world.

What is the explanation of its appearance in so many places during the same season can perhaps only be guessed at, and it really does not very much matter. It may have been distributed in seed sent by a Sydney house.

All who express any opinion in regard to it are loud in its praises as a nutritious grass, which produces an enormous quantity of feed. It seeds sometimes at a foot high, but usually it is a much larger plant, attaining a height of 6 feet and even more.

In Rajputana, India, Duthie states that it is considered a good fodder, though not plentiful.

" At the Hatch Experiment Station, in Massachusetts, U.S.A., the crop of this grass was very uniform, averaging 7 feet in height. The yield was at the rate of 11,207 lb. of straw per acre, and 66·7 bushels of seed. When sown for silage or for soiling, at the rate of 1 peck of seed to the acre, the yield was at the rate of from 15 to 18 tons per acre. A field sown on 26th July, after a crop of hay was removed, yielded 12 tons per acre. It is very much liked by stock, and is a valuable forage plant for feeding green or for the silo. It is not so well adapted for hay, as it is a coarse, succulent grass, and rather difficult to dry." (Lamson-Scribner.)

" In New Mexico it is found only as a weed on irrigated land, but one which is not difficult to keep down. The Mexicans cut it and feed it green while waiting for corn to mature.

" Opinion differs very much as to its value as a hay crop, some saying that it is an entirely worthless and troublesome weed, while others are as sure it is a valuable forage plant. In a moist climate it would have the disadvantage of being hard to cure, but in New Mexico's hot sun no such difficulty need be experienced. A field once sown to this grass would always supply a good crop of nutritious hay, since it re-seeds itself. Sown with *Eriochloa punctata* and *Pani-*

cum colonum after the wheat crop has been removed, it would give a crop of at least 2 tons of valuable hay per acre from land generally left to the weeds. If cut just as the seeds were beginning to form and thoroughly cured, such hay would be excellent to feed with Alfalfa (lucerne), and, if properly mixed, the two would make a first-class combination. A little corn added would produce an almost typical ration." (*Some New Mexico Forage Plants*, Bulletin No. 18, March, 1896, p. 65.)

The late Dr. George Vasey, in "*The Agricultural Grasses of the United States*," says of the Barnyard Grass :—"In the Northern States it is esteemed as a rough coarse weed ; in the South it is often utilised and considered a very useful grass. He quotes Dr. Charles Mohe, of Mobile, Alabama, who says :—' It grows luxuriantly, particularly in the lowlands of the coast, is greedily eaten by horses and cattle, and makes a hay of good quality. It is justly regarded as an excellent grass, particularly before it ripens its seed, as in the latter stages of its growth the long and stiff awns of its spikes tend to make it somewhat unpalatable.' He also quotes Professor Phares, of Mississippi, who says :—' In Louisiana, Mississippi, and some other States, it is mowed annually. Some farmers assure me that they harvest 4 or 5 tons of hay per acre. It may be cut twice each season by making the first mowing as soon as it begins to bloom. I know no one who plants it ; but it annually re-seeds the ground and requires no cultivation or other care, save protection from live stock and the labour of harvesting. Being a coarse grass, with long leaves and large succulent stems, it requires care to make into hay. In one county of Mississippi, hundreds of acres are annually mowed on single farms. Cows and horses are very fond of it whether green or dry. Farmers who have tested it most thoroughly for many years prefer it to the best corn fodder.' "

Here is a Canadian opinion of it :—" A tall coarse grass, producing a great quantity of succulent feed, which is highly relished by stock. It grows in low land and around dwellings throughout the country. In the early stages of growth it is excellent and nutritious feed ; but as it reaches maturity, in common with most grasses, it deteriorates rapidly—indeed somewhat more rapidly than any other." (Fletcher, *Bulletin* No. 19, Central Experimental Farm, Ottawa.)

Mr. Fletcher also gives an analysis of a Canadian specimen of this grass. The sample selected was in flower. Following is its percentage composition :—

	In fresh or green substance.	Calculated to water free substance.
Water	85·30	....
Ash...	1·64	11·16
Protein (albuminoids)	2·02	13·75
Fibre	4·48	31·09
Nitrogen free extract (carbo-hydrates)	6·25	41·87
Ether extract (fat)	·31	2·13
	100·00	100·00

It will be interesting to compare these analyses with those of three samples of grass of American growth, as quoted in Dr. Vasey's work :—

	In fresh or green substance.			Calculated to water free substance.		
	1.	2.	3.	1.	2.	3.
Water*	14·30	14·30	14·30	......	......	......
Ash	5·98	13·37	10·13	6·98	16·07	11·82
Albuminoids	6·66	3·42	10·80	7·77	3·99	12·60
Fibre	24·78	26·68	21·69	28·91	31·13	25·32
Nitrogen free extract ...	46·44	40·08	40·95	54·19	46·77	47·77
Fat	1·84	1·75	2·13	2·15	2·04	2·49
	100·00	100·00	100·00	100·00	100·00	100·00

* These samples were, of course, very much drier than the Canadian sample.

The percentages of total nitrogen, or non-albuminoids, and of nitrogen as non-albuminoid substances, are also given, and at page 139 an analysis by Wolff of the ash of this grass is given, but it will be sufficient to quote where they are to be found. The other analyses quoted by Dr. Vasey are by Clifford Richardson.

Speaking generally, it may therefore be said that the grass arrives at its greatest perfection in moist warm localities ; in colder climes it gives less satisfaction. I have shown that it will grow in many parts of our Colony, and I would recommend farmers to give every encouragement to it for horse and cattle feed. It is too coarse for sheep. An advantage of it is the freedom with which it seeds.

Other uses.—The grain is eaten by the poorer classes in India, and is also used for making into " khir." Duthie was informed that it was frequently used in the Lahore district as a food-grain. Lamson-Scribner alludes to a tall glabrous form, the seeds, which are produced abundantly, being collected by the Mohave Indians of the United States, ground into flour, and cooked for food. He also states that a variety introduced from Japan has been cultivated at some of the U.S. Experiment Stations, and treated as a millet.

Habitat and range.—Found in all the colonies except Tasmania. Perhaps truly indigenous only in the coast districts, but it is impossible now to define the area. A common weed in most hot and some temperate countries.

SERIES V.—MYUROIDEÆ.

Spikelets not silky, crowded and clustered in a dense continuous or rarely interrupted cylindrical spikelike panicle.

29. Panicum indicum, Linn.

Botanical Name.—*Indicus*—Latin, Indian—in allusion to the country from which the grass was first described.

Where figured.—Trinius.

Botanical description (B. Fl., vii, 480).—

Stems decumbent at the base, ascending to 6 or 8 inches in the smaller varieties, above 1 foot high in the larger ones.
Leaves narrow.
Spikelike panicle cylindrical, continuous or rarely interrupted, ½ to 1 inch, or in some varieties 2 inches long.
Spikelets crowded, narrow, acuminate, and more or less curved, 1 to 1½ or rarely 2 lines long.
Outer glume three-nerved, about half the length of the spikelet or rather more.
Second glume curved and gibbous at the base, often ciliate, seven or nine nerved.
Third glume the same length, but straighter and neither gibbous nor ciliate, with a small palea in its axil.
Fruiting glume considerably shorter.

Value as a fodder.—This is a moisture-loving grass, and hence valuable for cultivation or encouragement in very wet situations. We do not know much about its fodder value, but it is probably nutritious, like so many of its congeners.

Habitat and range.—Usually found in swamps and moist situations. Extends from the Illawarra along the Coast districts to Queensland and Northern Australia. It is also widely dispersed over tropical Asia and Africa.

Series VI.—Paniculatæ.

Panicle-branches usually more or less divided. Spikelets all ped cellate (except sometimes the first three species and a Queensland one, *P. inæquale*).

Panicle-branches scarcely divided ; spikelets few, rarely more numerous, scarcely under 2 lines long ; no male flowers.
Spikelets nearly or sometimes quite sessile (species approaching the *Paspaloideæ*).
Spikelets 2 to 2½ lines long, mostly distant along the branches   31. *P. foliosum.*
Spikelets rather under 2 lines, crowded on the lower part of the branches in a compact panicle, second and third glumes almost equal ...   . 32. *P. adspersum.*
Spikelets few, distinctly pedicellate in a loose spreading panicle.
Spikelets 2½ to 3 lines long, sprinkled with hooked hairs. Fruiting glume close above the others ...   . 34. *P. uncinulatum.*
Panicle narrow or spreading ; spikelets numerous, 1 to near 2 lines long ; shortly pedicellate, not clustered ; glumes acute or acuminate ; a male flower in the third glume. ...   ... 39. *P. repens.*
Spikelets ½ to ¾ line long ; no male flower ; diffuse or creeping ; panicle-branches few, spreading ; spikelets few and distant, ¾ line long, on short pedicels   ...   . 41. *P. pygmæum.*
Spikelets usually numerous, 1 to near 2 lines long, pedicellate ; no male flower.
Panicle narrow, branches usually few ; fruiting glume densely pubescent ...   . 44. *P. marginatum.*
Fruiting glume smooth and shining ; panicle 1 to 2 inches long ; spikelets about 1 line ; outer glume ovate, acute ; leaves glabrous   ...   . 46. *P. obseptum.*
Panicle spreading, with numerous capillary branches.
Panicle-branches scattered, neither clustered nor verticillate.
Spikelets 1 line long, acute ; outer glume acute ; a palea in the third glume   ...   . 48. *P. bicolor.*
Spikelets 1 line long, rather obtuse ; outer glume acute ; no palea in the third glume ...   . 49. *P. melananthum.*
Lower panicle-branches clustered, but scarcely verticillate.
Spikelets about 1 line ; outer glume acute, half as long as the spikelet ; a palea in the third glume ; nodes prominently ciliate ; ligula a ring of long cilia ...   . 50. *P. effusum.*

Panicum adspersum, Trin.

Spikelets of *P. effusum*, nodes glabrous, ligula very short ... 51. *P. Mitchelli*.
Spikelets about 1 line, outer glume short, broad, truncate,
   or scarcely acute, nerveless; a palea in the third glume 52. *P. decompositum*.
Lower panicle-branches verticillate, outer glume nearly as long
   as the others ; a palea in the third glume.
Ligula very short, with ring of cilia ... ... 53. *P. trachyrhachis*.
Ligula prominent, scarious, without cilia... ... ... 54. *P. prolutum*.

31. Panicum foliosum, R. Br.

Botanical name.—Foliosum, Latin for leafy or full of leaves, descriptive of this grass.

Botanical description (B. Fl., vii, 481).—

Stems 1 to 2 feet high, decumbent at the base.

Leaves rather broad, usually pubescent, the nerve-like margins often undulate.

Panicle loose, with few distant simple branches, the rhachis flexuose and slender, the lower branches sometimes 2 to 3 inches long.

Spikelets few, distant, almost sessile or distinctly pedicellate, and the lower pedicels sometimes bearing two spikelets, all above 2 lines long in the typical form, ovoid, acute, pubescent, or glabrous.

Outer glume about half as long as the spikelet, very broad, acute, with about seven nerves.

Second and third glumes nearly equal, five or seven nerved ; a rather broad palea in the third.

Fruiting glume minutely rugose without the point of *P. helopus* and its allies, but usually with a short callous incurved tip.

Value as a fodder.—This is more a Queensland grass than a New South Wales one, and I therefore quote the remarks of two Queenslanders in regard to it :—

" One of our most valuable perennial grasses, and admirably adapted for resisting very severe drought. Cattle of every description are fond of it. It delights in rich alluvial soil, where it attains a height of 3 to 4 feet." (O'Shanesy).

" A handsome, broad-leaved grass, found usually on broken land, the borders of scrubs and river sides, or amongst rocks. Of straggling habit, the whole plant clothed with short hairs; does not bear feeding off, for stock destroy it by pulling it up by the roots, it has so slight a hold of the ground." (Bailey).

Other uses.—It has been recommended for growth on river banks.

Habitat and range.—Northern New South Wales and Queensland, in the Coast districts.

32. Panicum adspersum, Trin.

Botanical name.—Adspersum—Latin for besprinkled, or scattered, referring to the scattered hairs on the spikelets.

Where figured.—Trinius, *Agricultural Gazette.*

Botanical description (B. Fl., vii, 481)—

Stems ascending to 1 foot or rather more, glabrous, except the ciliate nodes.

Leaves flat, rather broad and short, the sheaths broader upwards, prominently ciliate. The lamina almost cordate at the base, with a very short ciliate ligula.

Panicle narrow, rather dense, 1½ to 3 inches long, with several erect and slightly spreading branches, all glabrous, without any, or with very few small cilia under the spikelets.

Spikelets ovoid, rather acute, quite glabrous, 1½ to near 2 lines long, crowded or clustered in the lower part of the branches, singly sessile towards the end.

Outer glume one-quarter to one-third as long as the spikelet, rather acute, one or three-nerved.
Second and third glumes nearly equal.
Second broad, usually prominently seven-nerved.
Third narrower, with about five nerves, and enclosing a long palea.
Fruiting glume tipped with a minute point and minutely transversely rugose.

Value as a fodder.—This is a leafy and free-seeding grass, and doubtless produces a fairly bulky quantity of nutritious fodder. At the same time the records and observations in regard to its value for grazing are scanty in the extreme.

Habitat and range.—In the interior districts of this Colony and also of South Australia and Queensland. Found also in the West Indies (San Domingo).

Reference to Plate.—A, Part of panicle; B, Spikelet, showing the relative size of the outer glume (which is three-nerved); C, Spikelet dissected, showing outer and second (the larger) glume, the third glume; also, the fruiting glume and palea.

34. Panicum uncinulatum, R.Br.

Botanical name.—*Uncinulatum*—Latin, signifying "beset with little hooks," referring to the rigid hooked hairs on the glumes.

Botanical description (B. Fl., vii, 482).—Glabrous erect and much branched, attaining sometimes 8 feet.

Nodes often much thickened.
Leaves flat, narrow, tapering into fine points.
Panicle terminal, loose and slender, consisting of few distant spreading simple or scarcely divided branches.
Rhachis almost filiform.
Spikelets few and distant along the branches, usually purplish, 2½ to 3 lines long.
Outer glume lanceolate, about half the length of the spikelet.
Second and third nearly equal, acutely acuminate, seven or sometimes nine nerved, sprinkled with short, erect, rigid, hooked hairs; a small palea in the third.
Fruiting glume smaller, quite smooth.

Value as a fodder.—A grass usually met with in mountain scrubs, also amongst brigalow; it forms large tufts or tussocks, and furnishes in many places the principal scrub fodder both in New South Wales and Queensland. (Bailey.) It delights in the seclusion of our dense scrubs, where its wiry, perennial stems are found scrambling to a length of 9 to 10 feet, and its foliage, though scanty, is tender and nutritious, making a delicate repast for the innumerable wallabies and padamelons which inhabit those places. It is, perhaps, the tallest of ordinary fodder grasses. (O'Shanesy).

Habitat and range.—In our Colony, in the northern Coast district, extending to the interior. Found also in Queensland.

39. Panicum repens, Linn.

Botanical name.—*Repens*—Latin, creeping, referring to the rooting stems.
Vernacular name.—"Creeping Panic-grass."

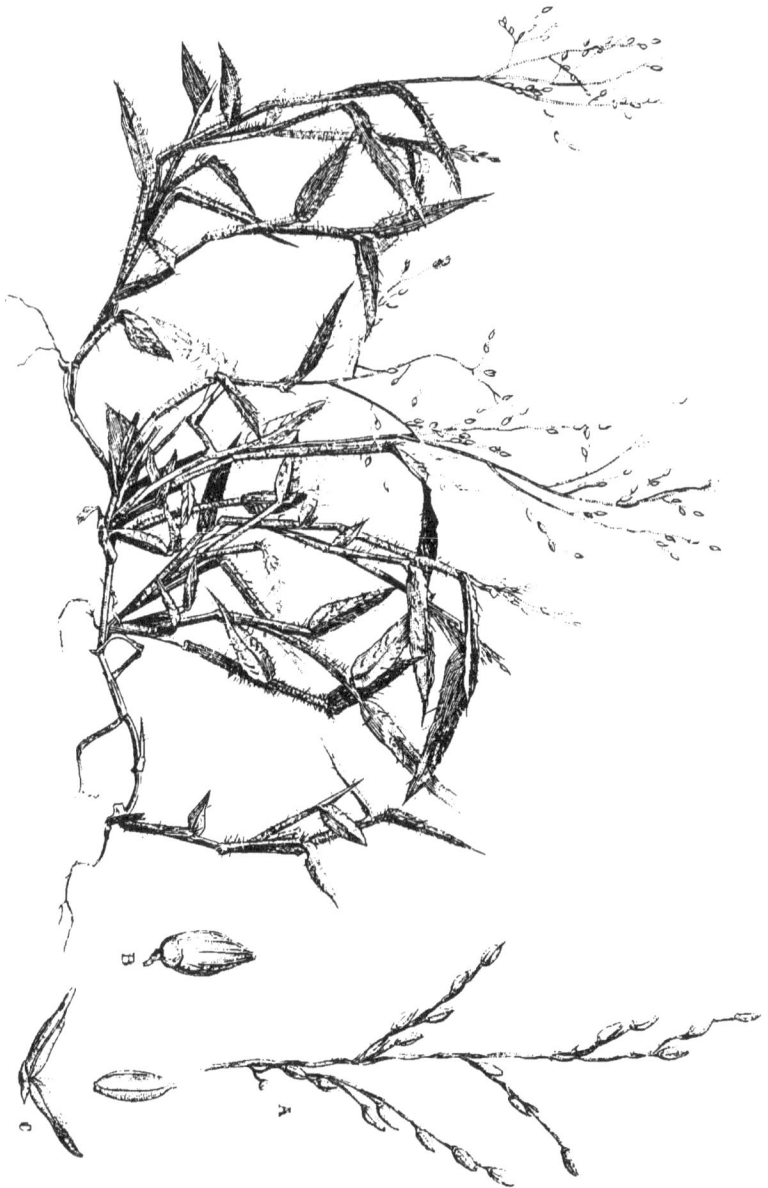

Panicum pygmæum, R. Br.

"The Pigmy Panic Grass."

Botanical description (B. Fl., vii, 484)—

Stems from a creeping and rooting base, ascending to 1 or 2 feet, rather stiff, the nodes glabrous.
Leaves narrow, more or less pubescent or hairy, or sometimes quite glabrous, ligula short, ciliate.
Panicle narrow, with a few long branches, erect or at length spreading, the spikelets shortly pedicellate, irregularly crowded on short secondary branches, with a filiform flexuose rhachis.
Spikelets 1½ lines long, glabrous, or the nerves of the glumes minutely ciliolate.
Outer glume less than half the length of the spikelet, acute, one-nerved.
Second and third glumes nearly equal, acute or acuminate, prominently three or five nerved ; a male flower in the third.
Fruiting glume acute, smooth or minutely rugose.

Value as a fodder.—Duthie quotes Royle and Roxburgh as stating that cattle are fond of this grass in India. Not much is known in regard to its fodder value in Australia. It will grow well in shady situations.

Other uses.—Lamson-Scribner asserts that it has no agricultural value, but that it is a natural sand-binder, stating that upon the sandy islands lying off the coast of the Gulf of Mexico it grows abundantly upon the outside of the dunes, protecting them from the action of the winds and waves.

Habitat and range.—In the Coast districts of this Colony, extending to Queensland and Northern Australia. Found also in Victoria. Common in maritime districts in Southern Asia, the Mediterranean region, apparently in Brazil, also in the Pacific Islands.

41. Panicum pygmæum, R.Br.

Botanical name.—*Pygmæum*—Latin, small or dwarfish. It is a small grass.
Vernacular name.—The " Pigmy Panic-grass."
Where figured.—*Agricultural Gazette.*
Botanical description (B. Fl., vii, 484).—A small species, creeping and rooting at the nodes, ascending to about 6 inches.

Leaves rarely above 1 inch long, linear or lanceolate, ciliate, and usually but not always sprinkled with long hairs.
Panicle short and spreading with a few capillary flexuose simple or slightly divided branches.
Spikelets few and distant, scarcely 1 line long, obtuse, glabrous.
Outer glume very short, broad, truncate, nerveless.
Second and third glumes equal, three or five nerved, both empty.
Fruiting glume smooth and shining.

Value as a fodder.—Probably small ; it is a dainty little grass which forms a dense, short turf even under the shade of trees, and hence valuable for such situations.
Habitat and range.—Coast district and Dividing Range from Port Jackson northwards through Queensland.

*Reference to Plate—*A, Portion of a panicle ; B, Spikelet, showing relative size of outer glume, which is very short, broad, and truncate ; C, Spikelet dissected, showing small outer glume, the 2nd and 3rd glumes, which are equal in size, and 3 and 5 nerved ; also the fruiting glume.

44. Panicum marginatum, R.Br.

Botanical name.—*Marginatum*—Latin, margined, referring to the leaves, which are prominently margined (showing a pale edge or margin).

Vernacular names.—I know of none; but, in order to distinguish it from the large number of other Panic-grasses, the half-botanical, half-vernacular name of "The Marginal-leaved Panic-grass" is suggested.

Where figured.—Trinius (type, also variety *strictum*), *Agricultural Gazette.*

Botanical description (B. Fl., vii, 485).—A rather slender but often rigid grass, decumbent, branching and often rooting at the base, ascending to 1 foot or more, glabrous except the cilia at the orifice of the sheaths, and the rhachis of the inflorescence often slightly pubescent.

Leaves flat, usually narrow, but exceedingly variable in size.
Panicle narrow, in the typical form 1½ to 3 inches long, of few erect or scarcely spreading simple or slightly divided branches.
Spikelets irregularly crowded along the branches, or sometimes almost in a single row, ovoid, obtuse, or scarcely acute, about 1¼ lines long.
Outer glume very thin, not one-third the length of the spikelet, one-nerved, or faintly three-nerved.
Second and third glume nearly equal and similar, both empty, membranous, three or five nerved, glabrous.
Fruiting glume rather short, slightly hardened, and densely silky-pubescent or villous, as well as the exposed part of the palea.

Botanical notes.—There is also a variety *strictum*, described by Bentham in the following words:—"Stems slender, rigid, much branched, with very short narrow leaves, the panicle narrow, very little branched, and sometimes reduced to a simple uninterrupted spike."

Bentham states, subsequently: "Some specimens seem to show that the var. *strictum* is rather an after-growth from plants that have been cut down than a distinct variety."

Whether extended observations should confirm that the cause is cutting down by man or herbivorous animals, I would add that I have specimens which show various stages between the normal species and the so-called variety. At the same time, I think it would be convenient to retain the name for the variety, as extreme forms of the species are very dissimilar in appearance.

As Bentham emphasises, the species is really known by the dense pubescence of the fruiting glume, which has not been observed in any other *Panicum.* Neglect of observation of this characteristic may cause the student to stumble, as some other grasses resemble this one a good deal in general appearance.

Bentham describes a coarse-growing variety of this species (*majus*) which is found in Queensland, and might be looked for in the northern parts of this Colony:—"The stems are tall, with broad leaves 6 inches long, the lower branches of the panicle 3 or 4 inches, and the spikelets above 1¼ line long."

Value as fodder.—Though not a grass of the first rank as a fodder-plant, I believe its value has sometimes been understated. I have

Panicum marginatum, R. Br.

"A Panic Grass."

47

seen cattle eat it many a time ; nevertheless, as it gets old, it becomes harsh and fibrous, and less acceptable to herbivorous animals, particularly where occurring in dry rocky places. On the northern rivers it is less succulent than further south—say from Port Jackson to Gippsland. Its decumbent joint-rooting habit renders it sometimes serviceable to form a first growth of grass on newly-made ground.

Habitat and range.—This grass is confined to the three eastern Colonies, extending from Eastern Gippsland as far as the southern parts of North Queensland. It is confined to the coast and coast-mountain districts, not extending far inland. Baron von Mueller records it from as far west as New England in this Colony.

Reference to Plate.—A and B, Portions of a panicle variously enlarged ; c, Spikelet, showing relative size and outer glume ; D, Spikelet dissected, showing outer glumes, silky, pubescent fruiting glume and palea ; E, front and back views of seed (grain). All variously magnified.

46. Panicum obseptum, Trin.

Botanical name.—*Obseptum*—Latin for "hedged in, or shut up against," perhaps in allusion to the ligula, which consists of a ring of cilia.

Botanical description (B. Fl., vii, 486).—A weak glabrous grass, decumbent at the base or creeping in the mud, and shortly ascending.

Leaves narrow, the *ligula* a ring of cilia.

Panicle narrow and loose, 1 to 2 inches long, of few simple or scarcely divided branches.

Spikelets few, pedicellate, the upper one of each primary branch solitary, the lower ones two or three together on short secondary branches, all narrow, ovoid, 1 to 1½ line long, quite glabrous, rather obtuse.

Outer glume short, broad, nerveless, truncate or shortly acute.

Second and third equal or nearly so, membranous, five-nerved, both empty.

Fruiting glume rather acute, smooth and shining.

Value as a fodder.—Unknown.

Habitat and range.—Confined to this Colony, as far as we know at present. Port Jackson to New England (coast to tableland) in muddy places.

48. Panicum bicolor, R. Br.

Botanical name.—*Bicolor*—Latin for two-coloured, referring to the spikelets.

Where figured. Agricultural Gazette.·

Botanical description (B. Fl., vii, 487).—Usually a small slender tufted grass, with much the habit of some species of *Aira* or *Agrostis*, but sometimes above 1 foot high, approaching in habit *P. melananthum.*

Leaves linear, usually very narrow, more or less hairy, especially at the orifice of the sheath, rarely quite glabrous.

Ligula very short, ciliate.

Panicle usually only 2 or 3 inches long, loose and slender, but rather narrow, but sometimes larger and spreading.

Branches capillary and flexuose, not clustered and not much divided.

Spikelets all pedicellate, about 1 line long, glabrous.

Outer glume acute, three-nerved, fully half as long as the spikelet.

Second and third glume nearly equal, acute, about five-nerved.

Third with a palea but not stamens.

Fruiting glume smooth and shining.

48

Value as a fodder.—A useful grass, hardy, and palatable to stock. Not frequently reported upon, probably because it has been confused with other species.

Habitat and range.—Found in New South Wales and Queensland. In our Colony, from north to south, from the coast to the tablelands. Speaking of Queensland, Bailey says it is always found on high stony dry land. In this Colony it is apparently more accommodating as to soil and situation.

49. Panicum melananthum, F.v.M.

Botanical name.—*Melananthum*, from two Greek words, *melan* black, and *anthos* a flower, referring to the dark colour of the flowers.
Vernacular names.—The " Black-seeded Panic-grass."
Where figured.—*Agricultural Gazette.*
Botanical description (B. Fl., vii, 488).—A glabrous grass of 2 feet or more, decumbent at the base and perhaps annual.

Leaves flat and rather broad.
Ligula exceedingly short, ciliate.
Panicle sessile, or nearly so, within the last leaf, large and loose, with very numerous much divided capillary branches scattered along the main rhachis, and very rarely clustered.
Spikelets all pedicellate, about 1 line long, acute, glabrous, often dark-coloured.
Outer glume ovate, acute, one or sometimes three nerved, nearly half the length of the spikelet.
Second and third glumes nearly equal, acute, rather broad, membranous, with usually five not prominent nerves.
Third quite empty, without any palea.
Fruiting glume smooth and shining.

Value as a fodder.—A moderately tall grass, yielding a fair amount of nutritious fodder. It may be distinguished by its panicle of nearly black seeds.
Habitat and range.—From Victoria to Queensland. In our Colony, from the Coast districts to the table-lands.

50. Panicum effusum, R.Br.

Botanical name.—*Effusum*, Latin, wide, open, spread out, referring to the panicle.
Where figured.—Trinius, *Agricultural Gazette.*
Botanical description (B. Fl., vii, 488).—An erect perennial; our specimens mostly under 1 foot, but said to attain 2 feet.

Leaves lanceolate or linear-lanceolate, scabrous, and hairy, as well as the sheaths.
Nodes bearded with long spreading hairs.
Ligula very short and ciliate.
Panicle much branched, sessile within the last leaf, 3 to 4 inches long when first in flower, at length twice as long, with filiform *divided branches* very spreading and flexuose, the lower ones densely clustered but not verticillate, the upper ones scattered and distant.
Spikelets all pedicellate, acute, about 1 line long, glabrous.
Outer glume acute, one to three nerved, about half the length of the spikelet, or rather more.
Second and third glumes nearly equal, five or seven‾nerved, a palea within the third, about half its length.
Fruiting glume smooth and shining.

Botanical notes.—Var. *convallium,* less hairy, and more or less glaucous.

Value as a fodder.—A useful grass, which has very extended geographical range, valuable alike in the coast country and in the dry interior. It is an excellent grass, nutritious, and palatable. Speaking of a test at the Wollongbar Farm, Mr. McKeown reports : " It is too light for pasture, being easily destroyed by stock."

Habitat and range.—Found in all the colonies, except Tasmania. In this Colony, from the Coast districts to the dry interior.

51. Panicum Mitchelli, Benth.

Botanical name.—*Mitchelli,* in honor of Major (afterwards Lieut.-Colonel Sir Thomas) Mitchell, an explorer, and for many years Surveyor-General of the Colony, who collected the grass on one of his journeys.

Botanical description (B. Fl., vii, 489).—An erect grass, decumbent at the base only, 2 or 3 feet high ; nearly allied to *P. effusum,* but larger ; quite glabrous, and the nodes not bearded.

Leaves often long.
Short ligula rather jagged than ciliate.
Panicle usually very large and spreading, with very numerous divided filiform branches, the lower ones clustered and rigid, the upper ones scattered.
Spikelets all pedicellate, usually several along the ultimate branches, rather above 1 line long, acutely acuminate, quite glabrous.
Outer glume acute, nearly half the length of the spikelet, one to three-nerved.
Second and third glumes nearly equal, acutely acuminate, about five-nerved.
Palea in the third sometimes very small, more frequently above half the glume.
Fruiting glume smooth and shining.

Value as a fodder.—An even more valuable grass than the preceding, to which it is closely allied.

Habitat and range.—In all the colonies, except Tasmania and Western Australia. In this Colony, from the coast to the interior, but more common in the dry country.

52. Panicum decompositum, R.Br.

Botanical name.—*Decompositum,* Latin, divided, or not set together, alluding to the branches and the panicle.

Synonyms.— *P. laevinode,* Lindl. ; also, *P. paludosum,* Roxb. (probably).

Vernacular Names.—" Native Millet," " Umbrella Grass." Sometimes called " Barley Grass." The seed used to be called "Cooly " by Western New South Wales aborigines, and "Tindil " by the aborigines of the Cloncurry River (North Queensland).

Where figured.—*Agricultural Gazette.*

Botanical description (B. Fl., vii, 489).—A semi-aquatic glabrous grass, often tall and stout.

Leaves mostly long, flat, and rather broad, especially when growing in water, narrow in drier situations.
Ligula very short and broad, ciliate.
Panicle 6 inches to 1 foot long, or even more, with numerous crowded filiform divided branches, the lower ones clustered, at first erect, and enclosed at the base within the last leaf sheath, at length sometimes very loose and spreading to the breadth of 1 foot.

D

Spikelets all on slender pedicels, narrow, acute, 1¼ to 1½ lines long, usually of a pale straw colour.

Outer glume very short, broad and truncate, thin and nerveless.

Second and third glumes nearly equal, acute, thinly membranous, five or seven-nerved, the third, with a palea from one-quarter or one-third its length, but no stamens.

Fruiting glume very smooth and shining.

Value as a fodder.—It affords a bulky, palatable, and nutritious fodder. It is worthy of extensive cultivation, particularly in the western country—an operation which is rendered the easier because it yields abundance of seed.

Other uses.—The aborigines convert the very small millet-like grains into cakes, which are really nutritious.

Alluding to this grass, Sir Thomas Mitchell (*Three Expeditions*, pp. 237 and 290), says :—" In the neighbourhood of our camp the grass had been pulled to a very great extent, and piled in hay-ricks, so that the aspect of the desert was softened into the agreeable semblance of a hay-field. The grass had evidently been thus laid up by the natives, but for what purpose we could not imagine. At first I thought the heaps were only remains of encampments, as the aborigines sometimes sleep on a little dry grass, but when we found the ricks, or hay-cocks, extending for miles, we were quite at a loss to understand why they had been made. All the grass was of one kind, and not a spike of it was left in the soil, over the whole of the ground. . . . We were still at a loss to know for what purpose the heaps of one particular kind of grass had been pulled, and so laid up hereabouts. Whether it was accumulated by the natives to allure birds, or by rats, as their holes were seen beneath, we were puzzled to determine. The grass was beautifully green beneath the heaps, and full of seeds, and our cattle were very fond of this hay."

Mr. E. Palmer, in describing the food-stuffs of the Cloncurry (Queensland) aborigines, thus refers to this grass :—" Has a fine yellow seed like lucerne seed, which is gathered when the seed is just opened from the sheath. It is winnowed and ground between two stones, mixed with water into a kind of paste or thick gruel, and poured into the hot ashes, making a sort of damp bread, very nourishing and satisfying."

Habitat and range.—A moisture-loving species, found in all the colonies except Tasmania. It is diffused throughout the Colony, but is most plentiful in the western districts. It has been doubtfully recorded also from Asia.

53. Panicum trachyrhachis, Benth.

Botanical name.—*Trachyrhachis*, from two Greek words—*trachys*, rough or harsh, and *rhachis*, the backbone (as applied to animals), the *rhachis* (in botany) or axis supporting a flowering stem. In this grass the *rhachis* is rough, and so are the branches and the panicle.

Vernacular name.—" Oo-kin " of the aborigines of the Mitchell River, Northern Queensland.

Where figured.—*Agricultural Gazette.*

Panicum trachyrhachis, Benth.

51

Botanical description (B. Fl., vii, 490).—A tall, erect, stout, glabrous plant, nearly allied to *P. decompositum.*

Leaves long and narrow.

Ligula reduced to a ring of cilia, the nodes glabrous.

Panicle large and loose, often 1 to 1½ feet long, with numerous long slender divided branches, the lower ones usually verticillate, scabrous as well as the *rhachis.*

Spikelets all pedicellate, nearly 1½ lines long.

Outer glume often as long as the others, three or five-nerved, tapering into a long point sometimes ciliate at the end.

Second and third glumes nearly equal, acutely acuminate, seven or nine-nerved, the third with a palea often nearly as long, but no stamens in any of the specimens examined.

Fruiting glume much shorter, obtuse, smooth, and shining.

Var., tenuior.—More slender, panicle not so large, and less scabrous, and the glumes less acute (the form found in this Colony).

Value as a fodder.—A coarser plant than *P. decompositum,* which, however, it resembles in value for grazing purposes.

Other uses.—"The fibre is peeled from the under surface of the leaf, by breaking it in the middle across with a sudden jerk while held between the fingers, and drawing the threads away. They are twisted up at once into twine by the Cloncurry (Queensland) natives. (E. Palmer.)

The aborigines sometimes used the grain for food.

Habitat and range.—Found in this Colony, and also Queensland and Northern Australia. With us it has only been found in the north-west of the Colony, but in the other colonies in the Coast districts.

Reference to Plate.—A, Portion of a panicle, note the pedicellate spikelets; B, Spikelet, showing relative size of outer glume; c, Spikelet dissected, showing outer glume, 2nd, and 3rd glume; D, Fruiting glume and its palea.

54. Panicum prolutum, F.v.M.

Botanical name.—*Prolutum*—Latin for soaked or drenched, the grass being usually found in damp situations.

Where figured.—*Agricultural Gazette.*

Botanical description (B. Fl., vii., 490).—

Stems from a branching base erect, rigid, 1 to 2 feet high.

Leaves rather rigid, the margins involute when dry, glabrous and glaucous.

Ligula very prominent, scarious, truncate, or slightly jagged.

Panicle 3 to 6 inches long, of numerous slender divided branches, the lower ones clustered, erect, and enclosed at the base by the last sheath, or at length exserted and spreading.

Spikelets on filiform pedicels, ovoid, acute, glabrous, about 1¼ lines long.

Empty glumes rather rigid, prominently nerved, the outer one obtuse, with scarious margins, more than half the length of the spikelet, three or five nerved, the second and third nearly equal, acute, five or seven nerved, no palea in the third.

Fruiting glume smooth and shining.

Botanical note.—Readily distinguished from all other members of the group by the much longer, non-ciliate ligule.

Value as a fodder.—Possessing much the same properties, and of much the same value as *P. decompositum,* and, like that grass, one of the most valuable of our interior species.

Other uses.—In former years, the seeds of this grass were gathered in large quantities by the aborigines as an article of food, and being ground between two stones, were converted into a kind of meal.

Habitat and range.—Found in all the colonies except Tasmania and Western Australia, in the interior.

O'Shanesy speaks in the following words of a Queensland grass, probably allied to the last few species :—" Also from the seeds of a tall grass (evidently a *Panicum*), known by the aborigines as 'Pawpa,' which is treated in a similar manner to the yellow-box seeds. Hats are made from the stem of this grass simply by sewing them together."

4. OPLISMENUS.

Spikelets with one terminal hermaphrodite flower and a rudimentary one below it, awned, clustered along the second distant branches of a simple panicle.

Glumes four, the lowest empty one not much shorter than the others, and with a longer awn, the flowering glume awnless and hardened with the palea round the grain as in *Panicum.*

Lower branches of the panicle ½ to 2 inches long ... ... 1. *O. compositus.*
All the branches of the panicle reduced to sessile clusters ... 2. *O. setarius.*

1. Oplismenus compositus, Beauv.

Botanical name.—*Oplismenus*, from the Greek, *oplei* armed (verb *oplizo*), perhaps in allusion to the slender but prominent awns ; *compositus*, Latin, composite or set together, the inflorescence being much more composite than *O. setarius*, and perhaps than all other species of *Oplismenus.*

Where figured.—Trinius, *Agricultural Gazette.*

Botanical description (B. Fl., vii., 491).—Usually a weak grass, softly pubescent or villous, but sometimes nearly glabrous.

Stems decumbent or creeping and rooting at the base, ascending sometimes to above 1 foot.

Leaves from linear-lanceolate to ovate-lanceolate, 4 to 5 inches long in the larger specimens, but more frequently under 2 inches.

Panicle slender, consisting of four to eight or rarely more distant one-sided branches or spikes, of which the lowest slender ones are 2 inches long in the most luxuriant specimens, scarcely ½ inch long in others, the upper ones or sometimes the greater number reduced to short clusters.

Spikelets glabrous, pubescent, or hirsute, rather above 1 line long, in distinct clusters of two or three each along the longer branches, crowded on the shorter ones.

Glumes, three lower ones membranous, five-nerved, the lowest not much shorter than the others, tapering into a rather long smooth awn ; the *second* with a small point or short awn, or only acuminate ; the *third* rather larger, awnless, with a small hyaline palea or rudimentary flower in its axil.

Flowering glume nerveless, smooth, and hard, as well as the palea round the grain.

Value as a fodder.—Affords a bite for stock, but it is so closely appressed to the ground that they do not often touch it ; it may also not be palatable.

Other uses.—It forms a dense turf under trees, possessing a considerable value for such a purpose in cases where it can get sufficient
moisture. It is a common weed in bush-houses.

Habitat and range.—Victoria to Queensland, in the moister parts.
In our Colony, confined to the Coast districts. Found also in Asia and
the Pacific Islands, and New Zealand.

2. Oplismenus setarius, Rœm. et Schult.

Botanical name.—*Setarius*—Latin, *seta*, a bristle, resembling *Setaria*
(the next genus).

Synonyms.—*O. compositus*, var. *setarius*, according to Mueller.
Panicum imbecille, Trin.

Vernacular name.—" Creeping Beard-grass."

Where figured.—Trinius and Buchanan, as *Panicum imbecille.*

Botanical description (B. Fl., vii., 492).—

Very near the slender forms of *O. compositus*, and perhaps rightly included in that
species by F. Mueller.

Spikes or branches of the panicle all reduced to single sessile clusters of spikelets, or
the lowest rarely slightly elongated into two distinct clusters.

Leaves always narrow lanceolate.

Value as a fodder.—Same as the preceding. Lamson-Scribner
speaks of it as having no recognised agricultural value. Buchanan
states that cattle eat it readily, but points out that their relish for it
must be considerably lessened by the large amount of foreign matter,
such as dead leaves, with which it is usually associated.

Other uses.—This grass also grows under the dense shade of trees,
and hence is very valuable for planting in such situations. It is,
therefore, of use for ornamental purposes, but it must have moisture.
" It can be propagated by pieces of the stem, which root at the joints,
and if cared for, will in a short time make a good turf. A closely-
allied grass of similar habit and growth, with variegated leaves
(*O. Burmanni*, Beauv.), is often grown in green-houses for its ornamental appearance." (Lamson-Scribner.)

Habitat and range.—Same as the preceding species.

5. SETARIA.

Spikelets with one terminal hermaphrodite flower and sometimes a
second male one below it, crowded in a cylindrical dense or rarely
interrupted spikelike panicle, not awned, but surrounded by numerous
awnlike barren branches, persistent on the main *rhachis*, the spikelets
sessile near the base of the branches, and falling away from them.

Glumes four, the outer one small, the second usually shorter than
the third; a palea, and sometimes three stamens in the axil of the
third.

Terminal or *fruiting glume* of a firmer consistence, transversely
rugose, with a perfect flower.

Styles distinct.

Grain enclosed in the hardened glume and palea, but free from them. Awnlike panicle-branches, scabrous, with erect teeth.

Panicle cylindrical, simple, 1 to 1½ inches long, the spikelets solitary
at the base of the awnlike branches ... ... 1. *S. glauca.*

Panicle dense or interrupted, 3 to 8 inches long, the spikelets
clustered near the base of the awnlike branches ... 2. *S. macrostachya.*

1. Setaria glauca, Beauv.*

Botanical name.—*Setaria*, from the Latin *seta*, a bristle, referring to the awn-like, barren branches of the panicle; *glauca*, Latin, grey or blue, or sea-green. In botany, glaucous, *i.e.*, a whitish, waxy-green, like the green of a cabbage-leaf.

Vernacular names.—" Pigeon-grass," " Yellow Foxtail," " Bottle-glass Foxtail " of the United States.

Where figured.—Trinius, Vasey, Hackel, *Agricultural Gazette.*

Botanical description (B. Fl., vii, 492).—An erect annual of a pale green, 1 to 2 feet high.

Leaves flat, with scabrous edges, and often ciliate, with a few long hairs.

Spikelike panicle, simple, cylindrical, 1 to 1½ inches long, the spikelets solitary at the base of numerous awn-like branches, many of which are barren, and all scabrous, with minute teeth directed upwards.

Spikelets ovoid, about 1½ lines long.

Outer glume very small, the second not quite so long as the third ; a *palea* and very rarely stamens in the third.

Fruiting glume more or less gibbous, marked with prominent transverse wrinkles.

Value as a fodder—It is a weed of gardens, orchards, &c., in many parts of the Colony, preferring low-lying situations where the ground has been newly broken up and is moist. It is of a spreading habit, green and succulent, and yields a fair quantity of fodder, which stock eat readily enough. It comes up in the summer months and dies down with the cold weather. Vasey says that it is very common in cultivated fields in the United States, especially amongst stubble after the cutting of grain. It is as nutritious as *S. italica*, but not so productive.

Duthie states that it is generally considered to be a fairly good fodder-grass in India, quoting Symonds, who says that it affords a moderately good fodder, but that it is unsuited for making hay. In the central provinces of India it is used as fodder.

Other uses.—The grain is used as food in the central provinces of India. (Duthie.)

Habitat and range.—Where truly indigenous, usually met with along river banks, &c., where the soil is rich. Found in all the Colonies except Tasmania. In this Colony it occurs in most districts. It is a cosmopolitan species.

---

* Sometimes this author's name is given in the contracted form as Palisot. His full name is A. M. F. J. Palisot de Beauvois, and he is the author of an important work on grasses published at Paris in 1812.

2. Setaria macrostachya, H. B. & K.

Botanical name.—*Macrostachya*, from two Greek words—*macros* long, and *stachys* an ear of corn, in allusion to the comparatively large, spike-like panicles.

Vernacular name.—" Barley Grass." (I have given the name " Barley Grass " to this kind on account of the resemblance it bears to barley grasses, being far greater than that of any of the numerous other grasses called by that name in Queensland. Bailey.)

Where figured.—Bailey.

Botanical description (B. Fl., vii, 493).—Much taller and stouter than *S. glauca.*

Leaves long, flat, often above ½ inch broad.

Ligula short, ciliate, otherwise quite glabrous in the typical form.

Spike-like panicle 3 to 8 inches long, compound, usually very compact and cylindrical, or the lower branches longer.

Spikelets numerous on the lower branches, few on the upper ones, in dense clusters, more or less interspersed with awn-like, barren branches, ovoid, acute, fully 1½ lines long, glabrous.

Outer glume about half the length of the spikelet, the second shorter than the third, but variable in proportion ; all membranous, with prominent nerves.

Fruiting glume often oblique or gibbous, always marked with prominent transverse wrinkles, as in *S. glauca.*

Value as a fodder.—A larger and better grass than the preceding. " Produces a great amount of feed, of which cattle are extremely fond. Frequently found in scrubs bordering rivers. Has a somewhat straggling habit in the scrubs, but when sown in the open field it has been seen to greatly improve, and from what I have seen of it I consider it equal, if not superior, to *S. italica.* Worthy of field culture, either for cutting for green fodder or for grazing." (Bailey.)

Mr. G. McKeown has tested it at the Experiment Farm, Wollongbar, and reports : "An annual grass which has produced a large yield of fodder, making hay of excellent quality, suitable only for cutting, as it would not withstand grazing."

" This is called ' Hungarian Millet,' but has no origin in Hungary. It grows with wonderful rapidity in warm weather, especially when irrigation can be applied, although it will grow on ordinary soils and under ordinary conditions in summer. It will reach a height of about 6 feet in two months in the hottest weather if a good shower or two of rain should fall during January. The fodder is very nutritious, and the seed can be sown at any time from October till February, and will produce a crop within eight or nine weeks." (*The Garden and Field*, vol. xv, p. 16.)

Habitat and range.—Found in all the colonies except Tasmania and Victoria. With us, only specifically recorded from the northern rivers. but from interior localities in the other colonies. Widely diffused in tropical Asia and America.

56

7. PENNISETUM.

Spikelets one-flowered, solitary or two or three together; sessile, or nearly so; each one enclosed in an involucre of several usually numerous simple or plumose bristles (probably awn-like branches of the panicle), the involucres crowded in a spike or spike-like simple panicle, falling off from the main rhachis with the spikelet and short peduncle.

Glumes four, the outer one shorter or sometimes minute.
Second and third both empty.
Fruiting glume usually smaller.
Palea perfect.
Styles distinct or united almost to the plumose stigmas.
Nut enclosed in the more or less hardened glume and palea; free from it.

1. Pennisetum compressum, R.Br.

Botanical name.—*Pennisetum*—Latin, *penna* a feather, and *seta* a bristle, each spikelet being enclosed in an involucre of feathery bristles; *compressum*, pressed close or flattish, the stem being flattish.
Synonym.—*P. japonicum*, Trin. "Closely allied to, if not identical, with this species." (B. Fl.).
Vernacular name.—"Swamp Foxtail Grass."
Where figured.—*Agricultural Gazette.*
Botanical description (B. Fl., vii, 495).—

Stems 2 to 3 feet high, erect, usually very scabrous and more or less hirsute under the panicle, glabrous and smooth lower down.

Leaves long and narrow, glabrous, the ligula prominent.

Involucres nearly sessile in a simple cylindrical dense spike of 3 to 6 inches, consisting of numerous very unequal bristles, the inner more rigid ones varying from ½ to 1 inch.

Outer ones much shorter and finer, mostly minutely scabrous-ciliate, but none of them plumose.

Spikelet solitary, within the involucre; narrow, terete, rather acute, about 3 lines long.

Outer glume under ½ line long, orbicular.

Second glume, from one-third to one-half the length of the spikelet.

Third many-nerved, empty.

Fruiting glume scarcely more rigid than the third.

Styles united up to the feathery branches.

Value as a fodder.—It is a coarse-growing, fibrous grass, little eaten by stock except when young and comparatively tender; when it is old it is as full of fibre as almost any sedge. It grows in large tufts, and when in flower is of an ornamental character.

Habitat and range.—Confined to New South Wales and Queensland, occurring from the southern districts of our Colony from the coast to the tableland. Often found on the margins of swamps, and frequently as tussocks in paddocks in cold districts.

8. CENCHRUS.

Spikelets with one terminal hermaphrodite flower, and sometimes a male one below it, not awned, singly or two or three together, within an ovoid or globular involucre of numerous bristles, the inner ones usually broad and flattened, connected at the base and hardened round the fruit, the involucres sessile or pedicellate in a simple spike or raceme, and falling off with the spikelets.

Glumes four, the outer one much smaller, sometimes minute, the second and third nearly equal, or the second shorter, a palea and sometimes three stamens in the third.

Fruiting glume more rigid than the other, but not so much hardened as in Panicum.

Styles usually very shortly united at the base.

Nut enclosed in the fruiting glume and palea, free from them.

1. Cenchrus australis, R.Br.

Botanical name.—*Cenchrus*, from a Greek word for "millet" (equivalent to the Latin *milium*); *australis*, Latin, southern,—in botanical names it frequently indicates Australian.

Vernacular names.—" Large Burr-grass," " Scrub or Hillside Burrgrass."

Where figured.—*Agricultural Gazette.*

Botanical description (B. Fl., vii, 497).—A stout glabrous grass, attaining 6 to 9 feet.

Leaves long and flat.

Ligula split into cilia.

Spike rather dense, 4 to 8 inches long.

Rhachis slightly scabrous, pubescent.

Involucres very shortly pedicellate, erect or at length reflexed, broadly ovoid, under 4 lines long.

Inner bristles, or lobes, about ten, flattened and very shortly united at the base, plumose in the lower half, scabrous in the upper part, with reversed asperities, one sometimes but not frequently longer than the others.

Outer bristles numerous, unequal, subulate and scabrous from the base.

Spikelets always (?) solitary in the involucre and shorter than the inner lobes.

Outer glume short, obtuse, hyaline, nerveless.

Second glume acute, three or five nerved.

Third rather longer, five-nerved, with a palea and sometimes a male flower in its axil.

Fruiting glume as long.

Value as a fodder.—A long, scrambling, undesirable grass. The herbage it affords is harsh and coarse, while its burrs cling to clothing and to the bodies of animals. There is no doubt that it affords a little feed when young, but I fancy most pastoralists consider that its disadvantages outweigh its advantages. O'Shanesy's statement is that it " is very nutritious, but that its long spikes of clinging seeds prevent cattle from feeding on it."

Habitat and range.—New South Wales and Queensland. O'Shanesy gives its habitat as on moist banks. Bailey says whole hillsides on the ranges may often be seen covered by this grass, both in New South Wales and Queensland. In our Colony it is found on the poorest soils to the best, but it prefers good soil in brush country on hillsides. Found from south (Mount Dromedary) to the north of our Colony in the Coast districts.

9. CHAMÆRAPHIS.

Spikelets with one terminal flower, usually female by abortion and a male one below it, few and distant or solitary on the filiform branches of a simple panicle, the partial rhachis produced into a long awnlike point beyond the insertion of the upper or only spikelet.

Glumes four, the outer empty one very small, the second and third nearly equal, membranous, or at length rigid, many nerved, often tapering to a point, but not awned ; the third with a palea, and three stamens in its axil ; the fourth, or fruiting glume, shorter and very faintly nerved.

Palea with inflected margins, but not auriculate.

Staminodia usually two, very slender, with small abortive anthers.

Styles very shortly united at the base.

Grain enclosed in the scarious, or rather rigid fruiting glume and palea, but free from them. Semi-aquatic grasses, glabrous, or nearly so.

Leaves flat, the ligula short.

Panicle spreading, with distant spikelets on filiform branches. Fruiting glume short and obtuse ... ... 1. *C. spinescens.*
Panicle spikelike but loose, the spikelets often two together on the lower branches. Fruiting glume acute. Outer glume half a line long, membranous ... ... 2. *C. paradoxa.*

1. Chamæraphis spinescens, Poir.

Botanical name.—*Chamæraphis*, Greek, *chamai* for " on the ground," and *raphis* a needle, referring to the awn-like point of the rhachis ; *spinescens*, derived from the Latin *spina*, a thorn or prickle, having much the meaning of *raphis* in the present connection.

Synonym.—*Panicum spinescens*, R.Br.

Botanical description (B. Fl., vii, 498) :—

Stems creeping at the base, and when in water forming large floating masses.

Leaves linear-lanceolate, flat, with loose flattened sheaths, quite smooth, or slightly scabrous.

Panicle, 2 to 4 inches long, with rather numerous filiform, flexuose, spreading branches produced beyond the last spikelet into an awnlike point always longer than the spikelet.

Spikelets few on each branch, distant, shortly pedicellate, but closely appressed in each bend of the rhachis, very narrow, about 3 lines long in the typical form.

Pedicels and rhachis usually minutely scabrous-ciliate.

Outer glume about ½ line long, thinly membranous, the second many-nerved, tapering to a long point ; the third usually rather smaller, with a shorter point and fewer nerves, enclosing the male flower.

Fruiting glume much shorter, obtuse, very thin, and remaining thin as well as the palea over the grain which readily falls out of them.

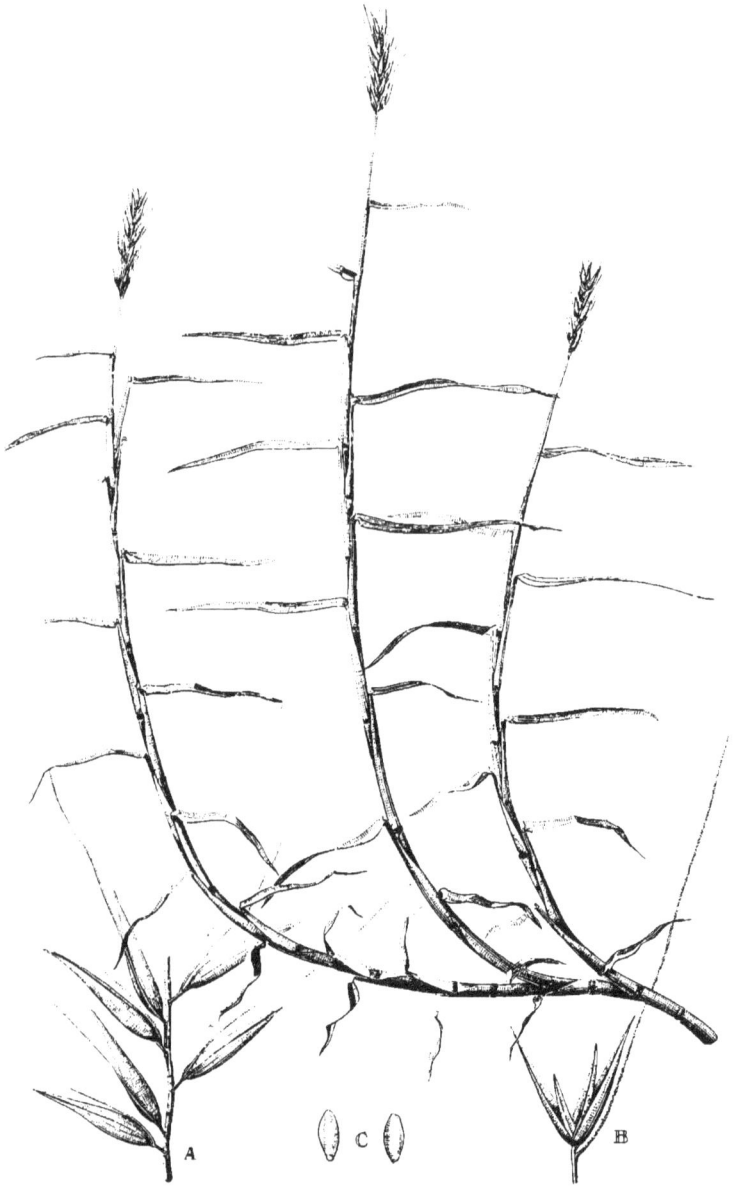

Chamæraphis paradoxa, Poir.

A "Mud-grass"

Value as a fodder.—A creeping grass found near water; forms a good sward, covering the land as the water recedes in waterholes. (Bailey). Believed to be nutritious; stock eat it readily.

Habitat and range.—A semi-aquatic, found in all the colonies except Tasmania ; and, as regards our own Colony, from the Coast districts on the ranges and table-lands to the driest districts. Found also in Asia.

2. Chamæraphis paradoxa, Poir.

Botanical name.—*Paradoxa*—Latin adjective, " something unusual or unexpected," a name first given to this grass by Robert Brown, who called it *Panicum paradoxum*, as it was abnormal in comparison with other species of that genus.

Synonym.—*Panicum paradoxum*, R. Br.
Where figured.—*Agricultural Gazette.*
Botanical description (B. Fl., vii, 499).—A smaller plant than *C. spinescens.*

Leaves mostly short and spreading.
Panicle almost reduced to a simple spikelike raceme.
Awnlike branches mostly bearing only a single spikelet near the base.
Lower ones only occasionally more elongated, with two distant spikelets.
Rhachis always produced into a long awn, exceeding the spikelet.
Spikelets acuminate, 4 or 5 lines long.
Outer glume broad, thinly membranous, about ½ line long, the second and third glumes nearly equal, striate with many nerves.
Fruiting glume oblong, acute, nearly 2 lines long, thin, and almost nerveless.

Value as a fodder.—Probably the same as that of the preceding species. These moisture-loving plants are frequently not appreciated to the extent they deserve, because the uncomfortable situations in which they are found, render careful examination and continued observation of them difficult for the greater part of the year.

Habitat and range.—Semi-aquatic; occurs from Victoria and Queensland. In our Colony it extends from the Coast district to the table-land. It is uncommon around Port Jackson.

Reference to plate.—A. Portion of a panicle, enlarged ; B. A spikelet, showing the rhachis produced into an awn longer than the spikelet ; C. Grain.

13. SPINIFEX.

Spikelets diœcious,* spicate or solitary on partial rhachises collected in dense globular heads, with a bract under each rhachis.
Male plant : Spikelets usually several to each bract, spicate or clustered, two-flowered.
Glumes four, nearly similar, two outer empty ones sometimes smaller, sometimes larger than the two flowering ones ; a perfect palea and three stamens within each flowering one.
Fertile plant : Spikelets solitary within each bract at the base of a partial rhachis, with one female or hermaphrodite flower, and an imperfect or rudimentary, or sometimes a male flower below it.

*Diœcious means having the male and female inflorescence on separate plants. This is very unusual in grasses.

Glumes four, as in the male, the third with a more or less developed palea, and sometimes three stamens or staminodes.

Palea in the fourth glume perfect.

Stamens three, often imperfect.

Styles two, distinct with long shortly-plumose stigmas.

Grain enclosed in the hardened glume and palea and free from them. Spreading or creeping hard branching grasses, the flowering branches subtended by leafy or lanceolate and concave bracts.

> Heads of spikelets several inches in diameter ; male spikelets in spikes of 1 to 1½ inches ; females at the base of rigid rhachises of 3 to 4 inches ; plant silky, pubescent, or villous ... ... 1. *S. hirsutus.*
> Heads of spikelets not above 1 inch diameter; male spikelets solitary or clustered within small bracts ; females within broad bracts, the rhachis shorter than the spikelet, and sometimes minute or obsolete ... ... 3. *S. paradoxus.*

1. Spinifex hirsutus, Labill.

Botanical name.—*Spinifex*, from the Latin, *spina* a thorn or prickle, in allusion to the spinous rhachis of the male spikelets; *hirsutus*, hairy, in allusion to the general appearance of the plant.

Vernacular names.—" Spiny Rolling Grass " appears to be, perhaps, the best name for this grass, but it is by no means in universal use, many people simply calling it " Sandstay " or " Sea-coast Grass." It is sometimes called " Porcupine Grass " in Tasmania. It is not to be confused with the so-called " Spinifexes " of the interior, which are botanically *Triodia*. They are far more prickly, and hence deserve the name of *Spinifex* better than the plants included in that genus. The genera *Triodia* and *Spinifex* are not closely related to each other.

Where figured.—*Labillardière*, Buchanan, Hackel, *Agricultural Gazette.*

Botanical description (B. Fl., vii., 503).—

> *Stem* stout, creeping in the sand, forming large tufts.
> *Leaves* often above 1 foot long with involute margins, clothed, as well as the whole plant, with silky or woolly hairs.
> *Male plant: Spikes* sessile or pedunculate, few or many in a terminal head or umbel, and often a cluster of two or three spikes, or a single spike lower down on the stem : each spike 1 to 1½ inches long ; the rhachis produced into a point usually exceeding the spikelets, and sometimes very long.
> *Bracts* under the spikes or peduncles, lanceolate, acuminate, concave.
> *Spikelets* sessile in the spike or scarcely pedicellate, 5 to 6 lines long.
> *Glumes* membranous, hairy, the empty ones five or seven nerved, usually as long as or longer than the flowering ones.
> *Fertile plant: Spikelets* very numerous, in a large dense globular head, each one solitary at the base of a spine-like rhachis of 4 inches or more, subtended by a much shorter linear-lanceolate bract, the spikelet 6 to 7 lines long, acute or acuminate.
> *Glumes* all nearly similar, with seven or more nerves, the two outer ones rather the largest, with more nerves than the others. A *palea* and sometimes three *stamens* in the axil of the third, and an *ovary* and three *stamens* or *staminodes* in the terminal one.

Value as a fodder.—Very small.

Other uses.—Its only use, though that is a great one, is as a sand-stay. The "Marram Grass" (*Psamma arenaria*, R. et. S.—a European

Spinifex hirsutus, Labill.

(Male Plant.)

Spinifex hirsutus, Labill.

(Female or Fertile Plant.)

species) is more valuable for resisting the encroachments of rolling sand than is the grass under present notice, but we should not neglect our indigenous plants. The "Spiny Rolling Grass," planted already by bountiful Nature along many parts of our coast, is capable of much good if landowners and public officers would only encourage its growth as a sandstay. Stock will rarely eat it, which circumstance is both an advantage and a drawback. It may be propagated readily, and it is of rapid growth. The "Spiny Rolling Grass" and the "Marram" are different in habit; the former is prostrate, while the latter is tall and erect, like rushes.

In this connection, the Newcastle sand-drift forces itself at once on our notice. At Newcastle and at other places on our coast (*e.g.*, Wollongong), the "Spiny Rolling Grass" has done much service, although it promises to fall into comparative neglect through the phenomenal success which has attended the introduction of the "Marram Grass" into Australia.

As has been pointed out in the course of an inquiry in regard to sandstays in India, no one plant is serviceable in all situations for the purpose; but where it is desired to utilise a grass, the "Spiny Rolling Grass" should always be given a trial. One advantage of it is its extensive geographical range, for it is practically indigenous all round the Continent. Sydney people will find quantities of it at the Spit, near Manly, and at Lady Robinson's Beach.

Many other of our native plants have been used as sandstays in addition to the grasses, *e,g.*, *Acacia longifolia*, Willd., var. *Sophoræ*, a golden wattle, with very spreading habit; several of the tea-trees, and particularly *Leptospermum lœvigatum*, F.v.M., together with several of the *Melaleucas*. Then, some of our *Casuarinas* are most valuable, particularly *C. glauca*, the swamp oak, and *C. Cunningham-iana*—the river oak. To cite but one instance, one of the islands in the Bega River would be washed away if the oaks on it were felled, and hence they are protected by the Forest Department. An allied species (*C. equisetifolia*) is very largely planted in India in almost pure sand, particularly in the Madras Presidency.

In other countries the question of preventing the encroachment of sea-sand upon adjacent land has often become of the greatest import-ance. The reclamation of the "Landes" of south-western France occurs at once to most of us. Here millions of acres of desert wastes have been transformed into valuable land through the success which has attended the planting of the Maritime or Cluster Pine (*Pinus pinaster*, or *maritima*), and not only has the problem of arresting the sand been solved, but the trees are tapped for resin, which is distilled for turpentine, forming the basis of a great industry.

Habitat and range.—Found round nearly the whole of the Australian Colonies, on the sea-shore. It extends also to New Caledonia and New Zealand.

Reference to Plates.—Male plant—1, creeping stem, with foliage ; 1*a*, inflorescence ; 2, spikelet. Female or fertile plant—1, creeping stem with foliage ; 1*a*, inflorescence ; 2, spikelet ; 3, ovary, with feathery stigmas.

3. Spinifex paradoxus, Benth.

Botanical name.—Paradoxus, Latin, something new or unexpected, an allusion by Bentham to the way in which the genus was overlooked by eminent botanists (*see* B. Fl., vii, 505).

Where figured—Icones plantarum, t. 1243, 1244.

Botanical description (B. Fl., vii, 504).—Glabrous divaricately branched, rigid, and brittle, but not so stout as the preceding species.

Branches in clusters of three to six, surrounded by short leaves with loose sheaths, the lower stem-leaves long and narrow ; the ligula a dense ring of cilia.

Male plant : Spikelets in a dense cluster or head of ½ to ¾ inch diameter, one to three outer bracts lanceolate and about as long as the head, the inner ones much reduced ; the spikelets about 3 lines long, the outer ones nearly sessile, the inner ones pedicellate and sometimes two on a pedicel, the pedicel or axis produced into a point shorter than the spikelet.

Outer empty glumes two, several-nerved.

Flowering glumes two, nearly equal, longer than the empty ones, each with a palea, and three stamens.

Female plant : Heads the size of the males when in flower, but the bracts larger and broader, and when in fruit the bracts variously enlarged, one or two often becoming curved, 1 inch long or more, broad with hard centres and scarious margins, sometimes all scarcely changed.

Spikelets almost sessile within each bract, the very short pedicel produced into a point much shorter than the spikelets, and sometimes minute or obsolete.

Empty glumes prominently seven or nine nerved, the two outer rather shorter than the third, which is either empty like them or contains a small palea.

Fruiting glume shorter, very acute, smooth, and shining.

Styles distinct.

Value as a fodder.—Not palatable to stock.

Other uses.—Excellent as a sand-binder for interior regions, as it withstands very high temperatures and protracted drought.

Habitat and range.—In the dry interior of all the colonies except Tasmania and Western Australia.

*Tribe ii.—*ANDROPOGONE.E.

Sub-tribe i.—Zoysieæ.

14. Zoysia.   16. Neurachne.

15. Lappago.   17. Perotis.

14. ZOYSIA.

Spikelets one-flowered, not awned, nearly sessile in a close spike, not distichous, the rhachis continuous.

Glumes two, the outer one broad, complicate, keeled, the inner flowering one much smaller, thin, and hyaline.

Palea still smaller.

Styles distinct.

Grain free, enclosed in the somewhat hardened outer glume.

1. Zoysia pungens, Willd.

Botanical name.—*Zoysia*, named in honor of Baron Charles de Zoys; *pungens*, Latin, "pricking," in reference to the sharp-pointed leaves.

Vernacular names.—" Coast Couch-grass" ; " Prickly Couch-grass" ; called " Porcupine-grass" by Bailey ; "Japanese Lawn-grass" (Lamson-Scribner).

Where figured.—Buchanan, *Agricultural Gazette.*

Botanical description (B. Fl., vii, 506).—

> *Rhizome* creeping in the sands to a great extent, with erect stems, rarely above 6 inches high.
>
> *Leaves* flat or convolute, with rigid subulate, often pungent, points; glabrous, except a few cilia at the orifice of the rather loose sheath.
>
> *Spike* terminal, 1 to 1½ inches long.
>
> *Spikelets* erect, closely appressed in the notches of the rhachis, 1½ to 2 lines long.
>
> *Outer glume* rather acute, broad, smooth, and shining ; the sides nerveless.
>
> *Flowering glume* completely enclosed, usually much smaller, thin and hyaline, but sometimes more than half the outer one and rather more rigid.

Value as a fodder.—Not inconsiderable, and it becomes the more important when it is considered that in sandy land, near the sea, very few grasses—at all events, edible grasses—will grow. It forms a compact turf, and is easily propagated. Its value as a sand-binder is even greater, and it may be readily propapated by division of the roots. It is palatable to stock, and should be encouraged in many places along our coast.

" Constant cropping appears to improve it, and to increase the density of the turf. In the foreign settlements of China and Japan it is prized as a lawn grass, especially for tennis-courts. It is finer-leaved than St. Augustine Grass,* and may prove superior to that grass for lawns in the Southern and Gulf States (U.S.A.). The habit of growth of Japanese lawn-grass (*Zoysia*) is very similar to that of Bermuda (our common Australian Couch-grass, *Cynodon dactylon,* J.H.M.), but the creeping stems are rather stouter and more rigid, and the upright branches or tufts of flowering stems are never so tall, rarely exceeding 6 inches. It may be propagated by root cuttings or by seed. Importations of both roots and seeds from Korea have been successfully grown in the United States, and the grass has proved hardy as far north as Connecticut. The leaves turn brown in the autumn, as do those of Bermuda." (Lamson-Scribner).

Habitat and range.—Found in Tasmania, Victoria, New South Wales, and Queensland, along the sea coast, and in salt marshes. It also extends to New Zealand, and is found in Asia.

15. LAPPAGO.

Spikelets one-flowered, not awned, two, or rarely three or four, together on very short pedicels along the continuous rhachis of a simple spikelike panicle.

---

* *Stenotaphrum americanum*, which is known in the Australian colonies as Buffalo Grass.

Glumes, usually three, the outer one, next the rhachis, very minute, and sometimes obsolete, the second empty, with five prominent nerves, armed with short, rigid, hooked bristles, the third or flowering glume and enclosed palea thin and hyaline.

Styles distinct, slender.

Grain enclosed in the thin palea and glume, and rigid outer glume, free from them.

1. Lappago racemosa, Willd.

Botanical name.—Lappago, from the Latin word for a plant with a burr. The Fuller's Teazle (*Dipsacus*) is one of the plants supposed to have been meant by the Ancients, though there are probably others. More indirectly, the name is from the Latin *Lappa*, the well-known Burdock of Europe (*Arctium lappa*), the burry fruits of which naughty school boys have collected from remote antiquity to put down one another's backs or to throw at the hair of school-girls. The burry appearance of the spikelets of our plant will be seen from the figure ; *racemosa*, with inflorescence in the form of a raceme.

Synonym.—Tragus racemosa, Desf. Authorities differ as to whom belongs the credit of this species. *Index Kewensis* gives Scopoli, Duthie gives Hall, Bentham and most Continental botanists quote Desfontaines.

*Vernacular name.—*The " Small Burr-grass," in contradistinction to the " Large Burr-grass " (*Cenchrus australis*).

*Where figured.—*Duthie, Hackel, *Agricultural Gazette.*

Botanical description (B. Fl., vii, 507).—An annual, spreading on the ground or ascending to from 6 inches to 1 foot in height, usually glabrous, except a few rigid cilia bordering the leaves.

Leaves flat, with loose sheaths.

Ligula small, split into cilia.

Spikelike panicle or raceme, 2 to 4 inches long, cylindrical and narrow, the very short peduncles bearing on their end two sessile narrow spikelets about 2 lines long, falling off together with the peduncle as little burrs.

The *second glumes*, with their hooked prickles, forming the principal part of the spikelets, the acuminate, almost aristate, *fruiting glumes* remaining enclosed within them.

*Value as a fodder.—*A useful grass for winter and early spring ; stock are fond of it. It is quite a small grass, usually not of much importance by itself for this reason, and also because it is not one of our most abundant grasses, but useful to supplement other fodder grasses. Bailey speaks of it as " a good little grass for winter."

Mr. W. Coldstream, quoted by Duthie, states that it is common at Hissar, India ; is too small to stock, but, being " a very nutritious grass," it is much grazed in the rains. Mr. Symonds states that cattle will not eat it, and Mr. Lowrie, of Ajmere, India, condemns it as a bad fodder grass.

No chemical analysis appears to have been made of this grass, but with us it is believed to be nutritious, and certainly both cattle and sheep eat it readily enough.

Its burrs are not usually complained of by the wool-grower.

Lappago racemosa, Willd.

"Small Burr Grass."

Habitat and range.—The original home of this grass is given in the *Index Kewensis* as the Mediterranean region and Afghanistan. It is common in the sandy soils of the plains of Northern India, and is described by Bentham as a common weed in most tropical and temperate regions in the new and old world. There is no doubt, however, that it is an indigenous Australian plant. The Baron informs us that up to the present it has been found in all the colonies, save only Tasmania and Western Australia.

This is one of those grasses which have been more widely diffused, though accidentally, by the agency of man. On the advent of the white man to this Colony it was found in the arid interior portions of it, but gradually it has worked its way coastwise, mainly, and perhaps entirely, through the burrs becoming entangled in the wool of sheep, or through the sweepings of the sheep-trucks containing seed-laden manure. So rapidly do sheep-trucks now come from such places as Hay, Narrandera, Gunnedah, &c., that the transmission of interior plants to the coast is proceeding at a rapid rate. To give but one instance; fettlers on the Southern line will inform you that the small introduced musk-melon *(Cucumis myriocarpus,* Naud.) constantly germinates on the permanent-way, distributed through the droppings from the sheep-trucks.

Our grass under notice I have traced on the railway line at different places, and finally near the Homebush sheep sale-yards near Sydney.

Reference to plate.—A, spikelike panicle ; B, part of the panicle enlarged ; C, a "burr," consisting of a pair of narrow spikelets opened out.

16. NEURACHNE.

Spikelets with one terminal hermaphrodite flower, and very rarely a second male one below it, sessile along the continuous rhachis of a simple ovoid or cylindrical spike.

Glumes four, the second the largest, fringed on each side, at least in the lower half, with long spreading cilia on the intramarginal nerve.

Third glume smaller and thinner, usually with a small palea in its axil.

Fruiting glume smaller, thin, and often hyaline.

The *palea* also very thin, as long as or longer than the glume.

Styles distinct.

Grain enclosed in the thin palea and glume, free from them.

Spike ovoid or oblong, ¾ to 1 inch long ; outer glume five- or seven-nerved, with long spreading hairs on the back ... .. 1. *N. alopecuroides.*

Spike narrow, 1 to 2 inches long. Outer glume with a transverse callosity on the back bearing long cilia, and below it an ovate very thin space, bordered by a thickened margin ... 2. *N. Mitchelliana.*

Spike narrow, 1 to 2 inches long. Outer glume thin, glabrous, or bordered by very few cilia... ... ... 3. *N. Munroi.*

E

1. Neurachne alopecuroides, R.Br.

Botanical name.—Neurachne, from two Greek words, *neuron,* a sinew or a nerve, *achne,* chaff (in botany, glume), referring to the nerves on the glumes ; *alopecuroides,* from *Alopecurus,* and *oidos,* like, denoting similarity to the genus of grasses known as *Alopecurus.*

Where figured.—Icones plantarum, t. 1,241 ; *Agricultural Gazette.*

Botanical description (B. Fl., vii, 507).—

Stems erect, 1 to 1½ feet high, with the nodes usually hairy, otherwise glabrous.

Leaves rather short, narrow and rigid, mostly at the base of the stem, glabrous, except the dense cilia of the ligula, the upper ones few and small.

Spike ovoid or oblong, ¾ to 1 inch long.

Spikelets numerous, densely crowded all round the rhachis, but spreading and very readily falling away, a few at the base of the spike barren and almost reduced to single ciliate glumes, but more persistent, and forming an involucre at the base of the spike. Each spikelet about 3 lines long, with a tuft of hairs at the base.

Outer glume rather shorter, five- or seven-nerved, tapering to a fine point, with a few spreading hairs on the back.

Second glume many-nerved, tapering to a fine point, densely ciliate with long hairs on each side.

Third glume rather shorter, with few nerves, sprinkled with a few short hairs.

Fruiting glume and *palea* thin and hyaline.

*Value as a fodder.—*Though coarse, it is a welcome fodder in summer, as the young leaves push out as long as there is any moisture in reach of their roots. (Tepper.)

Fungus found on this grass.—Ustilago Tepperi, Lind.

*Habitat and range.—*Found in all the Colonies except Tasmania and Queensland. An interior species.

*Reference to Plate.—*A, Portion of a panicle ; B, Spikelet showing relative size of outer glume, which is very broad and truncate ; C, Spikelet dissected, showing small outer glume, the 2nd and 3rd glumes, which are equal in size, and 3- or 5-nerved ; also the fruiting glume.

2. Neurachne Mitchelliana, Nees.

Botanical name.—Mitchelliana, in honour of Sir Thomas Mitchell, already alluded to.

Vernacular name.—" Mulga Grass," so-called because it is often found under Mulga *(Acacia aneura).*

*Where figured.—*Bailey ; *Icones Plantarum,* t. 1240 ; *Agricultural Gazette.*

Botanical description (B. Fl., vii, 508).—

Stems from a knotty woolly branching base, erect, leafy to the inflorescence or nearly so.

Leaves flat, short, spreading, ciliate with a few long hairs, or the lower ones woolly-hairy.

Spike narrow—cylindrical, 1 to nearly 2 inches long.

Spikelets about 2 lines long, with a tuft of hair at their base.

Outer glume as long as the others, many-nerved, ciliate, marked in the centre on the back with a tranverse callosity bearing long rigid horizontally spreading hairs, with a broad cavity underneath it, very thin, almost hyaline, bordered by a prominent nerve on each side.

Neurachne alopecuroides, R. Br.

Second glume broad to above the middle, pubescent on the back, and densely fringed on each side by long spreading hairs, the upper part narrow and glabrous, or nearly so.

Third glume shorter, thin, faintly nerved and not ciliate, either empty or enclosing a small palea.

Fruiting glume and *palea* thin and almost hyaline.

Value as a fodder.—An excellent grass, nutritious and palatable to stock. It grows under the shade of trees, and under the protection of shrubs and stones. It withstands severe drought, keeping up a growth when many other grasses are dried up.

Habitat and range.—Found in South Australia, Victoria, New South Wales and Queensland. An interior species.

3. Neurachne Munroi, F.v.M.

Botanical name.—*Munroi*, in honour of General William Munro, an eminent British authority on grasses.

Where figured.—*Icones Plantarum*, t. 1239.

Botanical description (B. Fl., vii, 508).—

Stems from a more or less woolly knotty base under 1 foot high.

Leaves narrow, convolute, or subulate, ciliate at the nodes and ligula, otherwise glabrous.

Spike narrow-cylindrical, 1 to nearly 2 inches long.

Rhachis pubescent.

Spikelets 2½ to 3 lines long, with a tuft of hairs at their base.

Outer glume nearly as long as the spikelet, thin, glabrous, or with a few marginal cilia.

Second glume more rigid, acutely acuminate, with about seven very prominent nerves, the marginal ones fringed in the lower half with long cilia.

Third glume shorter, much thinner, glabrous, about five-nerved, with a small palea.

Fruiting glume and *palea* thin and hyaline, the palea larger than the glume.

Value as a fodder.—A useful grass, believed to be nutritious, often affording a bite to stock in sheltered situations amongst scrub.

Habitat and range.—Found in South Australia, Victoria, and New South Wales. An interior species, found frequently amongst mulga scrub (*Acacia aneura* and allied species).

17. PEROTIS.

Spikelets one-flowered, sessile, or shortly pedicellate along the continuous rhachis of a loose simple spike or raceme.

Glumes three, two outer empty ones linear, rigid, tapering into long terminal straight awns, the lowest the longest.

Terminal flowering glume much smaller, thin, and hyaline, the palea still smaller.

Styles very shortly united at the base, the plumose stigmas short.

Grain narrow, free, longer than the terminal glume, enclosed in the two rigid outer ones.

68

1. Perotis rara, R.Br.

Botanical name.—*Perotis*, from the Greek *peros*, wanting or deficient, though the author of the genus gives no indication of what part he desires to indicate as deficient (supposing such to have been his idea); or, perhaps, from the Greek *otites*, eared, with long ears, and *peri*, around, referring to the long awns; *rara*, Latin, signifying seldom seen, or unusual. It is not a very common grass.

Vernacular name.—" Comet-grass," so called by Mr. Bailey because he noticed this grass to be very abundant in the pasture of the Comet River district, Queensland.

Where figured.—*Agricultural Gazette.*

Botanical description (B. Fl., vii, 509).—

Stems from a decumbent or branching base, slender, ascending to 1 foot or rather more.

Leaves linear, with subulate points, glabrous except a few marginal cilia especially at the orifice of the sheaths.

Ligula ciliate.

Spike or raceme in some specimens 3 to 4 inches, in others at least twice as long.

Spikelets always numerous, at first erect, at length reflexed, in some specimens almost sessile, in others on pedicels of ¼ to above ½ line long, often ciliate with a few hairs, the spikelets very narrow, 2 to 3 lines long without the fine awns, which are ½ to 1 inch long.

Outer glume with a prominent keel, sometimes glabrous, in a few specimens ciliate with rather long hairs.

Second glume similar, but rather shorter and narrower.

Value as a fodder.—This is a quick grower. Some observers say it is succulent, and stock are stated to be fond of it; but Mr. P. A. O'Shanesy, speaking of the dry summer of 1881, states that he has observed the goats will not eat it, even in places where there are no other grasses.

Bailey alludes to it as " a small decumbent grass, affording excellent sheep-pasture in open country, growing quickly after showers. The seeds, though sharp, are not very troublesome." He found it in much favour with the pastoralists of the Comet River, but in other places it was not so highly thought of.

Some of our stock-inspectors do not apppear to be able to appraise the value of this grass, and their attention might be drawn to it.

We know so little about the fodder value of *Perotis* that it may be interesting to note that, speaking of *P. latifolia*, Roxburgh says that cattle are not fond of this grass ; Mr. Lowrie, however, states that at Ajmere it is considered to be a good fodder grass." (Duthie.)

Other uses.—Its inflorescence is ornamental, and may be used for decorative purposes.

Habitat and range.—Found in South Australia, New South Wales, Queensland, and Northern Australia. It also occurs in Asia and the Pacific Islands. In New South Wales it is always an interior species. The Stock Inspector of the Bourke district says that it grows prolifically on sandy and red ground, and is not to be found on black soil anywhere.

Reference to Plate—A, Part of the spike, enlarged, to show the attachment of the spikelets ; B, A spikelet showing the two very long awns at the extremity of the glumes ; c, Unripe grain, very much enlarged.

Perotis rara, R. Br.

"Comet Grass."

Sub-tribe ii.—ROTTBOELLIEÆ.

19. HEMARTHRIA.

Spikelets in pairs, in the alternate notches of a simple spike, one sessile and half embedded in a cavity of the scarcely articulate rhachis with one hermaphrodite flower, the other on a closely appressed and often adnate pedicel reduced to two or three empty glumes, the spikes single on each peduncle above a sheathing bract, and often flattened.

Glumes in the sessile spikelet four, the outer one appressed and covering the cavity of the rhachis, the second thinner and concave or keeled, the third and fourth and the palea in the fourth thin and hyaline.

Styles distinct.

Grain enclosed in the glumes, but free from them.

1. Hemarthria compressa, R.Br.

Botanical name.—From the Greek words *hemi*, half, and *arthron*, a joint; half-jointed, referring to the spike. *Compressa*, Latin, flattened, referring to the spike of this species.

Synonym.—*Rottbœllia compressa*, Beauv.

Vernacular names.—"Mat Grass," "Mackay Sugar Grass" (in Queensland), "Needle Grass," "so called by me from the appearance of the spike just before flowering." (Bacchus.)

Allied grasses are known as "Rat-tail Grass" in the United States.

Where figured.—*Agricultural Gazette.*

Botanical description (B. Fl., vii, 510).—

> *Stems* decumbent or creeping at the base, rather rigid, ascending to 1 foot or rather more, slightly branched.
> *Leaves* narrow, glabrous, or the lower ones sprinkled with a few long hairs.
> *Spikes* solitary on the branches or nearly so, more or less compressed, rigid, 3 to 5 inches long, often 1½ lines broad.
> *Spikelets* all closely appressed, 3 to 3½ lines long.
> *Outer glume* many-nerved, tapering into a very variable point, sometimes very short and straight, especially in the sessile spikelet, sometimes elongated and fine or minutely hooked at the extremity, or in southern specimens especially towards the end of the spike, terminating in a rather long inflexed rigid hook. In the pedicellate spikelet the point of the outer glume is often longer, finer, and straight, but occasionally that also is hooked, and more rarely the second glume ends in a small hook.

Value as a fodder.—A strong rambling grass, with creeping roots, found on undrained heavy clay or wet, sour soils, and hence useful for encouraging in land of that description. Its inflorescence is not conspicuous, and hence many people do not distinguish this grass from others. Bailey describes it as "a rather harsh, wiry grass, the flattish stems often extending the length of 5 or 6 feet. It affords a coarse fodder around swamps and the margins of rivers, which is of value during very dry seasons. The flattened running stems are very sweet, and as the water dries up in the swamps, these are greedily eaten by stock; horses are said to leave all else for these stems." Bacchus, a

Victorian writer, describes it as "perennial, 1 to 2½ feet high. Common about salt marshes and lakes, vegetates late, keeps green through the hot weather, and is then a favourite food with stock, which do not seem to care about it in the winter. Often affected with rust." Roxburgh says that cattle are fond of it. (Duthie.)
Habitat and range.—Found in all the colonies. In New South Wales confined to the coast district of Dividing Range. Occurs also in South Asia and South Africa.

Sub-tribe iv.—EUANDROPOGONEÆ.

24. Heteropogon.	30. Imperata.
25. Ishæmum.	31. Chrysopogon.
27. Arthraxon.	32. Sorghum.
28. Pollinia.	33. Anthistiria.
29. Andropogon.	34. Apluda.

24. HETEROPOGON.

Spikelets one-flowered, monœcious, in pairs in the notches of the articulate rhachis of a simple one-sided spike; the females sessile, cylindrical, turned to one side of the spike; the males lanceolate, awnless, shortly pedicellate, imbricate on the other side of the spike.
Glumes in the female spikelet four; the outer one hard convolute, the second keeled, the third very thin and hyaline, fourth or terminal glume a hard twisted and bent awn, attenuate and flexuose, or narrow and hyaline at the base, as in *Andropogon.*
Palea very small and thin, or none.
Styles distinct.
Grain enclosed in the hardened glumes, but free from them.

1. Heteropogon contortus, Rœm. et Schult.

Botanical name.—*Heteropogon,* from the Greek *heteros,* irregular or variable, perhaps from the circumstance that the hairs on the outer glume and on the armed point of the flowering glume are different in colour and texture; *pogon,* a beard; *contortus,* entangled, referring to the twisted awns, which become entangled, and give the plant a matted appearance.
Synonym.—*Andropogon contortus,* Linn., in F.v.M. *Census.*
Vernacular names.—"Bunch Spear-grass," "Twisted Beard Grass."
Where figured.—Vasey, Duthie, *Agricultural Gazette.*
Botanical description (B. Fl., vii, 517).—

Stems ascending or erect, 1 to 2 feet high.
Leaves narrow, ciliate with a few long hairs, the sheaths flattened.
Spikes pedunculate, 1 to 2 inches long without the awns.
Male or barren spikelets 3 to 4 lines long, green, ciliate, closely imbricate in two rows along one side of the spike, almost concealing the females.
Female spikelets narrow, the outer glume hard, obtuse, convolute; the second narrow, with a hard centre, the hairs surrounding the spikelet brown and silky.
Awn protruding often to 2 inches, and very much twisted.

Value as a fodder.—A strong-growing grass, producing abundance of nutritious fodder when young, but becoming coarse when old. For this reason, as also because the barbed seeds are deadly to sheep, it is only suitable for large stock. These seeds are far more formidable than those of *Stipa setacea* (see page 114).

" In India it is largely used as fodder, both before and after it has flowered, but chiefly when it is young and tender. In Rajputana and Bundelkhand, where this grass abounds, it is cut and stacked after the rains are over. It is also cut for hay in the Hissar bir, and Mr. Coldstream states that it will keep good in stack for twelve years. On Mount Abu the people consider it is the best fodder-grass they have. In other districts it is said to be eaten only by buffaloes or by cattle when they are hungry and cannot obtain other kinds of grass." (Duthie.)

Other uses.—Much used in thatching in India. (Duthie.) Hackel suggests that the awns may serve as hygrometers. Lamson-Scribner points out that the strong rhizomes and tough roots of this grass commend it as a soil-binder for river-banks, dams, &c.

Fungus found on this grass.—*Cerebella andropogonis*, Ces.

Habitat and range.—In the North Coast districts of this Colony, extending through Queensland and Northern Australia; also extends over tropical and sub-tropical Asia, Africa, America, and the Pacific Islands.

25. ISCHÆMUM.

Spikelets in pairs in the alternate notches of the articulate flexuose rhachis of simple spikes, one sessile with one hermaphrodite terminal flower and a male one below it; the other pedicellate and either similar or with only one hermaphrodite or one or two male flowers or reduced to empty glumes.

Spikes either solitary or two or more, sessile or nearly so at the end of the common peduncle.

Glumes in the sessile spikelet four, the outer one the largest, awnless, truncate or two-toothed at the top.

Second glume keeled and sometimes produced into a short, straight awn.

Third glume rather smaller, thin, enclosing a palea and three stamens.

Terminal glume a twisted and bent awn, attenuate or hyaline and bifid at the base as in *Andropogon*.

Palea small and thin or none.

Styles distinct.

Grain enclosed in the glumes, but free from them.

Spikelets both two-flowered and awned ; outer glume rigid ; spikes two or three, rarely four, erect, often appressed so as to appear like one cylindrical spike ; nodes bearded.

 Stems 2 or 3 feet high ; awn exserted.

  Spikes 3 to 4 inches, spikelets 4 to 5 lines long ... ... 3. *I. triticeum.*

  Spikes 1½ to 3 inches, spikelets about 3 lines long ... ... 4. *I. australe.*

Stems creeping or diffuse, shortly ascending ; leaves hairy, rhachis
of the spike ciliate, outer glume wrinkled on the base,
awn shortly exserted ... ...   6. *I. ciliare.*
Sessile spikelet two-flowered, awned ; pedicellate spikelet unawned,
with a male or without any flower ; spike solitary.
Pedicellate spikelet without flowers ; spike slender ; sessile spikelets flat, closely appressed, pectinate-ciliate on each side ;
no awn ... ...8. *I. pectinatum.*
Pedicellate spikelets lanceolate, flattened, with two male flowers   10. *I. laxum.*

3. Ischæmum triticeum, R.Br.

Botanical name.—*Ischæmum*, said to be from *ischæmon*, a plant referred to by Pliny : " A herb like a hyrse, having sharp leaves and
moss ; it is good to stop blood." It is said that the woolly seeds of
one of the species were used as a styptic ; *triticeum*, Latin, wheat-like.

Vernacular Name.—" Wheat Grass."

Botanical description (B. Fl., vii, 519).—Very near *I. muticum*, but a
coarse plant, ascending to 2 or 3 feet.

Leaves mostly long and broad, contracted at the base or scarcely cordate, glabrous
or the lower sheaths hairy.

Spikes two together, 3 to 4 inches long.

Spikelets 4 to 5 lines long, more acuminate than in *I. muticum.*

Outer glume smooth and shining at the base, several-nerved, and often ciliate, with a
few hairs at the end, the wings of the lateral nerves often unequal.

Inner glumes rather rigid, the third with a rigid palea and male flower, the fourth
under the terminal flower more hyaline, shortly two-fid, the awn usually exserted
and sometimes ½ inch long.

Pedicellate spikelet nearly similar, but, as in *I. muticum* rather narrower, the wings
and nerves irregular, and the awn often shorter.

Value as a fodder.—A coarse grass, of but little value for fodder.

Habitat and range.—A common coast grass in Queensland and
Northern New South Wales.

4. Ischæmum australe, R.Br.

Botanical name.—*Australe*, Latin, southern (Australian).

Botanical description (B. Fl., vii, 519).—

Stems from a shortly decumbent base or creeping rhizome erect, 2 to 3 feet high, but
not stout.

Leaves rather narrow, glabrous or slightly hairy in the typical form, the nodes
always bearded, the upper sheaths very long.

Spikes two together on a long peduncle, sessile and erect, 1½ to 3 inches long, the
rhachis and pedicels slightly ciliate.

Spikelets 3 lines long or scarcely more, otherwise the same as in *I. triticeum.*

Awn of the sessile spikelet ¼ to ½ inch long, of the pedicellate spikelet shorter or
reduced to a short point.

Value as a fodder.—A coarse, harsh grass, only nutritious when
young ; when old, stock never touch it except when hard pressed.
Bailey remarks that it has a deep-running rhizome, and is thus enabled
to stand a length of dry weather, and continue to afford a bite for
stock after others have given up. Mr. Seccombe, with admittedly
limited experience of it, speaks of it as a valuable acquisition, growing

continuously through hot and cold weather, " for so far the winter has in no way affected its appearance or growth. It has, moreover, proved a continuous seed-producer."

Habitat and range.—Found near moist places from the Port Jackson district northward to Queensland and Northern Australia. Confined to the coast districts.

6. Ischæmum ciliare, Rctz.: *var.* podostachyum, Benth.

Botanical name.—*Ciliare*, Latin, *cilia*, the hairs of the eye-lids (eye-lashes), alluding to the hairy leaves and bearded nodes ; *podostachyum*, *pous*, *podus* a foot, and *stachys* an ear of corn, one of the spikes being attached lower down, giving the other a pedunculate appearance.
Botanical description (B. Fl., vii, 520).—

> *Stem*, in the specimen seen, slender, under 1 foot high, erect from a shortly decumbent or creeping base.
> *Leaves* short, glabrous.
> *Ligula* prominent.
> *Nodes* bearded.
> *Spikes* scarcely 1 inch long, two at the end of the peduncle, but one of them shorter and attached lower down, giving the other a pedunculate appearance.
> *Pedicels* ciliate.
> *Sessile spikelet* 3 lines long.
> *Outer glume* lanceolate, acutely acuminate, the nerves more conspicuous and not so smooth as in the typical *I. ciliare* and in *I. decumbens.*
> *Second glume* as long, but thinner, narrow, and keeled.
> *Third* nearly as long, very acute, with a male flower.
> *Fourth or terminal glume* hyaline, deeply two-lobed, with a slender awn not twice as long, enclosing the hermaphrodite flower.
> *Pedicellate spikelet* nearly similar, but containing only a male flower and no awn.

Value as a fodder.—It is occasionally used in India as a fodder-grass. (Duthie.)
Habitat and range.—As far as is at present known, confined to this Colony, and to the Hunter River district.

8. Ischæmum pectinatum, Trin.

Botanical name.—*Pectinatum*, Latin, combed or like a comb, from the supposed appearance of the spikelets.
Botanical description (B. Fl., vii, 521).—

> *Stems* tufted and leafy at the base, about 1 foot high or rather more.
> *Lower leaves* narrow, flat, under 6 inches long, those on the stem few, reduced to long close sheaths, with very short, erect laminæ.
> *Spike* single, pedunculate above the last sheath, rather slender, straight or slightly curved, usually about 2 inches, but sometimes twice that length.
> *Sessile spikelets* closely appressed and imbricate on one side of the rhachis, much flattened ; 2 lines long or rather more.
> *Outer glume* broad, truncate or retuse, thin but rigid, seven-nerved, the outer nerves close to the margin elegantly pectinate-muricate in the lower part, and produced upwards into short wings.
> *Second glume* narrower, acute, keeled.
> *Third glume* thin and hyaline, with a palea and male flower.
> *Terminal glume* with a hermaphrodite flower, shorter, rather broad, obtuse, very thin and hyaline, with a faint central nerve but no awn ; the palea similar but without the central nerve.
> *Pedicellate spikelet* reduced to a single few-nerved acuminate glume, slightly spreading.

Value as a fodder.—A very close-growing grass, forming on even dry, stony ridges a close turf. (Bailey.)
Habitat and range.—Extends from New South Wales to Northern Australia. In our own Colony found on the northern rivers, extending to the table-land. Found also in Ceylon and in the Indian Peninsula.

10. Ischæmum laxum, R.Br.

Botanical name.—*Laxum*, Latin for loose or slack, in allusion to the habit of the grass.
Vernacular name.—" Rat's-tail Ischæmum."
Where figured.—*Agricultural Gazette.*
Botanical description (B. Fl., vii, 522).—A rather slender grass of 2 to 3 feet, the Australian specimens quite glabrous.

Leaves narrow, often subulate.
Ligula short, ciliate.
Spike single, dense, sometimes slightly curved, 2 to 4 or rarely 5 inches long ; rhachis and pedicels ciliate.
Sessile spikelet narrow, scarcely flattened, 3 to 4 lines long.
Outer glume acutely acuminate, with two rather prominent nerves and obscure ones between them.
Second glume thin, produced into a long, fine, straight awn.
Third hyaline, with a male flower.
Terminal glume hyaline, narrow, bifid, with a long, bent awn.
Pedicellate spikelet more conspicuous, much flattened as well as the pedicel.
Glumes acutely acuminate, the outer ones broadly lanceolate, with five very prominent nerves.
Second thin, scarious, faintly three-nerved, two flowering glumes and paleas thin and hyaline, both with male flowers or the third empty.

Value as a fodder.—This is a coarse grass, often met with at the base of hills. Before seeding it forms a fair pasture for cattle, but is not adapted for sheep. (Bailey.) Mr. Lowrie says it is one of the best grasses in the Ajmere district of India. (Duthie.)
Habitat and range.—Extends from New England, New South Wales, to Northern Australia; occurs also in tropical Asia and Africa.

27. ARTHRAXON.

Spikelets one-flowered, sessile in the alternate notches of the articulate rhachis of simple spikes, with a short pedicel in the same notch usually without any spikelet, the spikes sessile or shortly pedunculate in a simple terminal panicle.
Glumes four, the outer one the largest, membranous, several-nerved; the second keeled, acute ; the third smaller, hyaline, all awnless ; fourth or terminal glume shorter than the second, hyaline but keeled, with a dorsal awn arising from the base, but twisted and bent as in *Andropogon.*
Palea very small and hyaline.
Styles distinct.
Grain enclosed in the outer glumes, but free from them.
Stems usually weak or slender with short broad leaves.

1. Arthraxon ciliare, Beauv : var. australe, Benth.

Botanical name.—Arthraxon, from the Greek *arthron* a joint, *axis* an axis or stem; jointed to the stem, the spikelets being sessile in the alternate notches of the articulate rhachis; *ciliare*, Latin, hairy.

Botanical description (B. Fl., vii, 524).—A broad-leaved, creeping, straggling, much-branched grass.

Stems slender, decumbent or creeping at the base, branching and ascending to about 1 foot.

Leaves ovate-lanceolate, acute, 1 to 1½ inches long, cordate at the base, the sheaths usually ciliate with long hairs.

Spikes usually three or four, shortly pedicellate, forming a little simple panicle of about 1 inch.

Rhachis and abortive pedicels glabrous.

Spikelets few, rarely above 6 inches, each branch or spike about 2 lines long.

Outer glume acute, with about seven equally prominent more or less muricate nerves; keel of the second glume ciliate towards the top.

Terminal or flowering glume obtuse, entire or very shortly two-lobed, the dorsal awn proceeding quite from the base, fine, and about twice as long as the spikelet.

Value as a fodder.—A straggling slender grass which, according to Bailey, seems to be well-liked by cattle. Duthie says it is considered to be a good fodder-grass in Rajputana, India.

Habitat and range.—Found in swamps; the only two Australian recorded localities being New England (New South Wales) and Toowoomba (Queensland). This grass requires the further attention of collectors.

Found also in Asia. In India the normal species is found in the plains of the north-west, and up to 7,000 feet on the Himalaya.

28. POLLINIA.

Spikelets one-flowered, in pairs in the alternate notches of the articulate rhachis of simple spikes, one sessile or shortly pedicellate, the other on a longer pedicel, but the two otherwise similar, the spikes sessile and clustered, or rarely solitary at the end of the common peduncle.

Glumes four or three; outer one the largest, membranous, awnless with a truncate toothed or ciliate tip; second usually thinner, keeled, acute or produced into a fine straight awn; third thin and hyaline or deficient; terminal or fourth glume a twisted and bent awn, contracted and flexuose or hyaline, dilated and two-lobed at the base as in *Andropogon*.

Palea small and hyaline or none.

Styles distinct.

Grain enclosed in the outer glumes and free from them.

Habit of *Andropogon*, section Gymnandropogon, the spikes silky-villous, rufous, or silvery-white as in *A. sericeus* and its allies, but the pedicellate spikelets are all, except sometimes at the base of the spike, fertile, which is never the case in *Andropogon*.

3. Pollinia fulva, Benth.

Botanical name.—Pollinia, in honor of Ciro Pollini, Professor of Botany at the University of Verona, and author of a *Flora Veronensis; fulva,* Latin, deep-yellow or tawny, such being the colour of the spikes.

Synonym.—Erianthus fulvus, Benth.: in F.v.M. *Census.* Variety of *P. Cummingii,* Nees (Hackel).

Vernacular names.—" Sugar Grass " is its most common name, owing to its sweetness. " Brown-top," " Red Grass," or " Red-ribbed Grass" allude to its rich brown-red silky spikes of flowers. It is sometimes known as " Bastard Mitchell Grass " in Queensland. " Aldroo " of the aborigines of Mt. Lyndhurst, South Australia (Koch).

Botanical description (B. Fl., vii, 526).—

Stems either slender and 1 to 1½ feet high, or stouter, more branching at the base, and attaining 2 to 4 feet, the nodes glabrous, or shortly bearded.

Leaves rather narrow, tapering to fine points, the orifice of the sheaths and ligula usually ciliate, and sometimes the sheaths hairy.

Spikes two or three, sessile, and near together in a terminal cluster, but not quite digitate, 1½ to 2½ inches long, covered with silky hairs of a rich brown.

Spikelets mostly about 2 lines long, but variable in size, all similar or the pedicellate ones rather narrower.

Outer glume truncate, or denticulate at the end, faintly nerved.

Second nearly as long, narrower, slightly keeled, truncate.

Third very minute, or more frequently entirely deficient.

Awn or terminal glume slender, rarely ½ inch long, contracted into a flexuose stipes, or slightly dilated at the base, hyaline and bifid.

Styles very shortly united.

Value as a fodder.—A showy, moderately tall grass, very abundant in some places. It is very nutritious and palatable to stock. A correspondent of Mr. Bailey says : " It is much more drought resisting than the Mitchell Grass, and springs up more quickly after rain." O'Shanesy speaks of it as a valuable grass for pastures.

Habitat and range.—Found in all the colonies except Tasmania. In this Colony extending from the table-lands to the western districts.

29. ANDROPOGON.

Spikelets one-flowered or empty, in pairs in the alternate notches of the articulate *rhachis* of simple spikes, one sessile hermaphrodite (or rarely female) and fertile, the other pedicellate and barren, either male or empty, the spikes either solitary or clustered and sessile, or very shortly pedunculate at the end of the common peduncle.

Glumes in the fertile spikelet four, the outer one the largest, awnless, several-nerved, but often two nerves near the margin much more prominent than the others; second glume keeled, rarely produced into a short straight awn ; third much smaller, very thin and hyaline, always empty; fourth or terminal glume under the flower, very slender, flexuose, and stipes-like at the base, or if dilated very thin and hyaline, entire or bifid at the top, with an awn either terminal or from the notch, rigid and twisted in the lower part, bent back and very fine above the middle.

Palea small and hyaline or none.

Glumes of the barren spikelets four or fewer, the outer one the largest and many-nerved, the second keeled, the third and fourth, when present, small, thin, and hyaline, all awnless.
Styles distinct.
Grain enclosed in the glumes, but free from them.
Grasses usually tall and often scented, simple or paniculately branched.

SECTION I.—GYMNANDROPOGON.

Spikes two, three, or more, clustered at the end of a peduncle without sheathing bracts, very rarely reduced to a single spike.
Spikelets concealed or nearly so under copious long silky hairs.
   Spikes about 3 inches, spikelets about 3 lines long   ...   ... 1. *A. erianthoides.*
Spikes not above 2 inches, spikelets scarcely 2 lines long.
   Long silky hairs on the back of the outer glumes as well as
      on the rhachis and pedicels ...   . 2. *A. sericeus.*
   Long silky hairs only or chiefly on the rhachis and pedicels.
      Glumes not pitted...   ...   . 3. *A. affinis.*
      Outer glumes marked with a pit on the back...   ...   ... 4. *A. pertusus.*
Spikes silky-hairy, but the hairs not covering the spikelets.
   Spikes numerous, the common axis elongated   ...   . 7. *A. intermedius.*

SECTION II.—CYMBOPOGON.

Spikes two together on each peduncle within or above a sheathing bract.
   Spikes both sessile at the end of the peduncle. Awns slender,
      short and glabrous or deficient.
   Silky hairs long, concealing the spikelets or nearly so. Spikes at
      length spreading or reflexed. Awns none or very fine
      and scarcely projecting   ...   . 11. *A. bombycinus.*
   Hairs minute. Spikes soon reflexed. Awns very short or none .. 13. *A. refractus.*
   One spike affixed lower down than the other, slightly hairy.
      Awns 1 to 3 inches long, hairy on the lower part ... 14. *A. lachnatherus.*

1. Andropogon erianthoides, F.v.M.

Botanical name.—*Andropogon*—Greek, *andros*, of man (man's), *pogon*, a beard, in allusion to the tufts of hairs on the inflorescence, thought to resemble a man's beard. *Erianthoides*, from two Greek words signifying resembling a grass of the genus *Erianthus.*

Vernacular name.—" Satin Top," or " Satin-topped Grass " ; " Blue Grass," the leaves having a somewhat bluish tinge.

Where figured.—Bailey, *Agricultural Gazette.*

Botanical description (B. Fl., vii, 529).—An erect glaucous grass of 2 or 3 feet, glabrous except the inflorescence, the nodes not bearded.
   Leaves rather narrow.
   Spikes usually three or four, nearly sessile at the end of a peduncle without sheathing
      bracts, erect or scarcely spreading, about 3 inches long.
   Spikelets concealed under the very copious long silky hairs surrounding the sessile
      spikelet on the pedicels and a few on the outer glumes.
   Sessile spikelet about 3 lines long.
   Outer glume nearly equally many-nerved, with a short scarious often notched tip.
   Second glume rather shorter, keeled, three-nerved, acute.
   Third thin and hyaline.
   Awn or terminal glume fine, not above twice the length of the spikelet, contracted
      at the base into a flexuose stipes, with sometimes a very slight hyaline dilatation.
   Pedicellate spikelet reduced to one or two empty glumes.

Value as a fodder.—An excellent grass, nutritious and palatable, yielding a large quantity of rich fodder.

" This is one of the most remarkable of the Queensland grasses. Anyone seeing it when in flower would be surprised if told it was probably, for Downs country, one of the best that could be grown; yet nevertheless such is the case. The flowering stalks attain 4 or 5 feet in height, but its shortly creeping root-stock forms a very close leafy turf, before and even when the plant is in flower." (Bailey.)

S. M. Tracey, in *Bulletin* No. 20, Mississippi Experiment Station, U.S.A., writes :—" Australian Blue-grass (*Andropogon erianthoides*) is a perennial species from Australia, which has been cultivated in a few localities for a number of years, and advertised to a considerable extent, but its growth has not been very satisfactory here. It is so tender that it barely lives through the winter in this latitude, and starts into growth late in the spring, though it makes an excellent growth during summer and will give two good cuttings of fine, tender, and nutritious hay. The leaves are killed by a moderate frost, and it fails to hold the ground against the encroachment of other grasses. Several other species of *Andropogon* from Australia and from India have also been tested, but this appears to be the best of the genus, and the only foreign one which makes any promise of final success."

Habitat and range.—Found in New South Wales and Queensland. In this colony it is principally found in the Western districts, but it is also recorded from the Monaro.

2. Andropogon sericeus, R.Br.

Botanical name.—*Sericeus*—Latin, silky, in allusion to the appearance of the spikes.

Vernacular names.—The " Blue-grass" *par excellence* of Queensland and New South Wales ; has been sent from Mudgee under the name of " Canary-grass."

Where figured.—Bailey, *Agricultural Gazette.*

Botanical description (B. Fl., vii, 529).—Perennial,

Stems erect, branching at the base, usually rather slender and 1 to 2 feet high, with narrow leaves chiefly at the base, but sometimes twice that height with larger leaves, the nodes bearded.

Spikes in the typical form two or three or rarely twice as many, sessile at the top of a slender peduncle, without sheathing bracts, all 1 to 2 inches long and densely clothed with long silky hairs on the outer glumes, as well as on the rhachis and pedicels.

Spikelets scarcely two lines long, the pedicellate one reduced to a many-nerved silky-hairy glume enclosing a second small hyaline lanceolate one.

Outer glume of the sessile spikelet rather rigid, obtuse or nearly so, about five-nerved, with long silky hairs on the back, and a short scarious ciliate tip.

Second glume keeled, acute, glabrous.

Third very small, broad, thin, and hyaline.

Awn or terminal glume ¾ to 1½ inches long, without any hyaline dilatation at the base.

Value as a fodder.—One of the best and most widely diffused of our grasses. Valuable alike for pasture and for hay. Very fattening, and much liked by stock of all kinds.

Habitat and range.—Found in all the colonies except Tasmania, in all the districts of this colony, and in all sorts of soils and situations. Very widely distributed. Occurs also in Asia, the Phillippine Islands, and New Caledonia.

3. Andropogon affinis, R.Br.

Botanical name.—Affinis—Latin, contiguous to, in allusion to its affinity to *A. sericeus.*
Vernacular name.—A " Blue-grass."
Where figured.—Agricultural Gazette.
Botanical description (B. Fl., vii, 530).—Very near *A. sericeus* and perhaps a variety, with the same habit; the nodes less bearded and sometimes quite glabrous.

Spikes usually three or four, not quite sessile, 1½ to 2 inches long.
Spikelets rather longer and narrower than in *A. sericeus* and not so closely imbricate, the long silky spreading hairs only on the pedicels and at the base of the sessile spikelets, not on the back of the glumes.
Third glume more developed in the spikelets examined, the awn ¾ to 1½ inches long.

Value as a fodder.—The remarks under *A. sericeus* will apply here very well.
Habitat and range.—Occurs from Victoria to Queensland. In this colony it extends from south to north, both in the coast districts and on the tablelands and Dividing Range.

Andropogon pertusus, Willd.

Botanical name.—Pertusus—Latin, having holes, in allusion to the little pit or depression in the outer glume. (See *A. intermedius.*)
Vernacular names.—Sometimes called " Blue-grass ; " known as " Sour-grass " in the West Indies.
Where figured.—Agricultural Gazette.
Botanical description.—(B. Fl., vii, 530).—A rather tall grass,

Stems slender, 1 to 2 feet high, the nodes glabrous.
Leaves chiefly at the base of the stem, narrow, glabrous.
Spikes two to five, sessile or nearly so at the end of the peduncle without sheathing bracts, 1 to 2 inches long, silky-hairy as in the preceding species, with long hairs on the pedicels and at the base of the sessile spikelets.
Spikelets fully 2 lines long, rather obtuse.
Outer glume marked above the middle with a small pit which assumes inside the appearance of a projecting gland.
Awn slender, about ¾, rarely 1 inch long.
Pedicellate spikelet usually containing a male flower.

Value as a fodder.—An excellent grass, standing drought well, and yielding abundant and palatable, nutritious feed.
" Excellent for pastures, yielding a large quantity of forage, and it stands constant grazing better than most grasses with which I am acquainted." (O'Shanesy.)
" This grass, which is met with all over the plains of Northern India, is universally esteemed as a good fodder-grass, both for grazing and stacking." (Duthie.)
The following account of West Indian experience with this grass is interesting :—" The ' sour-grass ' is the chief fodder-grass of Barbados, where it is cultivated almost to the exclusion of all others. In the driest districts and most exposed places, this hardy and excellent fodder-plant, which grows from 18 inches to 2 feet high, seems to

thrive and be at home, furnishing at the time of the year, when other fodder is scarce, food for the animals employed on the sugar estates. If cut shortly after it flowers, just as the fruit is setting, it forms valuable food for horses, cattle, and mules, who then seem to eat it with relish, but if it is allowed to get over-ripe the stems become hard and unpalatable, the animals then only eating the leaves and tender parts, unless it is chaffed up and given them with the addition of oil-cake and molasses. It is propagated by root-cuttings, the cuttings being placed in holes about 1 foot apart each way, when it soon spreads, covering the whole surface of the land. It goes on ratoon-ing for many years, giving two and sometimes three cuttings annually. The yield varies with the soil, rainfall, and manurial treatment, but the average yield, without manure, may be set down from 5 to 7 tons per acre per annum. With the application of manure the yield is greatly increased, an acre then giving from 10 to 12 tons of fodder yearly." (*Kew Bulletin*, September, 1895.)

Habitat and range.—Occurs in South Australia, Victoria and Queensland, as well as our own Colony. With us it is very widely diffused, extending over most parts of the Colony. It is also found in tropical Asia.

7. Andropogon intermedius, R. Br.

Botanical name.—*Intermedius*—Latin, between, in allusion to its affinities with *A. ischæmum* and *A. pertusum*, which causes it to be intermediate, in some respects, between these species.

Synonym.—*A. punctatus*, Roxb., in Mueller's *Census*.

Where figured.—*Agricultural Gazette*.

Botanical description (B. Fl., vii, 531).—An erect grass of 2 feet or more, with the narrow leaves and general habit of *A. ischæmum*, the nodes varying with or without beards.

Spikes slender, 1 to 1½ inches long, usually numerous, all shortly pedicellate in an oblong terminal panicle of 3 or 4 inches without sheathing bracts ; the common Rhachis glabrous and always more or less elongated, the pedicels and base of the sessile spikelets more or less ciliate.

Spikelets under 2 lines long, narrow and acute or scarcely obtuse, and often purplish, as in *A. ischæmum*.

Outer glume often, but not always even in the same spike, marked with a dorsal pit, as in *A. pertusus*.

Awn small and slender.

Pedicellate spikelet more developed than in *A. ischæmum*, and often enclosing a male flower.

Botanical notes.—Outer glume often, but not always even in the same spike, marked with a dorsal pit, as in *A. pertusus*. This is alluded to in the synonymic name (*A. punctatus*) of *A. intermedius*.

Value as a fodder.—A rather coarse grass which yields, when young, a large quantity of nutritious fodder. It has been recommended by Bailey for planting river sides.

Habitat and range.—Found in all the Colonies except Tasmania. Is said to be common on springy land on the borders of rivers in Queensland. In our own Colony it does not appear to be very common. It occurs from the tableland to the interior. It is also found in Asia.

81

11. Andropogon bombycinus, R.Br.

Botanical Name.—Bombycinus—Latin, silken, or made of silk, in allusion to appearance of the inflorescence.

Vernacular names.—" Woolly-headed Grass," or " Silky-heads."

Where figured.—Bailey, *Agricultural Gazette.*

Botanical description.—(B. Fl., vii, 533).—An erect rigid perennial grass of 1½ to 3 feet, usually glabrous, except a little silky pubescence on the lower leaf-sheaths, the nodes glabrous or shortly bearded.

Leaves narrow, flat, rather rigid, the *ligula* very prominent, entire.

Panicle shortly branched, 3 to 6 inches long, with sheathing bracts of 1 to 2 inches under the branches.

Peduncles usually shorter than the bracts, bearing each a narrow sheathing bract and two very densely woolly-hairy spikes of ½ to 1 inch, at first erect, but soon spreading and reflexed.

Sessile spikelets two to five, concealed by silvery-silky hairs.

Outer glumes acute, many-nerved, but the two lateral nerves much more prominent, especially as the flowering advances, and the intermediate ones becoming almost obliterated or visible only towards the end of the glume.

Second glume thin, with a prominent keel, produced into a short point; *third* very thin, faintly three-nerved ; *terminal flowering glume* very thin and hyaline, shortly bifid, with a very fine awn scarcely exceeding the spikelet, or entire without any awn.

Pedicellate spikelets reduced to a single narrow many-nerved glume of 2½ to 3 lines.

Value as a fodder.—Some pastoralists speak highly of this grass, and when it is young there is no doubt it yields most nutritious pasturage. It is highly drought-resisting. Queensland observers speak of it in qualified terms. O'Shanesy says it is not at all relished by stock, and Bailey says it is only cropped by stock in early growth. It is well known that stock avoid grasses with much silky or woolly vesture if they can.

Habitat and range.—Found in all the colonies except Tasmania. It occurs in shifting sand and in the hottest interior districts; but it is also found east to the tableland.

13. Andropogon refractus, R.Br.

Botanical name.—Refractus—Latin, broken, in allusion to the broken or reflexed appearance of the inflorescence.

Vernacular names.—Often called " Kangaroo-grass" because of its resemblance to the true kangaroo-grass (*Anthistiria ciliata*). " Broken-spiked Grass" is a name coined by Bailey. It is the " Turpentine-grass" of O'Shanesy, so called owing to the odour of its roots.

Where figured.—Bailey, *Agricultural Gazette.*

Botanical description (B. Fl., vii, 534).—A glabrous erect grass of about 2 feet, with the narrow leaves, paniculate inflorescence, and sheating bracts of *A. schœnanthus*, and the spikes similarly two together, about ½ inch long, on short bracteate peduncles, but much more divaricate, soon reflexed, and glabrous except a small tuft of short hairs at the base of the sessile spikelets.

Sessile spikelets, two to five, 2½ to 3 lines long.

Outer glume acute, many-nerved; *second,* narrow and keeled; *third,* thin and hyaline ; *terminal or flowering glume* hyaline, narrow, either two-lobed with an awn slightly exceeding the spikelet, or more frequently entire or nearly so and awnless.

Pedicellate spikelets neuter, or rarely with a male flower ; the *outer glume* many-nerved.

F

Value as a fodder.—An excellent grass, nutritious and palatable, and making great growth if reasonably conserved. Many people look upon it as but little inferior in value to the true kangaroo-grass. In the northern territory of South Australia, the Rev. J. E. Tenison-Woods thus refers to it : " It was usually a coarse jungle-grass, more like a rush or sedge, and often completely concealing the horses. The species was most commonly *A. refractus*, a worthless, weedy grass, only good when young and green. In the dry state the horses would not touch it." This unfavourable report refers to a tropical locality.

Other uses.—The roots (in common with those of other species of the genus) are aromatic, and perhaps for that reason the coarse hay of the species is used by Fijians for mattresses. Hackel states that in Tahiti the natives prepare a cosmetic oil, "monoi," from it.

Habitat and range.—Found in Victoria and Queensland, besides New South Wales. It occurs in most parts of the Colony, right from the coast districts to the west. It is also a native of the Pacific Islands and of Japan.

14. Andropogon lachnatherus, Benth.

Botanical name.—*Lachnatherus*—Greek, *lachne*, soft woolly hair ; *ather*, an ear of corn, in reference to the vestiture of the spike.

Synonym.—*A. filipendulinus*, Hoch., in Muell. *Census.*

Where figured.—*Agricultural Gazette.*

Botanical description (B. Fl., vii, 534).

Stems rather slender, erect, about 2 feet high.

Leaves narrow, glabrous or sprinkled with long hairs.

Nodes not bearded.

Panicle looser than in the preceding species, with slender but not very long branches, solitary or clustered within sheathing bracts or floral leaves.

Peduncles exceeding the last sheathing bracts, bearing each two spikes, but not digitate, one attached lower down than the other, each ½ to ¾ inch long without the awns.

Sessile spikelets three or four, the lowest sometimes containing only a male flower, the others with a hermaphrodite flower, 2 to 2½ lines long, slightly hairy.

Outer glume obtuse, about nine-nerved.

Second rather shorter, obtuse, three-nerved.

Third very narrow, thin, and hyaline.

Awn or terminal glume on a short filiform base, 1 to 2 inches long, the lower part rigid and hirsute with rufous hairs.

Pedicellate spikelets narrow, acute, 2½ to 3 lines long, usually containing a male flower.

Outer glume many-nerved, often produced into a fine point.

Value as a fodder.—We have little knowledge as to its value for this purpose in New South Wales. It probably resembles most of its congeners, in being a very useful grass when young and tender.

Speaking of Queensland, Bailey says : " During the early part of summer it affords a fair amount of herbage, after which it sends up a number of flattened long stems, the greater part of which is occupied with the branching dry inflorescence, which is seldom touched by stock."

Habitat and range.—Found in New South Wales and Queensland. In our Colony it extends from the north coast to New England, being usually found in poor, stony ground. It is also found in East Africa.

30. IMPERATA.

Spikelets with one or rarely two flowers, usually in pairs, one sessile the other pedicellate, along the slender continuous *rhachis* of the short branches of a long cylindrical spike-like panicle, densely silky, with the long hairs surrounding and seated on the spikelets.

Glumes four, all thin, hyaline, and awnless, two outer empty ones usually hairy, the third empty or rarely enclosing a flower smaller and without hairs, terminal flowering glume still smaller.

Palea usually truncate and jagged at the top.

Stamens two, or one only in species not Australian.

Styles distinct.

Grain small, free, enclosed in the outer glumes.

1. Imperata arundinacea, Cyr.

Botanical name.—Imperata, in honour of Ferrante Imperata, a Neapolitan botanist of the sixteenth century; *arundinacea*—Latin,. reed-like.

Vernacular name.—" Blady-grass."

Where figured.—Duthie, *Agricultural Gazette.*

Botanical description (B. Fl., vii, 536).—A stiff, erect perennial, 1 to 3 feet high, glabrous except sometimes a tuft of hairs at the nodes, which however is not so common in Australian as in Indian specimens.

Leaves erect, narrow, often longer than the stem.

Spike-like panicle very dense, 3 to 8 inches long, regularly cylindrical, silvery white, with the long silky hairs concealing the glumes, the dark-coloured stigmas and oblong linear anthers alone protruding.

Spikelets 1½ to near 2 lines long.

Outer glume five- or seven-nerved.

Second, three- or five-nerved.

Third, usually empty.

Value as a fodder.—This is a grass very easily recognised, and many people look upon its presence as indicating poor land. They also look upon the grass as worthless for feed, but this is by no means the case. In Bengal it forms the principal pasturage, and with us, if burnt over, it produces plenty of feed, although it may not be of the best quality. In our colony enormous areas of coarse blady grass are systematically burnt over for cattle-feed. When old it is so fibrous that only a camel could digest it.

Other uses.—"The Telingas, of India, make use of it in their marriage ceremonies." (Duthie.)

The strong broad leaves were often used for thatching in Australia in the early days, a use to which it is often put in India and the Malay Archipelago. Mr. O'Shanesy says that it is preferred by brickmakers to any other grass for a thatch to protect their bricks when wet.

Mr. Bailey has suggested that it might be found useful for paper-making.

Lamson-Scribner recommends it for binding river-banks, the sides of dams, and loose coast sands.

Habitat and range.—This grass is usually found on damp, sour soils ; often it grows on poor, rocky soils, but by no means on worthless soils as a rule. It furnishes the principal grass of the Alang Alang fields of the Malay Archipelago. It is found in most parts of New South Wales, and in all the colonies. It is also a native of Europe, Asia, Africa, and America—an almost cosmopolitan grass.

31. CHRYSOPOGON.

Fertile spikelets one-flowered, sessile between two pedicellate male or barren spikelets at the end of the filiform unequal simple or divided branches of a terminal panicle, with sometimes one to three pairs of spikelets on the branch below the terminal three.

Glumes of the fertile spikelets four, the outer one the largest, awnless, membranous, and many-nerved, or more rigid with the lateral nerves prominent and often muricate ; second glume narrow, keeled, pointed or produced into a fine straight awn ; third much smaller, very thin, and hyaline ; fourth or terminal glume under the flower slender, flexuose, and stipes-like at the base, or dilated hyaline and two-lobed, with a short or long awn terminal or from between the lobes, twisted in the lower half and bent back above the middle as in *Andropogon*.

Palea very small or none.

Styles distinct.

Grain enclosed in the glumes, but free from them.

Pedicellate spikelets awnless with reduced glumes and usually one male flower.

Spikelets 3 to 5 lines long, one fertile and two pedicellate ones to each branch ; second glume of the fertile one awned ; awn of the terminal one long and rigid ...   . 1 *C. gryllus.*
Spikelets scarcely 1½ lines long, one to three fertile besides the pedicellate ones on each branch, second glume awnless   ...   ... 2 *C. parviflorus.*

1. Chrysopogon gryllus, Trin.

Botanical name.—*Chrysopogon*, from two Greek words signifying "golden beard," the tuft of hairs under the spikelet being sometimes of a golden colour (very marked in *C. gryllus*). Gryllus—Latin, a cricket. Trinius took the specific name from Linnæus (*Andropogon gryllus*), but it is not evident why the species is connected with a cricket.

Synonym.—*Andropogon gryllus*, Linn., in Mueller's *Census.*

Where figured.—Duthie (sectional drawing).

Botanical description (B. Fl., vii, 537).—An erect glabrous grass of 2 to 4 feet.

Leaves long and narrow, with a small ligula.
Panicle loose and spreading, 3 to 6 inches long, of numerous capillary simple branches mostly verticillate, of very unequal length, each bearing a single hermaphrodite spikelet, sessile between 2 pedicellate male ones, with a tuft of hairs at the base of the sessile one and on the pedicels.

Chrysopogon parviflorus, Benth.

"A Scented Grass."

Sessile spikelet narrow, 3 to 4 lines long, outer glumes rigid, acute, five- or seven-nerved, the lateral nerves more prominent and muricate or hispid, with a few short conical or rigid hairs.

Second glume narrow, hispid only at the end, the keel produced into a fine straight awn.

Third thin and hyaline.

Awn or terminal glume, long, rigid, and twisted in the lower part, the hyaline base narrow, with short lobes sometimes obsolete.

Pedicellate spikelets 3 to 5 lines long.

Outer glume membranous, tapering into a short fine awn, the inner ones unawned.

Value as a fodder.—A very good pasture-grass, not, however, abundantly diffused in this Colony. O'Shanesy says it improves much under cultivation.

Other uses.—C. R. Dodge *(Useful Fibre Plants)* says:—" Known in Italy as Barbone and Pollinia. From the fibrous roots horse-brushes and other coarse brushes, mats, &c., are said to be made ; also used for thatch material."

Habitat and range.—Found in all the Colonies except Tasmania, and extending in New South Wales from the tableland to the interior. It is also found in Europe, Asia, and Africa. In India it is specially found in the hilly parts of North India.

2. Chrysopogon parviflorus, Benth.

Botanical name.—*Parviflorus*, from two Latin words signifying " small-flowered."

Synonyms.—C. *violascens*, Trin., is the oldest name, according to the *Index Kewensis.* (The inflorescence has a violet or purplish cast.) Baron von Mueller, designating it an *Andropogon*, adopts the name *A. micranthus*, Kunth., in the *Census* (2nd ed.) and that of *A. montanus*, Roxb.,) an Indian-grass in the *Census* (1st ed.) Certain it is that the two grasses are very closely allied, and their properties are probably identical.

Vernacular names.—" Scented grass," owing to the sweet smell of the panicle, which is particularly observable when crushed between the fingers.

Where figured.—*Agricultural Gazette.*

Botanical description (B. Fl., vii, 537).—Stems 2 or 3 or even nearly 4 feet high ; the nodes usually but not always bearded.

Leaves narrow, scabrous, glabrous, or the lower sheaths pubescent or hairy.

Panicle 4 to 8 inches long, with very numerous capillary branches, mostly clustered and divided, the ultimate branches bearing in the typical form each a single hermaphrodite spikelet between two pedicellate male ones, the pedicels and base of the sessile spikelet ciliate.

Spikelets scarcely 1½ lines long.

Outer glume acute, not awned, finely many-nerved.

Awn capillary, 3 to 6 lines long, without any basal dilatation.

Mr. F. M. Bailey has described a variety, *flavescens*, of this grass, and says of it : " This lovely and very distinct form is in some localities upon the Darling Downs, Queensland, plentiful. Instead of the usual purplish colour, the inflorescence is of a pleasing yellow."

Var. *spicigera*, Benth. Ultimate branches of the panicle bearing one or two sessile spikelets below the terminal one, each accompanied by a pedicellate male.

Value as a fodder.—It is of too harsh a nature to be generally valuable for fodder, except when young. Cattle are, however, fond of it before it gets wiry. The general characteristic of this and other *Chrysopogons* may be stated as tall, slender grasses, only tender when young, but dry, wiry, and indigestible when old, not forming a dense pasture-growth.

Mr. A. R. Crawford points out that usually, in this Colony, it grows along fences, where stock cannot get at it. Mr. W. H. Walker remarks that it is to be found for miles in the Tenterfield district within the railway fence chiefly,—testimony to its appreciation by stock. O'Shanesy says it is a good fodder in Queensland.

Referring to *C. montanus*, Trin., J. F. Duthie (quoting *C. parviflorus* as a synonym), says :—" This is found in the hilly parts of Northern India. On Mount Abu I found several patches of this very elegant grass. It is said there to be an excellent fodder grass." Holmes (quoted by Mueller), says that this species resists fire better than many other grasses, which is a recommendation to us in this Colony.

Speaking of the closely-related *C. serrulatus*, Trin., Mr. S. M. Tracy (*Mississippi Agricultural Experimental Station, Bull.* No. 20) says :— " This is a perennial grass, the seed of which was received from India, and which is one of our most valuable importations. Although nearly related to our native broom-sedge(? *C. nutans*, Benth.), it starts into growth much earlier in the spring, produces a heavier growth of leaves, and will yield two cuttings of excellent hay, besides a considerable amount of winter pasturage. It has been entirely free from any injury from cold, and from all attacks of fungus diseases, and is spreading well by self-sown seeds. It grows 4 to 5 feet high, and more than one-half of the hay is made up of the leaves, the stalks being rather small."

I think that both *C. parviflorus* and *C. gryllus*, as well as several of the exotic species, are well worthy of careful experimental cultivation.

Other uses.—In Rajputana the grain is sometimes collected and eaten by the natives.

Habitat and range.—Extends from Victoria to Northern Australia, occurring in our own Colony in the coast districts, in sheltered situations on the Dividing Range and spurs, and on the tablelands. It is partial to rich flats.

Mr. W. H. Walker states that it is common at Tenterfield and for miles south within the railway fence.

In the more southern parts of New England it is common. It extends also to Asia and the Pacific Islands.

Reference to plate.—1. Part of a panicle, showing the inflorescence ; 2. Showing the two pedicellate male spikelets and sessile hermaphrodite spikelet undeveloped (much enlarged). In *C. gryllus* the inflorescence is much larger, is more hairy under the inflorescence, and the second glume of the fertile spikelet is awned.

Sorghum halepense, Pers.

"Evergreen Millet."

32. SORGHUM.

Fertile spikelet one-flowered, sessile between two pedicellate male or barren ones, at the end of the simple or divided branches of a terminal panicle, with one to five pairs or triplets of spikelets below the terminal three.

Glumes on the fertile spikelets four, the outer one the largest, awnless, lanceolate or broad, hard and shining, obscurely nerved ; second glume rather hard, keeled and acute ; third glume shorter, very thin and hyaline ; fourth or terminal glume very thin, hyaline and two-lobed at the base, with an awn between the lobes, twisted in the lower half, bent above the middle as in *Andropogon*.

Palea very small or none. Styles distinct.

Grain enclosed in the hard and shining outer glumes, but free from them.

Nodes glabrous or scarcely pubescent. Fruiting spikelets lanceolate, nearly glabrous. Awn short and fine ...   . 1. *S. halepense*.
Nodes bearded. Fruiting spikelets lanceolate, 2½ to 4 lines long, villous. Awn usually long. Ovary glabrous ...   . 2. *S. plumosum*.

To this genus belongs Planter's Friend or Imphee, Amber Cane, and other fodder plants. They have, from time to time, been reputed to have caused the death of stock, and the deaths have been attributed either to hoven, or to the presence of a specific poison (not hitherto isolated) in the plant. A note on the subject will be found at page 251 of the *Agricultural Gazette* of New South Wales, for April, 1896. Attention has again been drawn to the subject by the publication of a paper by Veterinary-Captain H. T. Pease, in the *Agricultural Ledger* (1896, No. 24), Veterinary Series No. 23, published by the Indian Government, entitled " Poisoning of Cattle by the Juar Plant (*Andropogon Sorghum*)." This is a synonym of *Sorghum vulgare*, and the poisoning is attributed to the large deposits of nitrate of potash that, under certain conditions, are thrown down in the stems. The death of stock by eating sorghum has not been attributed to this cause before, I believe, and the matter is worthy of careful consideration. At the same time, I believe that the matter has not reached finality, and we require absolute confirmation of Mr. Pease's results.

1. Sorghum halepense, Pers.

Botanical name.—Sorghum, stated by some to be derived from an Indian word for a grain belonging to this genus ; but I cannot trace, with certainty, the Indian word. *Halepensis*, Aleppo (adjectival form).

Synonym.—Andropogon halepensis, Sibth.

Vernacular names.—" Evergreen Millet " is a name in use in the Sydney market (also in California), while Johnson-grass is the most widely-used name given to it in the United States. It is a much-named grass. As regards the names " Aleppo-grass," and " Johnson-grass," neither the former, after a place in Asia Minor, nor the latter, after the name of a gentleman who introduced its cultivation from one part of the United States to another (South Carolina to Alabama), would seem to be a suitable name for an Australian grass. A. A. Crozier, of

Michigan, U.S.A., in his monograph on millets, gives the following common names :—Australian Millet, Morocco Millet, Arabian Millet, Arabian Millet-grass, Arabian Evergreen Millet, Mears'-grass, Guinea-grass (erroneously), False Guinea-grass, Egyptian-grass, Egyptian Millett, Green Valley-grass, Cuba-grass, Alabama Guinea-grass, Syrian-grass, St. Mary's-grass.

Where figured.—Duthie, Vasey, Hackel, *Agricultural Gazette.*

Botanical description (B. Fl., vii, 540).—Stems erect, varying from 2 or 3 to 8 or 10 feet high, the nodes glabrous.

Leaves long and flat, often rather broad, the midrib usually white and prominent.
Panicle from 3 or 4 inches to above 1 foot long, loose and often much branched.
Fertile spikelets lanceolate, varying from 2 to above 3 lines long, pale-coloured or scarcely purple, not rufous, with a few hairs at the base.
Outer coriaceous glume faintly many-nerved, at length smooth and shining.
Second glume rather smaller, five-nerved, usually sprinkled with a few hairs.
Terminal glume hyaline, broad, ciliate, two-lobed, the awn from the notch very fine and short, rarely nearly twice as long as the spikelet.

Mr. W. H. Walker, of Tenterfield, who has made many experiments in the cultivation of both indigenous and introduced grasses, writes that he is sending down 10 lb. of seed of this grass to his Winton Station, 30 miles below Goondiwindi, and is having a small paddock ploughed for it. He adds that it seems to grow well at Goondiwindi, and gives green feed for horses and cattle when other grasses have little growth in them.

Value as a fodder.—It is best known as a fodder-grass in the United States, and as regards experience in that country, we cannot do better than quote Vasey: " This grass is best adapted to warm climates, and has proved most valuable on warm, dry soils in the Southern States. Its chief value is for hay, in regions where other grasses fail on account of drought. If cut early the hay is of good quality, and several cuttings may be made in the season; but if the cutting is delayed until the stalks are well grown, the hay is so coarse and hard that stock do not eat it readily. The seed may be sown at any time when the soil is warm and not too dry. Failures often occur from sowing the seed too early. If there is danger that the soil should dry out before the seed can germinate, soaking the seed may be resorted to with good results. Thick seeding gives a heavier yield, and a better quality of hay. From 1 to 2 bushels are usually sown per acre, according to the quality of the seed. In case of failure to get a good stand, the crop may be allowed to go to seed the first year, after which the vacant spaces will be found to be self seeded. On small patches, in such cases, the ground is sometimes ploughed up, and the underground stems scattered along the furrows over the vacant spots. In most localities it is generally considered desirable to plough the land about every third year, otherwise the root-stocks become matted near the surface, and the crop is more affected by drought. Ploughing causes it to grow more thickly and vigorously."

In another work, " Report on the Grasses of the South," Dr. Vasey further says :—"Mr. N. B. Moore has cultivated this grass for forty years, and prefers it to all others. It is perennial, as nutritious as any other, difficult to eradicate, will grow on ordinary soil, and yields abundantly."

" Horses and cattle are fond of it, both in its dry and green condition.
Probably no grass gives better promise for the dry arid lands of the west."
" In California it is known as Evergreen or Arabian Millet. It roots
deep in the sub-soil, and where that is at all alkaline it grows
enormously, but at the same time absorbs so much of the unpalatable
alkali that stock will not eat it. It is excellent for dry hills, free from
alkali."

It is common all over Northern India, in cultivated and uncultivated
ground, and is considered to be a good fodder grass both for grazing
and hay.

The Department of Agriculture of Victoria distributed some of the
seed of this grass to farmers in 1888, and following are extracts from
the circular issued at the time :—" Superior both as a grazing and hay
grass ; has abundance of roots, which decay, thereby enriching the
ground rather than exhausting it. The best results follow sowing the
seed in August and September, enabling the seed to get a good root
by the autumn, and forming a better turf the following season. Sow
broadcast at the rate of a bushel an acre, and cover with a light brush,
or sow just before a heavy rain. Three good crops the following season
will be the result if the season is favourable."

Baron von Mueller quotes J. L. Dow, of Victoria, as stating that it
keeps green in the heat of summer ; also, Mr. Hollingsworth, that it
is not eaten out by pasture animals. The Baron adds : " It will also
grow in drift sand of the coast, and will keep growing during the dry
season, when most other grasses fail, but improves much on irrigation ;
the roots resist some frost ; three tons can be cut from one acre in a
single season ; it yields so large a hay-crop that it may be cut half a
dozen times in a season, provided the land be rich. All kinds of stock
have a predilection for this grass."

Objections to this grass.—" The greatest objection to this grass is
the difficulty of eradicating it. Care should be taken not to introduce
it into fields intended for cultivation. It spreads rapidly, both by root
and seed, and it is apt to enter fields where it is not wanted. The
grass is not well adapted to pasture, and close pasturing is one of the
means of getting rid of it. Its succulent subterranean stems are
usually well liked by hogs after they have become accustomed to them,
and by keeping hogs closely confined on it, it may be eradicated. There
has been much discussion in the papers of the Southern United States
as to this grass, some considering it a great blessing, others a curse,
the fact being that it is a blessing where a permanent grass is desired,
and a great pest in land intended for general cultivation." (Vasey.)

Duthie points out that various reports indicate its injurious effects
on cattle if eaten when too young, or when the plants are stunted by
drought. He adds that the same results have been observed to take
place in the case of *Sorghum vulgare.* Dr. Stewart was told in Hazara
that cattle, after eating it, are often attacked by fatal head affections.
In other districts it is said to be poisonous until the rains are over,
when cattle eat it with impunity. (See *ante,* page 87.)

A gentleman in the Inverell district wrote to the Department some
time ago asking for directions how to eradicate it, and there is no

doubt it may become a pest in cultivated ground. I only bring it again under notice at the present time because I think it is not as generally known as it should be, and if it escapes into cultivated ground, if pigs be carefully enclosed, they will eradicate it. That it is poisonous in the ordinary sense I do not believe; but I have seen it so rampant and succulent that I can readily understand that stock, unused to it, might do themselves injury by gorging themselves with it.

Other uses.—Duthie says that the seed of this grass is collected in Bikanir, India, ground and mixed with the flour of *Pennisetum typhoideum*, and eaten by the poorer classes. He also states that native pens are made from the stems.

Habitat and range.—This is a truly Australian grass, being indigenous to Western Australia, New South Wales, and Queensland, In our own Colony it is found as far west as New England. It also occurs in the Pacific Islands, the countries around the Mediterranean, and is largely distributed in Asia. It is not a native of America, although it is so much cultivated in the United States, from which country most of the seed sent out by seedsmen has been originally obtained. I doubt whether any seed is collected from the indigenous New South Wales grass, which appears to be confined to the coast districts.

Most of the remarks which have been made in regard to this grass have been based upon non-Australian forms of it, and I trust that it will be thoroughly tried in the arid regions of the west. I fancy it has been tried in the vicinity of the artesian bores; but, if not, it would appear to be of singular promise for such situations. It flourishes in alkaline soils, and it could readily be ascertained in what localities it takes up so much alkali as to be distasteful to stock.

In experimenting with such a grass as this in arid places, disappointment might at first result through seed being used which was raised in the moist coast lands of Australia, or any other country; but, with care, drought-resistant seed might be saved in a very few seasons. It bears such a good reputation for droughty localities that it is worth taking some pains over.

This grass (imported seed) has been introduced into New South Wales for many years, although, as already remarked, it is far from being generally known even yet. A few years ago, the late Rev. Dr. Woolls (who lived at one time near the Hawkesbury), stated that the settlers in that district looked upon it as a recent importation, and that the seed had been distributed under the name of *Panicum spectabile*—quite a different grass.

At the present time the catalogues of most of our leading seedsmen offer it, so that good seed is readily available. I have noted all the warnings that can be given in regard to the grass; but its good qualities far outweigh any possible bad ones, and I would again submit it to careful attention.

Reference to plate:—(A), Portion of panicle; (B), Showing female spikelet, and one male (stalked) spikelet. A second male spikelet has been broken off where shown; (c), Female spikelet opened out, showing awn and three glumes.

2. Sorghum plumosum, Beauv.

Botanical Name.—*Plumosum*—Latin, full of feathers, in allusion to the fruiting spikelets, which are villous.

Where figured.—*Agricultural Gazette.*

Botanical description (B. Fl., vii, 540).—A tall grass, closely resembling *S. halepense*, but with the nodes bearded with a dense tuft of hairs, and the leaves much narrower. Inflorescence and structure of the spikelets the same, but the smaller branches, pedicels, and spikelets more or less villous, with hairs usually rufous, besides the dense tuft at the base of the sessile spikelets.

> *Spikelets* varying from 2½ to 4 lines long, lanceolate as in *S. halepense*, but less flattened, and usually narrower.
> *Outer glume* at first several-nerved, at length rigid, shining, and apparently nerveless, except two ciliate nerves near the top, often turning almost black when ripe.
> *Awn* often short and capillary, but usually longer and stouter than in *S. halepense*, though never so long as in *S. intrans.*
> *Ovary* glabrous.

Value as a fodder.—This is a coarse grass, not liked by sheep-farmers, but on a cattle-run it is a very good grass. (Bailey.)

Habitat and range.—Found in all the Colonies, except South Australia and Tasmania. In our Colony it occurs from the Coast district to the tableland.

33. ANTHISTIRIA.

Spikelets one-flowered or empty, seven (rarely six) in a spike or cluster, four male or barren, either sessile or pedicellate in a whorl at the base of the hairy rhachis, two, or sometimes one, pedicellate and male or barren on the top of the rhachis, with an intermediate sessile fertile one.

Glumes in the barren spikelets usually two, the outer one several-nerved, the inner thin and hyaline, in the male spikelets usually a third smaller hyaline one ; in the fertile spikelet glumes four, the two outer ones nearly equal, usually rigid and coriaceous, the outer one obscurely five- or seven-nerved, the second with two prominent nerves, the central one very faint, third glume much smaller, very thin and hyaline ; fourth very narrow and thin at the base, thickened into a long twisted awn, usually bent above the middle.

Palea very small and hyaline, sometimes scarcely conspicuous.

Styles distinct.

Grain free, enclosed in the hardened outer glumes. Erect leafy branching grasses, the spikes or clusters singly pedunculate within sheathing bracts, or sessile in the bracts and collected many together in compound clusters, forming short almost cyme-like leafy panicles.

> The four-whorled barren spikelets sessile. Awn very long and rigid.
> Spikelets in dense compound clusters, sessile within the bracts.
> Bracts glabrous. Barren spikelets glabrous or sprinkled with long cilia. Fertile spikelet glabrous or shortly pubescent at the end .. .. 1. *A. ciliata.*
> Spikelets with the surrounding barren ones on slender pedicels within the sheathing bracts. Barren spikelets glabrous. Fertile one densely villous with brown hairs ... ... 3. *A. avenacea.*
> The four whorled barren spikelets pedicellate, all the spikelets glabrous.
> Awns very fine ... ... 4. *A. membranacea*

92

1. Anthistiria ciliata, Linn.

Botanical name.—Anthistiria, from the Greek *Anthisteri*, very stiff stubble, the grasses often being coarse looking and tussocky ; *ciliata* (Latin), bearing hairs, or bearded, in allusion to the spikelets, which are often ciliate.

Synonym.—Themeda Forskalii, Hack.

Vernacular names.—The " Common Kangaroo Grass." " It forms tussocks, which habit, combined with its nodding clusters of flowers, probably procured its local name" (Bailey.) Perhaps, however, it was so called because kangaroos and other marsupials feed on it. The " Rooi Grass " of South Africa.

Where figured.—Bailey ; *Agricultural Gazette ;* Hooker, *Fl., Tas. ;* Duthie (figure and flower) ; Hackel.

Botanic description (B. Fl., vii, 542).—

Stems 1 to 3 feet high.

Leaves narrow, glabrous or the sheaths hairy.

Ligula very short, sometimes ciliate.

Spikes or clusters of spikelets not numerous, sessile or the lower ones pedunculate in a short terminal leafy panicle, the leafy bracts subtending each spike sheathing at the base, and tapering into points longer than the cluster, the short rhachis bearded with long brown hairs.

Spikelets narrow, 4 to 5 lines long, four male or barren sessile at the base of the bearded rhachis, two or one pedicellate at the top, glabrous or sprinkled with a few long hairs.

Outer glume the largest, acute, many-nerved.

Second shorter, thin, and three -or five-nerved.

Third thin and hyaline.

Fertile terminal spikelet glabrous, or shortly pubescent at the end.

Outer glume broad, obtuse, rather thick, about seven-nerved.

Second rigid, rather shorter and narrower, with two prominent lateral nerves and a faint central one.

Third narrow-oblong, very thin and hyaline.

Awn, or fourth glume, very long and rigid, the attenuate base not dilated.

Value as a fodder.—This is, perhaps, the best known and most appreciated of all our native grasses. It is readily identified, for its characteristic inflorescence freely forms if it has a chance to recuperate, and it grows in tussocks or tussocky masses, which frequently grow closely together. The grass has been so much appreciated by stock that it is now virtually extinct in many districts in which it was formerly plentiful. It forms so much inflorescence that a paddock of it, with its nodding flowers, has the appearance of a cultivated crop, but only those who have endeavoured to collect seed of it know how difficult it frequently is to collect even a few fertile grains. Hence one difficulty in propagating it ; but it can be so readily propagated from living plants that it seems a great pity that farmers and pastoralists do not more frequently introduce it into their paddocks than they do at present. Of course, they would require to fence patches of it for a season ; in fact, it would be desirable to permanently maintain nursery patches of it, in order that a supply of roots might always be available. This is, of course an amplication of the advice so often given to landowners to periodically rest the whole or portions of their paddocks, in order to enable the grasses to contend against the danger of extermination through overstocking. Hooker wrote in 1859 : " This is the best fodder grass in Australia," and the dictum remains true to this day. Mac Owan says: " This is the best native fodder we have in South Africa." In western New South Wales it is less succulent than in the eastern districts more favoured with rain, and, hence, there it sometimes becomes harsh and unpalatable to stock.

Following is a Victorian account of this grass :—" Perennial ; average height under 3 feet, on rich unstocked land much higher, with strong penetrating fibrous roots ; in flower during December. This grass is found in all parts of Australia. It forms generally but few perfect seeds, and these do not germinate readily. Some plants are much better seed-bearers than others. It is the finest and most useful of all the indigenous grasses. Here it commences to vegetate early in November, when all stock should be taken away until it is in flower. From then until winter it proves an excellent fattening grass. It keeps green during the summer, but turns a little brown in autumn, when its nutritive qualities are at the highest. In the early days of the Colony, I have ridden the same horse 20 to 40 miles, on a journey of several hundred miles, turning him out to graze on pasture of which this grass formed the principal part, and the horse kept his condition. With a sufficiency of this grass, a little turned by the sun, the working powers of horse and cattle can be taxed to the utmost. They keep in better condition doing hard work on this than on any other description of native forage. If closely grazed by sheep or cattle (the former in particular) all the year round, it soon dies out. Other varieties of this valuable grass might be obtained by cultivation." (Bacchus.)

Other uses.—The aborigines of Lake Tyers, Victoria, used to make fishing-nets of this grass. A figure of the mesh, and an account of the method of employing the net, will be found in Brough Smyth's *Aboriginals of Victoria*, i, 389.

Habitat and range.—Found in all the colonies, and, in New South Wales, all over the Colony. It is eaten out in many districts where it was once known to be plentiful. It attains its greatest luxuriance in the good soils of the coast and mountains. Found also in tropical Africa and Asia ; common on the Himalaya.

3. Anthistiria avenacea, F.v.M.

Botanical name.—*Avenacea*, Latin, oat-like, in allusion to the appearance of the spikelets.

Synonym.—*Themeda gigantea*, Hackel, var.

Vernacular names.—The " Tall Oat Grass " of the Darling Downs, Queensland. Sometimes called simply " Oat Grass," and even "Kangaroo Grass."

Where figured.—*Agricultural Gazette.*

Botanical description (B. Fl., vii, 543).

Stems from a more or less silky-hairy or woolly base, 2 to 3 feet high.

Leaves very narrow, glabrous.

Sheathing bracts narrow, membranous, glabrous, 1 to 2 inches long.

Spikes or clusters all on rather long, slender, glabrous, or ciliate peduncles, within the last bract.

Barren spikelets either reduced to a single several-nerved rigid glume, with a small hyaline one inside, or more developed, enclosing a male flower, the four involucral ones sessile.

Fertile spikelets about 4 lines long.

Rigid outer glumes, especially the lowest, densely villous with brown hairs.

Awn long and rigid as in the two preceding species.

Value as a fodder.—Undoubtedly a valuable grass, chiefly for the dry country and dry tablelands. It is of a tussocky habit, and produces a large quantity of palatable and nutritious food.

Few men could have been better acquainted with this grass than O'Shanesy, but his account, which follows, is not very favourable ; he probably refers to the old growths :—

" It is perennial, and grows in large tufts, but its foliage is very harsh, and, therefore, rejected by cattle as well as by the kangaroo."

Habitat and range.—Found in all the colonies except Tasmania. In New South Wales it prefers good soil and occurs from the tableland to the interior.

4. Anthistiria membranacea, Lindl.

Botanical name.—*Membranacea*, Latin, like parchment, in allusion to the translucency of the glumes.

Vernacular names.—" Landsborough Grass," " Barcoo Grass" (both named after Queensland localities), " Red Gulf Grass " (in allusion to its growth in the Gulf of Carpentaria country).

Where figured.—Bailey. *Agricultural Gazette.*

Botanical description (B. Fl., vii, 543).—Quite glabrous, sometimes forming dense leafy tufts of 6 inches, the branching stems often elongated to 1 or 2 feet.

Leaves flat, appearing almost articulate on the short, flat, prominently striate sheaths.
Floral leaves or bracts with coriaceous sheaths and short lanceolate laminæ.
Panicles small, dense, almost cyme-like, as in *Apluda*, with very numerous small spikes or clusters, each subtended by a scarcely longer bract.
Spikelets scarcely 2 lines long, glabrous, the four involucral ones pedicellate, the fertile one rather longer than the two pedicellate barren ones beside it.
Glumes all thin, the outer one acute with several green nerves, the second with one or three nerves.
Awn very fine, scarcely more than as long again as the spikelet.

Value as a fodder.—This is mainly a Queensland grass, and Bailey says of it :—

" When under cultivation, it makes a dense intricate growth from $1\frac{1}{2}$ feet to over 2 feet in depth, and being very leafy and full of seed should make good, nutritious hay. It is the rule to cut grass for hay when in flower, but with a grass like this, this rule cannot be strictly adhered to, for, from an early period of its life, it continues to flower and mature seed. When closely fed, it bears good seed on stems only 2 or 3 inches high, and, although a tropical grass, has been found to thrive admirably in the Brisbane district. . . . Probably no grass, indigenous or foreign, is so relished by stock. . . . It is very brittle when approaching maturity ; thus it is much broken by stock, but it is said that cattle are so partial to it that they often lick the broken pieces off the ground." Information in regard to New South Wales experience with this grass, and in regard to its distribution, would be very acceptable.

Habitat and range.—Found in all the colonies except Tasmania and Victoria. It is suitable for hot districts, occurring only in the dry interior.

34. APLUDA.

Spikelets with one fertile flower, and a male one below it, sessile between two flattened pedicels, bearing each a rudimentary or barren spikelet, the whole embraced by a sheathing bract, the bracts clustered on the branches of a leafy panicle.

Outer glume of the sessile spikelet concave, striate, awnless ; second glume acute, awnless, thin but stiff ; third, very thin and hyaline ; fourth or terminal glume, very thin and hyaline, entire or bifid at the top, awnless, or with a slender twisted terminal awn.

Palea very thin, or none.

Styles distinct.

Grain enclosed in the outer glumes, free from them.

1. Apluda mutica, Linn.

Botanical name.—*Apluda*, Greek for chaff, the inflorescence resembling chaff in appearance ; *mutica*, Latin, blunt, perhaps, in allusion to the outer glume.

Synonym.—All species of *Apluda* are reduced by Hackel to forms of *A. varia*, Hackel.

Where figured.—Duthie (sect. figure).

Botanical description (B. Fl. vii, 544).—

Stem creeping or climbing, several feet long, with erect branching flowering shoots.

Leaves long, usually glabrous.

Panicle loose and leafy, 1 to 2 feet long.

Bracts subtending the spikelets 3 to 4 lines long, very concave, striate, with short, sometimes awn-like points, in clusters of five or six.

Sessile spikelet shorter than the bract.

Pedicellate spikelets either reduced to a rudimentary glume or more developed and protruding beyond the bract.

Awns of the terminal glume very minute or entirely deficient.

Value as a fodder.—So little is known of the economic value of this *Apluda* that the following note on an allied species (*A. aristata*)* is interesting :—"In hedges and bushes it usually assumes a climbing habit. In forest land it often constitutes a large portion of the undergrowth. It is considered to be a fairly good fodder grass, and is readily eaten by cattle when young." (Duthie.)

Habitat and range.—Found in New South Wales and Queensland. In our Colony found only in the interior, but rare, and worthy of the best attention of collectors. Found also in Asia, Africa, and the Pacific Islands.

---

* Really a form of the same species, according to Hackel.

Sub-tribe v.—Tristegineæ.

35. ARUNDINELLA.

Spikelets with one terminal hermaphrodite flower and often a second male one below it, in a loose terminal panicle.

Glumes four, the three outer ones often pointed but not awned, the third with a palea or a male flower in its axil; terminal flowering glume smaller, thinner, with a fine awn twisted in the lower part and bent back at or below the middle.

Palea smaller.

Styles distinct.

Grain enclosed in the more or less stiffened glume and palea, free from them.

1. Arundinella nepalensis, Trin.

Botanical name.—Arundinella, diminutive of *arundo,* a reed, the grass being like a thin reed; *nepalensis,* adjective for Nepal, India, the country whence it was originally recorded.

Where figured.—Hackel (after Trinius).

Botanical description (B. Fl., vii, 545).—An erect glabrous perennial, attaining 6 to 8 feet.

Leaves narrow.

Ligula short, minutely ciliate.

Panicle narrow, dense or loose, erect or slightly spreading, varying from 4 to 6 inches in the smaller specimens to above 1 foot in luxuriant ones, the lower branches densely clustered.

Spikelets all or mostly pedicellate, narrow, about 2 lines long, the three outer glumes usually five-nerved, tapering into short points, the lowest rather shorter than the others, the third rather thinner, with a male flower in its axil.

Terminal flowering glume smaller and thinner at the time of flowering, slightly notched with minute obtuse or acute points on each side of the awn not produced into bristles.

Palea auriculate on each side near the base.

Value for fodder.—When mature this is a harsh, rush-like or cane-like grass which stock cannot eat. When young they nibble it in conjunction with other and better grasses which are also available at a similar period of their growth. I give three opinions of it, remarking that it is better known in Queensland than with us. Duthie remarks that nothing definite is known in regard to its value for fodder in India.

"Usually a dry grass, particularly when grown on poor land, but affording better fodder in the tropics and on better soil." (Bailey.)

"Commences its growth in the spring weather, and continues to increase during the whole summer, forming a dense mass of foliage, which grows as fast as it is fed off or cut." (Mueller.)

"It is useless for thatch, uninteresting to the settler, it being one of those grasses which cattle of every description appear to reject." (O'Shanesy.)

Habitat and range.—Found in New South Wales and Queensland. In our own Colony from Windsor, Hawkesbury River, northwards. Bailey says, "Met with usually on poor land, such as ironbark ridges," while O'Shanesy states that it is chiefly confined to inundated places, bordering on creeks and rivers, where it grows to a height of 5 to 6 feet.

It is also found in Asia and South Africa.

B.—Poaceæ.

---

38. LEERSIA.

Spikelets one-flowered, flat, articulate, on short pedicels along the filiform branches of a terminal panicle.
Glumes two, complicate and keeled, the outer one the largest.
No two-nerved *Palea.*
Stamens six or in species not Australian three or fewer.
Styles short, distinct.
Grain enclosed in the slightly hardened glumes, free from them.

1. Leersia hexandra, Swartz.

Botanical name.—*Leersia,* in honor of J. D. Leers, a German botanist; *hexandra,* Greek *hexa,* six ; *aner, andros,* a man (botany, stamen), in allusion to the six stamens.
Vernacular name.—" Rice Grass."
Where figured.—Bailey.
Botanical description (B. Fl., vii, 549).—An erect though weak glabrous grass, attaining several feet, often rooting in the mud at the lower nodes.

Leaves rather narrow, flat when fresh, mostly erect.
Panicle oblong, 2 to 4 inches long, with erect or slightly spreading filiform flexuose branches.
Spikelets narrow-ovate, about 1½ lines long.
Glumes membranous, acute, the outer one with a prominent nerve on each side besides the marginal one ; the inner glume nearly as long, but narrower, with only one nerve on each side near the margin.
Stamens six.

Value as a fodder.—This grass is closely allied to that which produces rice. It is a semi-aquatic grass which is so sparingly distributed in this Colony that we know but little of it from a pastoral point of view, but it is not likely ever to be important to the raiser of stock. It is, however, a tender grass, much liked by stock, and Duthie quotes Symonds as stating that cattle are fond of it in India.
" A widely-distributed perennial swamp-grass found in warm regions of both hemispheres. In the Philippine Islands it is regularly cultivated, under the name of Zacate, for the purpose of supplying food

G

for domestic animals. It is treated like rice, being transplanted to wet and previously ploughed meadows. Bailey found it to be one of the most relished by cattle amongst the aquatic grasses of East Australia. In Singapore it is regularly gathered in waste places as a green fodder for cattle and horses."—(*Kew Bulletin*, 1894, p. 382.)

Fungus found on this grass.—*Thecaphoria inquinans*, B. & Br.

Habitat and range.—New South Wales and Queensland, from Port Jackson north. It is a semi-aquatic plant. It is especially common along the watercourses of Queensland, to a less extent on those of the northern parts of this Colony. It is found throughout the entire tropical zone.

40. POTAMOPHILA.

Spikelets one-flowered, polygamous, not flattened, articulate on very short pedicels along the filiform branches of a terminal panicle.

Glumes four, two outer ones very small membranous, nerveless, two upper ones much larger, membranous but prominently nerved, the outer one the broadest.

No two-nerved *palea*.

Stamens six.

Styles short, distinct.

Grain enclosed in the larger glumes, free from them.

1. Potamophila parviflora, R.Br.

Botanical name.—*Potamophila*, Greek *potamos* a river, *philo* I love, in allusion to the habitat of this grass; *parviflora*, *parvus* small, *flora* (*flos*, *floris*) flower, small-flowered.

Where figured.—Trinius.

Botanical description (B. Fl., vii, 550).—An aquatic glabrous grass of 3 to 5 feet.

Leaves narrow and erect, convolute when dry, scabrous; ligula prominent, jagged.

Panicle narrow, 1 to 1½ feet long, or even more.

Spikelets very numerous, about 1¼ lines long, pale-coloured or purplish, ovoid-oblong, the males and females very similar and variously intermixed, with a few barren ones reduced to empty glumes.

Larger glumes membranous, rather acute, concave, the outer one five-nerved, the inner one three-nerved.

Value as a fodder.—A tall, pale-coloured, erect, cane-like grass, forming large tussocks in the water several feet in diameter. It is cropped by cattle wherever they can reach it, and is probably a very nutritious grass.

Habitat and range.—Confined to this Colony, and only recorded from the Hastings and Williams Rivers. I found it in my recent expedition to Mount Seaview, occurring for many miles in the Lower and Upper Hastings. It is found in the stony bed of the limpid stream, always more or less submerged, probably because cattle have eaten it out close to the bank.

42. MICROLÆNA.

Spikelets one-flowered, on filiform pedicels in a narrow loose panicle, the *rhachis* of the spikelet articulate above the two outer glumes.

Glumes six, two outer short and persistent, third and fourth long, narrow and awned, fifth and sixth shorter, acute, unawned, all keeled.

Flower terminal.

No *palea.*

Lodicules large, very thin.

Stamens four or two.

Styles distinct.

Grain enclosed in the larger glumes, but free from them.

1. Microlæna stipoides, R. Br.

Botanical name.—*Microlæna*—Greek, *micros*, small; *lenos*, wool—in allusion to the small woolly flower-stalks; *stipoides*, Stipa-like (*oidos*), resembling the grasses known as *Stipa*.

Synonym.—*Ehrharta stipoides*, Labill., in F.v.M. *Census.*

Vernacular names.—" Weeping-grass," Meadow Rice-grass" of N.Z., " Wire-grass;" the " Star-grass" of Bacchus, and the " Nodding Feather-grass," of Bailey.

Where figured.—Labillardiere, as *Microlæna stipoides;* Bailey; Buchanan; *Key Victorian plants* (Mueller); Hooker (*Flora Tasmania*); *Agricultural Gazette.*

Botanical description.—(B. Fl., vii, 552).

Stems from a perennial rhizome, erect or ascending, 1 to 2 feet high.

Leaves usually rather short, flat or convolute and very acute, glabrous or slightly hairy.

Panicle narrow, 3 to 6 inches long, with filiform erect branches and pedicels.

Spikelets narrow, 4 to 5 lines long without the awn, two outer persistent glumes minute; third and fourth glumes narrow, rigid, with three prominent scabrous nerves, tapering into a fine awn, with a tuft of hairs at their base on the slightly elongated *rhachis*, the fourth rather longer than the third, and its awn sometimes much longer; fifth glume rather shorter, acute but not awned, the nerves not prominent; sixth shorter, very narrow and thin but stiff.

Stamens, 4.

Value as a fodder.—This is an excellent pasture-grass for the moister districts of the colony. In depressions in pasture-land, and in other situations where it can obtain the necessary moisture, it grows in patches, affording a tender green growth, 6 inches to 1 foot high, for many months of the year. Though not one of our best grasses, it is believed to be nutritious. Cattle crop it readily, and the dairy farmer should give it every encouragement. It is not a very conspicuous grass, hence it may be readily passed over even when in inflorescence.

Bacchus says of it :—" Where the Kangaroo-grass grows this grass is generally found also ; it does not, however, suffer so much from overstocking as the former. It is a good fattening grass."

Habitat and range.—Found in all the Colonies, including New Zealand. In our Colony it is widely diffused, except in the interior.

43. TETRARRHENA.

Spikelets one-flowered, sessile or very shortly pedicellate in a simple spike or in a scarcely branched spike-like panicle; the *rhachis* of the spikelet articulate above the two outer glumes.

Glumes six, two outer small and persistent, the third various, the fourth usually the largest and rigid, the fifth similar but usually smaller, the sixth narrower but keeled like them, none of them awned.

Flower terminal.

No *palea*.

Lodicules large, very thin.

Stamens four.

Styles short, distinct.

Grain enclosed in the larger glumes, but free from them.

2. Tetrarrhena juncea, R.Br.

Botanical name.—*Tetrarrhena*—*tetra*, Greek for four; *arrhen*, man (stamen), the flowers having four stamens; *juncea*—Latin, rush-like.

Synonym.—*Ehrharta juncea*, Spreng., in F.v.M. *Census*.

Vernacular name.—" Wire-grass."

Where figured.—Hooker, *Fl. Tasmania.*

Botanical description (B. Fl., vii, 554).

Stems either long, slender, and slightly branched, or more branched and entangled, scrambling over bushes to the height of 8 to 12 feet. (F. Mueller.)

Leaves narrow, glabrous or pubescent, with short rigid hairs.

Spike or *raceme* simple, 1 to 2 inches long, the rhachis flexuose.

Spikelets distant, sessile or nearly so, 2 to 2½ lines long. Two outer glumes short but unequal, obtuse, faintly-nerved, third glume nearly equal to the fourth and fifth, all three obtuse, prominently three- or five-nerved, sixth glume enclosing the flower, very narrow and hyaline.

Value as a fodder.—It must be very little, perhaps affording a bite for stock, with other grasses, in the spring. Its tough stems and straggling habit would preclude stock walking amongst it even if it were otherwise desirable. It is a hindrance to travellers in the districts in which it grows. Stirling, speaking of the Australian Alps, says that even the dreaded thorns and the "Climbing Lawyer" *(Smilax australis)* are less objectionable than the finely serrated stems and leaves of this grass.

Habitat and range.—Found in Tasmania, Victoria, and New South Wales. In our Colony, from the Blue Mountains, in a southerly direction, to Victoria.

44. ALOPECURUS.

Spikelets one-flowered, flat, densely crowed into a cylindrical spike or spike-like panicle.

Glumes three, two outer complicate, keeled, acute, but not awned, third under the flower shorter, keeled, with a short slender dorsal awn.

No two-nerved *palea* or *lodicules*.
Stamens three.
Styles distinct.
Grain enclosed in the scarcely hardened glumes, but free from them.

2. Alopecurus geniculatus, Linn.

Botanical name.—*Alopecurus*, from the Latin *Alopecurus* (indirectly from the Greek), signifying a plant like a fox-tail; *geniculatus*, Latin, knotty and jointed (like a knee).

Vernacular names.—"Knee-jointed Fox-tail Grass," because it is bent at the joints; "Water or Floating Fox-tail Grass"; the "Common Fox-tail" of England.

Where figured.—Buchanan, Sowerby, *Agricultural Gazette*.

Botanical description (B. Fl., vii, 555).—A perennial or sometimes annual only, glabrous except the spike.

Stems usually procumbent at the base, bending upwards at the lower nodes, sometimes only 3 or 4 inches, often 1 foot high or more.

Leaves narrow, the upper sheaths broad and loose.

Spike 1 to 2 inches long, closely imbricate but slender.

Outer glumes hairy on the keel, scarcely pointed, usually but little more than 1 line long, free or scarcely united at the base, the hair-like awn of the flowering glume not projecting above 1 line beyond them.

Value as a fodder.—Perennial fodder-grass, valuable for swampy or moist ground. Stock eat it readily enough with other grasses, but whether it is nutritious or not in Australia we can only make inferences.

Bailey alludes to it in these terms: "This rather weak grass is valuable as producing, on the South-western Downs, a quantity of herbage during the winter when many other grasses are at a standstill."

It should be well-known in Europe, but the testimonies of eminent British authorities in regard to it are contradictory, as the following extracts will show :—

"It is an extremely valuable pasture-grass, being relished by all cattle, and yielding a good crop of stems and foliage, and on stiff soils is perhaps the most reproductive of all our native (English) species, but is perhaps not so well adapted for hay as for pasture on account of the stems being few." (Sowerby.)

"It does not appear to be eaten with much relish by either cows, horses, or sheep. Its nutritive powers are not considerable, and its sub-aquatic natural place of growth excludes any recommendation of it for cultivation. (Sinclair, *Hortus Gramineus Woburnensis*.)

As regards the United States, Vasey reports: "It seldom reaches more than a foot in height. It is of no value for cultivation, being useful only for the amount of grass it may contribute to the wild forage of the place in which it grows."

Fungus recorded on this grass.—*Sclerospora macrospora, Sacc.,* has been recorded on the leaves of an *Alopecurus*.

Habitat and range.—It is usually found near shallow lagoons and water-courses, often actually floating in water. It is found in all the

colonies, and is a cosmopolitan grass in addition. In New South
Wales it is found in most parts of the Colony. The following note
from a correspondent from Myall Plains, near Jerilderie, explains one
of its habitats :—
"Only growing on some land that was cleared and burnt off last
January, and only in the stump holes and ashes where the trees were
burnt, and as thick as it can grow. It is quite unusual for grass to
grow here for several years where large trees or heaps of wood or
scrub are burnt, but this grass seems to come up at once, and do well
where the most ashes are found. It grows so high and rank that you
can trace where every portion of the tree has been burnt."

47. HIEROCHLOE.

Spikelets with one terminal hermaphrodite flower and two male
flowers below it, in a pyramidal or narrow terminal panicle, the rhachis
articulate above the two outer glumes.

Glumes six, thinly scarious; two outer acute, keeled, with a more or
less distinct short nerve on each side; third and fourth obtuse or emarginate, the keel sometimes produced into a short awn, each enclosing
a narrow palea and three stamens; fifth shorter, broad, obtuse, five-
nerved, the keel rarely produced into a short point, enveloping the
sixth which is narrower with a central nerve or keel.
No two-nerved *palea* to the terminal flower.
Stamens two.
Styles distinct.
Grain enclosed in the two upper glumes.

Spikelets crowded on the branches of the panicle; outer glumes
as long as the male ones ... ... 1. *H. redolens.*
Spikelets all on slender pedicels; outer glumes shorter than the
male ones ... ... 2. *H. rariflora.*

1.—Hierochloe redolens, R.Br.

Botanical name.—*Hierochloe* or *Hierochloa,* from two Greek words—
hieros, holy; *chloe,* grass. It is generally and properly spelt *Hierochloa,*
but Gmelin, author of the genus, spelt it *Hierochloe; redolens*—Latin,
smelling sweet.
Vernacular name.—"Sweet-scented Grass."
Where figured.—Labillardière, as *Disarrenum antarcticum ;*
Buchanan.
Botanical description (B. Fl., vii, 558).—Stems tufted, erect, branching, leafy, 2 to 3 feet high.

Leaves flat, rather rigid, slightly scabrous, otherwise glabrous, the ligula scarious,
entire.
Panicle rather dense, secund or nodding, 4 to 10 inches long in the larger forms, the
spikelets crowded along the primary branches, forming spike-like secondary
panicles of 1 to 1½ inches, the upper ones sessile, the lower distant on clustered
filiform peduncles.

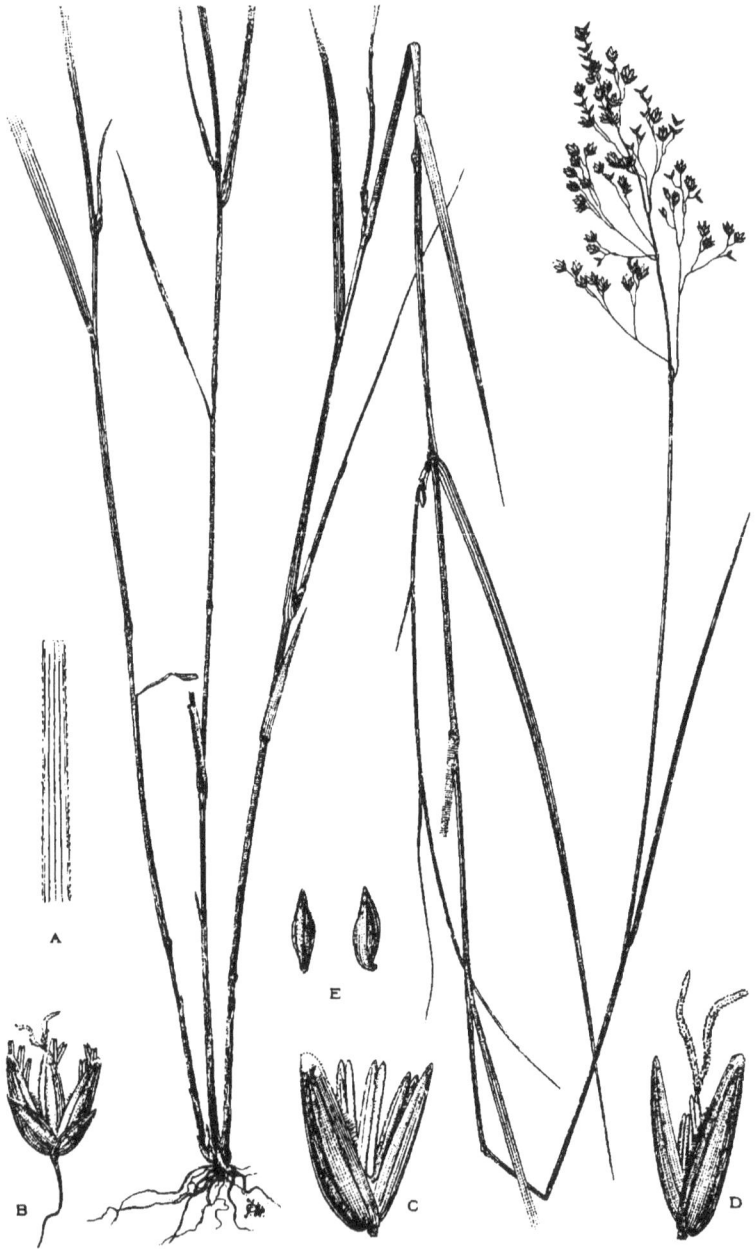

Hierochloa rariflora, Hook. f.

Glumes all thin, almost hyaline, rather shining; outer empty ones in the typical form about 3 lines long, the short lateral nerve on each side more prominent in the second than in the outermost one.

Third and fourth glumes each with a male flower, nearly as long as the outer ones, ciliate on the margins and keels, with a short awn arising from a little below the tip, the rhachis of the spikelet shortly lengthened between and above the male glumes.

Fifth and sixth glumes enclosing the grain obtuse and perfectly glabrous, or the fifth slightly hairy at the end with the keel produced into a minute point.

Value as a fodder.—Believed to be nutritious as a fodder, but quite harsh when old. It is one of the few grasses which grow in cold moorland, and hence valuable in that respect. Its odour of Coumarin (pleasing to cattle when not too strong), renders it an acceptable ingredient of hay, and it often renders damaged hay more palatable to stock.

Habitat and range.—Found in Tasmania, Victoria, and New South Wales. In our own Colony it is found in the southern mountain districts. It also occurs in New Zealand and Antarctic America.

2. Hierochloe rariflora, Hook., f.

Botanical names.—*Rariflora*, from two Latin words, signifying thin or loose (inflorescence), in allusion to the panicle. The word *rarus* is the opposite of the word *densus*, which signifies *dense*.

Vernacular names.—Usually known as " Scented-grass " but sometimes as " Wire-grass " for obvious reasons.

Where figured.—Hooker, *Fl. Tasmania ; Agricultural Gazette.*

Botanical description (B. Fl., vii, 559).

Stems slender, branching, 2 to 3 feet high.

Leaves narrower than in *H. redolens,* tapering into long subulate points.

Panicle loose and spreading, 2 to 3 inches long.

Spikelets all on slender pedicles, often variegated from the contrast of the purplish outer glumes and pale-coloured upper ones.

Glumes.—*Outer persistent glumes* broad, obtuse, the lowest about 1½ lines long, the second rather large and three-nerved ; *intermediate male glumes* about 2 lines long, rather rigid, five-nerved, obtuse, and awnless, finely and shortly ciliate on the margins, and sometimes on the keel.

Fifth glume very broad, thin, obtuse, glabrous, five-nerved.

Sixth glume much narrower, keeled, but the lateral nerves scarcely visible.

Botanical note.—Dr. (now Sir Joseph) Hooker, who first described this grass from a Tasmanian specimen, speaks of it as " a very distinct species, conspicuous for its slender, branched, leafy, knotted culms, 2 to 3 feet long, its narrow, strict rigid leaves rough to the touch, and small loose panicles of small spikelets on long flexuous branches." This is a brief popular description which could not readily be improved upon.

Value as fodder.—We have practically no data as to the specific fodder-value of our Scented-grass, and therefore we must fall back upon comparisons with other grasses belonging to the same genus. All *Hierochloes* have a certain value as sweeteners of musty or other hay, the pleasant odour they impart being grateful to most herbivorous animals ; but I express the opinion at once that our scented grass is of no agricultural importance. It is true that it is probably fairly nutritious ; but its foliage is sparse, the whole plant is wiry, the seed is less abundant than in the other Australian (and in most other) species ; and, supposing for a moment that anyone in the Colony thinks of propagating it, the warning of Mr. Fletcher, of Canada, as to the tendency of a closely-related species to become (in Manitoba) a noxious weed, should be borne in mind.

Speaking of a native *Hierochloe*, Mr. Bacchus states : " I am aware that stock eat the grass, but know nothing of its merits for grazing.

We will now inquire what is the opinion held in regard to *Hieroch-loes* in older countries.

Under the name of *Holcus odoratus*, there are some interesting notes on *Hierochloe borealis* in Sinclair's *Hortus Gramineus Woburnensis* (2nd ed., p. 167). There are some data as to the product per acre of this grass, dried and green, and at different seasons. Mr. Sinclair proceeds : " Though this is one of the earliest flowering grasses, it is tender, and the spring produce of herbage is very inconsiderable, the flowering straws rising up in a manner destitute of leaves. This deficiency of produce is much to be regretted, as the nutritive qualities of the grass are greater than in most of the early spring grasses. It sends forth but a few flower straws, which are of a slender structure compared with the size of the leaves. In no instance that I have observed was this grass eaten by the hares and rabbits which preyed upon many of the other grasses. The powerful creeping roots of this grass, its tender nature, and the great deficiency of foliage in the spring, are demerits which discourage the idea of recommending it further to the notice of the agiculturist."

H. borealis is dedicated to the Virgin Mary on account of its sweet-ness, and is strewn about Catholic Churches in Northern Europe on festival days. Hence the name Holy-grass. The odour it emits is much more powerful when it is trampled upon. It is often called Vanilla-grass, on account of its perfume. This is the grass stated by Don to be indigenous to Scotland, as well as to Sweden, Norway, &c. No one else found it in Scotland, and it was dropped out of lists, until Robert Dick, the baker, botanist, and geologist, of Thurso, rediscovered it in that country, and an account of the discovery is pleasantly recounted by Samuel Smiles in his life of that worthy.

Hierochloe borealis is common along the streams and rivers in the mountainous districts of Montana, U.S.A., frequently occupying ex-tensive areas to the exclusion of all other grasses. (Prof. Scribner, quoted by Dr. Vasey.) Dr. Vasey says that this grass is known in the United States as Vanilla or Seneca Grass, and Holy-grass. " It is a perennial grass of northern latitudes, growing in moist meadows near the coast, also in low marshy ground in some parts of Illinois and other States bordering the great lakes, and in the mountains of Colorado and northward. . . . In our country it does not appear to be adapted to general cultivation."

According to Mr. James Fletcher (*Bulletin* No. 19, *Central Experimental Farm, Ottawa*), this grass is known in Canada as Indian Hay, and he makes the following observations in regard to it:—" When cut or fed off, it keeps continually producing young leaves. When once established, however, it is very persistent, and in Manitoba is rapidly becoming a noxious weed most difficult to eradicate. It cannot, therefore, in any case be recommended for cultivation there, and should be introduced everywhere with caution. Our analyses prove it to be a very rich grass. Horses and cattle eat it readily. " This is the grass of which the leaves are used by the Indian women to weave the scented ' Indian hay ' baskets and mats."

No analysis of our Scented-grass has yet been made. It will, therefore, be useful to peruse the two accompanying analyses of *H. borealis*. No. 1 is a Canadian grass, gathered with the seeds half ripe. No. 2 is from the United States. It will be observed that the Canadian specimen was very moist. The albuminoids (the flesh-forming constituents of plants) are unusually high.

	In Fresh or Green Material.						Calculated to Water-free Substance.				
	Water.	Ash.	Albuminoids.	Fibre.	Nitrogen--Free Extract.	Ether Extract (Fat).	Ash.	Albuminoids.	Fibre.	Nitrogen—Free Extract.	Ether Extract (Fat).
No. 1 ...	75·32	1·64	4·93	6·14	10·68	1·29	6·63	20·00	43·25	24·88	5·24
No. 2 ...	14·30	7·99	12·12	19·73	43·28	3·48	9·32	14·15	23·02	49·45	4·06

Other uses.—None, except that there would be a limited sale for small baskets and other plaited work made out of it.

Since the above was written, Mr. W. H. Walker, of Tenterfield, has found this grass at his Boonoo Boonoo Out Station in very swampy country. This discovery (see *Agricultural Gazette*, February, 1896, p. 81) brings the range of the grass several hundreds of miles further to the north, Boonoo Boonoo being in the mountainous country near the Queensland border ; and I feel sure that only further search is required to find this interesting species within Queensland territory. In a letter subsequent to the communication originally forwarding the grass, Mr. Walker writes :—" I saw this grass on Bookookoorara, close to the top of the main range (say) about 4,000 feet above the sea ; and as the grass I saw had no seed on it, I asked my head stockman to bring in a specimen in seed or flower. He says there is lots of it on both the eastern and western watersheds of the main range. Stock are very fond of it in the winter and early spring months of the year. He did not know it was scented until he got the specimens. From what I can hear it is a valuable winter and early spring grass, but useless when old."

Tribe v.—STREPTATHERÆ.

Sub-tribe i.—*Stipaceæ.*

48. Aristida. | 49. Stipa.

48. ARISTIDA.

Spikelets one-flowered on filiform pedicels, or nearly sessile in a terminal panicle, the *rhachis* of the spikelet articulate above the two outer glumes.

Glumes three, narrow; two outer usually persistent, keeled, empty, and unawned ; terminal or flowering glume narrow, rigid, rolled round the flower, entire, with a terminal trifid awn.

Palea small, enclosed in the flowering glume.

Styles distinct.

Grain narrow, enclosed in the hard upper glume but free from it, the whole falling off with the stipes and awn as in *Stipa.*

All Australian species glabrous, with convolute more or less subulate leaves.

Fungus found on Aristida sp.—*Ustilago segetum,* Bull.

Section I.—*Arthratherum.*—*Awn* articulate on the glume, entire and spirally twisted below the branches ; *flowering glume* much shorter than the outer ones.

Awn about 1½ inches below the branches, which vary from 1½ to 2½ inches   2. *A. stipoides*

Awn ½ to ¾-inch below the branches, which vary from 1 to 3 inches   3. *A. arenaria*

Section II.—*Chætaria.*—*Awn* not articulate, and divided to the glume into three branches, the glume itself when barren sometimes twisted, but not the awn ; *flowering glume* about as long or longer than the outer ones.

Panicle short, broad and dense ; glumes ½ inch long ; awns long ...   4. *A. Behriana*

Panicle branches very long, at length spreading, with few spikelets on long pedicels ; glumes at least ¼ inch long   5. *A. leptopoda*

Panicle loose, at length pyramidal ; pedicels short ; outer glumes 2 to 3 lines long ; flowering glume much longer ; awns short...   6. *A. vagans*

Panicle narrow, rather loose ; outer glumes as long as the flowering one.

Glumes scarcely 3 lines ; awns under ½ inch long   7. *A. ramosa*

Glumes 4 to 5 lines long ; awns ¾ to 1 inch long   8. *A. calycina*

Panicle narrow, dense ; spikelets sessile and crowded on the short branches ; glumes 3 lines, or the flowering one rather longer ; awns 4 to 6 lines   9. *A. depressa*

2. Aristida stipoides, R. Br.

Botanical name.—*Aristida,* from the Latin *arista,* the beard of an ear of corn ; *stipoides,* from two words, *stipa, oidos* (Greek for like, or similar to), signifying resembling the genus *Stipa.*

Aristida stipoides, R. Br.

"A Wire Grass."

Vernacular name.—"Wire-grass" is the only name known to me for this grass, and the reason for its use is obvious. This is one of the grasses which is only a useful native plant at an early period of its growth.

Where figured.—*Agricultural Gazette.*

Botanical description.—(B. Fl., vii, 561).—A perennial grass, with rigid subulate leaves, and with the sheaths minutely ciliate at the orifice.

Panicle long, with a slender *rhachis*, the lower short erect branches usually bearing two spikelets, the upper spikelets singly distant on short erect pedicels.

Outer glume one-nerved, about ½ inch long, glabrous or minutely pubescent.

Second glume rigid, convolute, ¾ inch.

Flowering glume scarcely smaller than in *A. hygrometrica*, but the awn much finer, about 1½ inches below the branching, the branches 1½ to 2 inches long.

Value as a fodder.—This is a harsh, dry, wiry grass, which is, as a rule, but little relished by animals of any kind. When burnt off it produces a moderate quantity of tender feed, but this soon becomes of a hard, fibrous nature. The awns (three-pronged) with "spears" at the end, are bad for sheep, hence the grass is looked upon with disfavour by the squatters at seed-ripening time.

Habitat and range.—It is found in all the colonies, except Victoria and Tasmania. While mainly an interior species, it extends to the north coast, and to the islands adjacent thereto. In our own Colony it is found in the interior, on sand-ridges.

Reference to plate.—A, Spikelet showing the trifid awn; B, Showing articulation of awn with glume.

3. Aristida arenaria, Gaud.

Botanical name.—*Arenaria*, Latin, belonging to sand—*i.e.*, growing in sandy, sterile places.

Botanical description.—(B. Fl., vii, 561).

Very near *A. stipoides*, and reduced to that species by F. Mueller, Fragm. VIII, 111, but a smaller plant, the—

Stems usually not above 6 inches below the inflorescence, rarely slender, leafy, and nearly 1 foot long.

Leaves much finer, almost filiform.

Panicle narrow and spikelike, scarcely branched, or more frequently reduced to a simple raceme, 3 to 4 inches long, without the awns.

Outer glumes very narrow and fine pointed, usually dark coloured, the lowest nearly ½ inch long, the 2nd ¾ inch.

Flowering glume rather smaller than in *A. stipoides*, the *awn* under 1 inch and usually ½ to ¾ inch below the branching, the *branches* very fine, varying from 1 to 3 inches.

Value as a fodder.—A dry, wiry grass, bad for sheep on account of its sharp awns, becoming harsh when old, and only useful for fodder when young.

Habitat and range.—Poor, sandy, or sour land in all the colonies except Tasmania. In New South Wales it is confined to the dry western districts.

108

4. Aristida Behriana, F.v.M.

Botanical name.—Behriana, in honour of Dr. Herrmann Behr, a German botanist long resident in South Australia.
Botanical description (B. Fl., vii, 562).

Stems ascending, usually under 1 foot below the inflorescence.
Leaves subulate at the end, somewhat dilated at the base, and the upper sheaths often rather broad and loose.
Panicle dense, 2 to 3 inches long, and almost as broad, the *spikelets* nearly sessile.
Outer glumes nearly equal, the lowest fine-pointed, the second usually rather longer than the flowering glume.
Flowering glume about ½ inch long, with three nearly equal, sessile awns, fine and above 1 inch, sometimes nearly 2 inches long.

Value as a fodder.—Same as *A. arenaria.*
Habitat and range.—Found in South Australia, Victoria, and Queensland, besides our own Colony. In New South Wales it is usually found in the interior, but it also occurs on the Dividing Range and spurs at least as far south as Mudgee.

5. Aristida leptopoda, Benth.

Botanical name.—Leptopoda, from two Greek words, *leptos, pouspodos*, signifying slender-stalked.
Botanical description (B. Fl., vii, 562).

Stems rather stout, from scarcely 6 inches to 2 feet long.
Leaves long and subulate, with rather broad loose sheaths.
Panicle very loose, 6 inches to 1 foot high, with numerous long rigidly filiform branches at first erect, at length spreading horizontally, bearing few spikelets on filiform pedicels.
Outer glumes unequal, with long points, the longest usually about as long as the flowering glume.
Flowering glume 6 to 8 lines long, on a very short scarcely ciliate stipes, with three nearly sessile awns ½ to 1 inch long.
Palea small and rigid.

Value as a fodder.—Same remarks as under *A. arenaria.*
Habitat and range.—Found in South Australia, Victoria, and Queensland, as well as New South Wales. In our Colony it extends from the tableland to the interior. It is often found on good soil.

6. Aristida vagans, Cav.

Botanical name.—Vagans—Latin, straggling, in allusion to the inflorescence.
Vernacular name.—" Wandering Three-awned Spear-grass."
Botanical description (B. Fl., vii, 562).

Stems slender, erect, and 1 to 2 feet high, or diffuse and much branched.
Leaves slender, almost filiform, usually short.
Panicle 3 to 6 inches long, at first narrow, at length branching and pyramidal, the pedicels very short.
Outer glumes usually dark-coloured, 2 to 3 lines long, the second longer than the lowest, both with one prominent nerve.
Flowering glume always longer than the outer ones and often twice as long.
Awns sessile, about 4 lines long.
Palea very short.

It is sometimes not easy to distinguish this species from *A. ramosa*. *Value as a fodder.*—" In some places this grass affords good pasture, growing through the year and forming a good leafy bottom. The awns of this species are shorter and less troublesome than some others of the genus." (Bailey).

" Found with *A. calycina*, which it somewhat resembles, but it is a superior pasture kind." (Mueller.)

At the same time it is an inferior grass, wiry, and providing but little nutriment for stock under the most favourable circumstances. It is one of the best of the *Aristidas*, but no Australian member of the genus is worth conserving as a fodder plant.

Habitat and range.—It is found in Victoria and Queensland, and also extends from south to north of our Colony, in the coast districts and table-lands. It prefers dry rocky situations.

7. Aristida ramosa, R.Br.

Botanical name.—*Ramosa*—Latin, full of branches, in allusion to the inflorescence.

Botanical description (B. Fl., vii, 563).

Very nearly allied to *A. calycina*, and almost intermediate between that and *A. vagans*.

Panicle narrow, with erect or scarcely spreading branches, and the outer glumes as long as the flowering ones or nearly so, as in *A. calycina*, but the *spikelets* much smaller, the *glumes* scarcely above 3 lines, and the awns under ½-inch long.

Value as a fodder.—A dry wiry grass, and sometimes very tough and full of fibre. During the winter months affording some pasture, but in summer bearing too much seed and flower-stalks to be of much use as feed.

Habitat and range.—Found in South Australia, Queensland, and New South Wales. In our Colony it occurs in the coast districts and tablelands, its most southern locality appearing to be the Clyde-Braidwood district. In the western districts it has been sparingly recorded as far west as the Darling River. It is also found in New Guinea.

8. Aristida calycina, R.Br.

Botanical name.—*Calycina*—Latin, adjective from *calyx* a cup (in Botany, calyx), hence, having a prominent calyx or outer glumes (as regards the present species).

Botanical description (B. Fl., vii, 563).

Stems tufted, erect, 1 to 2 feet high.

Leaves very narrow, mostly subulate.

Panicle narrow, often above 6 inches long, with few short erect branches, rarely at length spreading, each bearing one or two, or the lower ones several, but few sessile or shortly pedicellate spikelets.

Spikelets in the typical form 4 to 5 lines long without the awns.

Outer glumes with fine points, the second as long as or longer than the flowering glume.

Awns slender, sessile, ¾ to 1½ inches long.

Palea rather long.

Value as a fodder.—Usually a very dry coarse grass, rarely affording a bite to stock. Its sharp awns are very injurious to sheep.

Mr. Forester Kidston, of Condobolin, thus alludes to it: "The celebrated No. 9 grass, the most hurtful of all our grasses, the seed going
right through to the paunch." No. 9 is, of course, an allusion to the
gauge of fencing-wire, and other *Aristidas, Xerotes longifolia,* and
other plants with exceptionally tough leaves are also referred to by
country people as No. 9 or No. 10.

Habitat and range.—Found in all the colonies except Tasmania,
principally on the sand-hills in the arid districts.

9. Aristida depressa, Retz.

Botanical name.—*Depressa*—Latin, weighed or pressed down, signifying, in a botanical sense, spread out or flattened down, referring to
the panicle.

Vernacular name.—" Beardy grass."

Botanical description (B. Fl., vii, 563).—A very variable grass,
distinguished by its narrow spikelets crowded and almost imbricate
along the short erect branches of a narrow compact panicle.

Stems, in the Australian specimens, ascending or erect, above 1 foot high.
Leaves narrow, ending in subulate points.
Panicle from 2 to 3 inches long and spikelike, to 6 or 8 inches and interrupted at the
base.
Spikelets sessile along the branches and often purplish.
Outer glumes about 3 lines long.
Flowering glumes usually longer.
Awns sessile, varying from 4 to 6 lines or rather more.

Probably the same as the tropical American *A. dispersa,* Trin. et
Rupr. (Benth.)

Value as a fodder.—Usually a dry unpalatable, innutritious grass.
" Opinions vary as to the value of this grass for fodder. Stewart
described it as a favourite fodder for cattle in the Punjab. Symonds
says that it is a troublesome grass which cattle will not eat. Colstream
states that it is grazed, but is too short and light to stack; that it covers
the Hussar bir in vast sheets, is too fine to cut with a scythe, but is
nutritious, and particularly relished by cattle. In the Jhang Settlement Report it is stated to be a grass of average quality, and is
found growing in Kallar. Neither at Ajmere nor at Jeypur is it
considered to be a good fodder grass." (Duthie.)

Habitat and range.—Found on sandy or light loamy soils in New
South Wales, and in Queensland. In our own Colony occurring in the
dry country, and found sparingly on the tableland, Dividing Range,
and northern coast district from Hunter River. It is also a native
of Europe, Asia, Africa, and America.

49. STIPA.

Spikelets one-flowered, on filiform pedicels or nearly sessile in a
terminal panicle, the *rhachis* of the spikelet articulate above the two
outer glumes.

Glumes three, narrow; two outer, usually persistent, membranous,
keeled, empty, unawned; terminal or flowering glume narrow, rigid,

rolled round the flower, with a terminal undivided bent awn spirally twisted below the bend.
Palea enclosed in the flowering glume.
Lodicules usually large.
Anthers usually tipped with a tuft of hairs.
Styles distinct.
Grain narrow, enclosed in the hard upper glume, but free from it. A short continuation of the *rhachis* of the spikelet above the articulation forms usually a stipes to the flower and fruit, falls off with it, and is usually ciliate with short hairs ; the awn is more or less distinctly articulate on the flowering glume, but usually remains attached to it after it falls.

The genus *Stipa* contains about 100 species. Australia claims fifteen, New Zealand two, one* of which is also found in Australia, while the others are natives of America and Asia. The United States has twenty-three species, and some of these have well marked varieties. In that country they are not, at least at present, accounted of much importance to the grazier, and no experiments appear to have been undertaken to determine their specific fodder value.

Flowering glume glabrous or slightly hairy at the end, very shortly
    produced into hyaline lobes or entire. Palea very small or
    rarely half as long as the glume.
  Panicle branches long and plumose. Spikelets 4 to 6 lines long...1. *S. elegantissima.*
  Panicle very much branched, glabrous or slightly pubescent.
    Spikelets scarcely 1½ lines long ... ... 2. *S. micrantha.*
Flowering glume silky hairy, the hyaline margins at the end produced
    into a small lobe on each side of the awn. Palea nearly as
    long as the glume. Panicle narrow and compact.
  Outer glumes acute, under ½ inch, usually yellowish brown. Lobes
    of the flowering glume very small... ... ... 3. *S. flavescens.*
Flowering glume silky-hairy, the margins not dilated under the awn.
    Palea nearly as long as the glume.
  Ligula elongated, not ciliate. Panicle loose. Leaves slender, filiform   8. *S. setacea.*
  Ligula short, ciliate. Panicle dense, 6 to 10 inches long. Awn
    plumose hairy in the lower part, 1½ to 4 inches long... ... 9. *S. semibarbata.*
  Ligula short, ciliate. Awn glabrous or slightly pubescent.
  Lowest glume usually slightly dilated and truncate or toothed at
    the end. Flowering glume narrow. Panicle dense or at
    length long and loose   ... ... 11. *S. pubescens.*
  Lowest glume usually three-pointed. Flowering glume rather
    broad. Panicle very loose... ... ... 12. *S. aristiglumis.*
  Lowest glume always fine pointed. Leaves slender, glabrous or
    pubescent, the upper sheaths sometimes dilated. Panicle
    loose ... . 15. *S. scabra.*

1. Stipa elegantissima, Labill.

Botanical name.—Stipa—Latin for "tow," in allusion to the feathery awns of the original species (*S. pennata*). In some species the awn is naked. *Elegantissima*, superlative of *elegans*, signifying handsome. This is a most beautiful grass.
Where figured.—Labillardière.

---

* Two, if *S. Petriei* be reducible to *S. setacea.* See Bentham, *Proc. Linn. Soc.,* xix., 288.

Botanical description (B. Fl., vii, 565).

Stems from a horizontal rhizome erect and branching, rigid though rather slender,
2 to 3 feet high.
Leaves narrow, mostly erect, convolute when dry, glabrous.
Panicle very loose, 6 to 8 inches long, at length broadly spreading, the *rhachis* and
long filiform branches elegantly plumose, with fine spreading hairs.
Outer glumes 4 to 6 lines long, equal or the lower much shorter, acutely acuminate.
Flowering glume shorter, on a short hairy stipes, but glabrous, the involute margins
shortly hyaline at the end, and produced into a very short obtuse lobe on each
side of the awn.
Awn 1 to 1½ inches long, or sometimes even longer.
Palea less than one-third as long as the glume.

Value as a fodder.—Probably very little.

Other uses.—This grass is often cultivated for ornamental purposes.
The elegantly plumose branches of the panicle render it a charming
object.

Habitat and range.—Found in all the Colonies except Tasmania. In
our own colony it occurs from the tableland to the interior.

1a. Stipa Tuckeri, F.v.M.

Botanical name.—*Tuckeri*, in honour of G. A. Tucker, who first
sent the grass to Baron von Mueller.

Botanical description (Fragmenta xi, 129).—Described as a small
grass, but according to specimens in the herbarium, Botanic Gardens,
Sydney, scarcely less than 2 feet high.

Leaves flat, with the stalks, sheaths, and nodes velvety-pubescent.
Spikelets small.
Panicles—the branches much spreading, soft, covered with short soft hairs " whitish
and patent " (F.v.M.).
Outer glumes short.
Flowering glume glabrous.
Awns about 1 to 1½ inches long.

[See also *Key to System of Victorian Plants*, p. 491.]
Value as a fodder.—Unknown.

Habitat and range.—In our own Colony it has been recorded from
the Lachlan and Darling Rivers and Liverpool Plains. Further search
may greatly augment this list. It also occurs in Victoria and South
Australia.

2. Stipa micrantha, Cav.

Botanical name.—*Micrantha*, from the Greek, *micros*, small, *anthon*
a flower, in reference to the small spikelets.

Synonym.—*Stipa verticillata*, Nees, according to Bentham. (See
Dichelachne sciurea.)

Vernacular name.—" Bamboo-grass."

Botanical description (B. Fl., vii, 566) :—

Stems several feet high, not stout but rigid, sometimes spreading or scrambling with
the branches in dense clusters, sometimes long and little branched.
Leaves very slender, the sheaths often long and loose, glabrous.
Panicle loose, but often narrow, from under 6 inches to above 1 foot long, with very
numerous capillary glabrous branches.
Spikelets the smallest in the genus, pedicellate on the ultimate branches.
Outer glumes linear, very thin, nearly equal, scarcely 1¼ lines long.
Flowering glume shorter, nearly glabrous, on a very short and ciliate stipes, entire
at the top, the awn very slender, about ½ inch long.
Palea not above half the length of the glume.

Stipa setacea, R. Br.

"A Spear Grass or Corkscrew Grass."

113

Value as a fodder.—Although rather a rigid grass, it is always, at all events when young, cropped by cattle and horses. It is a tall tufty grass, met with in various situations, on hill sides and on the banks of rivers.

Habitat and range.—Found in New Zealand, Queensland, and New South Wales. In our Colony, confined to the coast district and Dividing Range north of Port Jackson.

3. Stipa flavescens, Labill.

Botanical name.—*Flavescens*—Latin, growing yellow, in allusion to the general colour of the inflorescence.

Where figured.—Labillardière.

Botanical description (B. Fl., vii, 566).—An erect rather slender grass of 1½ to 3 feet, quite glabrous, or the lower leaves slightly pubescent.

Lower leaves sometimes flat at the base, but all otherwise convolute when dry, very narrow or almost subulate, often rigid.
Ligula very short, not ciliate.
Panicle narrow and dense, 6 inches to above 1 foot long, the erect branches and pedicels glabrous.
Outer glumes 4 to 6 lines long, acute.
Flowering glume on a rather long hairy stipes, scarcely 3 lines long, silky hairy, the hyaline involute margins ending in a small very thin lobe or tooth on each side of the awn, often difficult to distinguish from the hairs.
Awn usually pubescent, 1½ inches long or more.
Palea nearly as long as the glume, hairy towards the top.

Value as a fodder.—Only of value when young.

Habitat and range.—Found in all the Colonies except Queensland. In New South Wales it is found on the Monaro, and also on the Dividing Range and spurs as far north as the Mittagong district. It prefers rocky situations.

8. Stipa setacea, R. Br.

Botanical name.—*Setacea*, bristly, in allusion to the fine leaves. *S. setacea* is found pretty well all over Australia, and hence it is not surprising that it varies a good deal. For instance, the leaves vary in width, and also in length, and we have figured both narrow and broad-leaved forms.

Vernacular names.—A "Spear-grass," owing to the spear-shaped ripened seed, to which is attached a long awn. Called "Corkscrew-grass," owing to the twisted, corkscrew-like appearance of the lower part of the awn.

Where figured.—*Agricultural Gazette*, Hooker, *Fl. Tasmania.*

Botanical description (B. Fl., vii, 568).—

Stems slender, 1 to 2 feet high, or rarely more.
Leaves fine and short, tufted at the base of the stem ; those on the stem few, with long sheaths.
Ligula elongated, not ciliate, often broken off from dried specimens.
Panicle loose, 4 to 10 inches long, glabrous.
Outer glumes very thin, narrow, acuminate, 4 to 5 lines long.
Flowering glume much shorter, pubescent or villous, entire at the top.
Awn glabrous, very fine, 1½ to above 2 inches long.
Palea as long as the glume, often hardened when ripe.

II

The wide diffusion and variability of this grass have already been
alluded to. In some forms the panicle is much looser than shown in
our drawing; in others, the amount of twist (" corkscrewness") of the
awn varies, and other points of variation might be mentioned.

Value as fodder.—Although this is a rather coarse grass, it is useful
on account of its drought-resisting qualities. It is much relished by
stock of all kinds, and is very nutritious while young and tender. Mr.
Bacchus says of it : " By reason of its early growth of nice tender
herbage, which stock are fond of, it constitutes a useful part of the
supply of early annual grasses." There is no doubt at all that it is a
really valuable grass before the " seeds" (" spears") ripen, and hence
it is admissible into the category of " useful plants"; but a sad drawback to its value is the danger to sheep and wool from these seeds.
They are produced in large quantities, are caught up by the wool, and
by the mouth and nostrils. The structure of the " seeds" is sufficiently shown in the drawing, and they work home as certainly as a
corkscrew or a gimlet. Mr. Bacchus says : " I once lost 800 out of
2,000 lambs by placing them on a part of the run which had been
rested for some time where this grass abounded, and was just beginning to shed its seeds, which penetrated the skin in hundreds ; and,
but for being able to get them shorn at once, I believe nearly all the
lambs would have died." Mr. Alfred Hawkesworth, who has had a
good deal of experience in such matters, has been kind enough to give
me the following note on the terrible havoc spear-grass sometimes
works with sheep :—" Of all grasses and weeds, spear-grass seeds are the
most damaging to sheep and wool. Being straight, and with sharp-
pointed ends, when once they get attached to the wool they lie
parallel with the staples and fibres, and by the movement of the animal
they work their way on to the skin. In extreme cases the fleece is
composed of fully 75 per cent. of spear-grass seeds, so persistently do
they hold on to the wool. When once they get a hold, they never
fall out. In the same way, when these sharp-pointed seeds enter the
skin, they work through it, right into the sheep, until they come in
contact with the vital organs, which results in certain death. I have
seen them in the heart of a sheep, and even having a hold on the
bones, from which they could not be pulled ; they would break off.
I once saw a mob of sheep that had travelled from Hughenden to
Townsville (Queensland), where they were slaughtered, and the spear-
grass seeds were so dense and tenacious that they had to be cut
through, in order that the skins might be released ; also, all through
the body, to the intestines and lungs, they were present in large
quantities. The face, also, suffers greatly, making the sheep blind in
a very short time. I am of opinion that spear-grass country is only
fit for cattle." This bad character must not be borne entirely by
S. setacea, as some other Australian species of *Stipa* contribute to
this result, and the blame must be borne by them jointly. Spear-
grasses are also credited with destroying a large number of young
chickens.

Stipa spartea is also injurious to sheep in Manitoba, Canada. Mr.
R. M. Christy observes (*Proc. Linn. Soc.* 1883-6, p. 57) :—" This

widespread species forms a more succulent grass than any other of the prairie grasses, and is locally known as buffalo-grass, spear-oat, &c. The fruits ripen in July, and the awns penetrate the hides of sheep and dogs, causing much damage to the settlers. There are very like those of *S. pennata*, but about ½-inch in length, with an awn nearly 2 inches long, twisted nine or ten times. Rather more than 3 inches beyond, it is produced into a delicate bristle, which does not twist, and many small teeth pointing upward; when wet, the whole awn is perfectly straight. The author experimented in August, November, and December upon *S. spartea* and *S. pennata*, and found that actual penetrative power was possessed by the hygrometric awned seeds. Butchers repeatedly find these seeds embedded about half an inch beneath the skin of animals slaughtered by them, and animals have not infrequently to be destroyed on account of their being infested with these fruits."

Other uses.—Nil. This and other species have toughish stems when old, but none of them approach the *Esparto* (*S. tenacissima*), in this respect.

Habitat and range.—Found in every one of the Colonies, from the coastal districts to the deserts of the centre of the Continent.

References to plate—Stipa setacea 1. The long ligule ; 2. Spikelet (opened out a little) ; 3. Outer or empty glumes ; 4. One empty glume, showing venation ; 5. Flowering glume, with awn ; 6. Flowering glume, entire at top. All variously magnified. A, filiform leaves (type form) ; B, an old plant from western New South Wales.

9. Stipa semibarbata, R.Br.

Botanical names.—*Semibarbata*—Latin, *semi*, half; *barbata*, bearded, the awn being only partially (often for half its length) plumose.

Where figured.—Hooker, *Fl. Tamania.*

Botanical description (B. Fl., vii, 568).—

Stems 1½ to near 3 feet high.

Leaves narrow, convolute, often almost subulate, glabrous, or shortly pubescent, the ligula very short and ciliate.

Panicle oblong, rather dense, 6 to 10 inches long, with erect branches.

Outer glumes 6 to 9 lines long, tapering into very thin, long, acute points.

Flowering glumes silky-hairy, scarcely three lines long, entire at the top.

Awn varying from under 2 inches to near 4 inches long ; shortly plumose-hairy to the bend, or sometimes nearly to the end.

Var. *mollis*, Benth.—A coarser grass of 2 to 3 feet, the foliage usually softly pubescent, the other characters the same. Coastal New South Wales ; also, the Wimmera, Victoria.

Value as a fodder.—A bad Spear-grass. (Fl., Tas.)

Habitat and range.—Found in all the Colonies. In New South Wales it is found in the coast districts and tablelands, and as far west as the Lachlan and Darling Rivers.

11. Stipa pubescens, R.Br.

Botanical name.—Pubescens—Latin, downy, the nodes of the stem being pubescent.
Botanical description (B. Fl., vii, 569).—

Stems 2 to 3 feet high, with pubescent nodes.
Leaves narrow, convolute, the ligula very short, usually ciliate.
Panicle rather loose in the typical form, very loose in some varieties.
Outer glumes unequal, the longest about ½ inch, scarious at the end, and often, but not always, truncate notched or three-toothed, rarely very acute.
Flowering glume much shorter, hairy, entire at the top.
Awn above 2 inches long, pubescent in the lower part or glabrous.
Palea rather long.

Value as a fodder.—A tall, tufty grass, rather coarse, and a cattle-grass rather than one for sheep. It is, however, believed to be nutritious. It is a bad spear-grass.
Habitat and range.—Found in all the Colonies. In New South Wales it occurs from the coast to the tableland.

12. Stipa aristiglumis, F.v.M.

Botanical name.—Aristiglumis—Latin, *arista*, the beard of corn ; *gluma*, the husk or chaff of corn (glume), alluding to the outer glume being produced into fine points.
Botanical description (B. Fl., vii, 570).—Very nearly allied to *S. pubescens*, and should probably be added to its varieties.

Habit and foliage the same.
Panicle much looser.
Spikelets smaller.
Outer glume usually produced into one to three fine points.
Fruiting glume broader.
Awn of S. pubescens, but usually glabrous.

Value as a fodder.—The remarks under *S. pubescens* will apply here.
As found in Queensland, Bailey speaks of it as a "strong-growing grass, producing a large quantity of excellent fodder; indeed, it is one of the very best species found on the Downs ; the seeds, also, are not so troublesome as some others of the genus."
Habitat and range.—Found in all the Colonies except Western Australia and Tasmania. In New South Wales it extends from the coast districts to the interior.

15. Stipa scabra, Lindl.

Botanical name.—Scabra—Latin, rough, the grass being somewhat harsh. Mitchell, the discoverer, writes, *Tropical Australia*, p. 31 : . . . . . "A new species of *Stipa*, remarkable for its fine, silky ears, and coarse *rough* herbage."

Botanical description (B. Fl., vii, 570).—

Stems in the typical form, slender, tufted, 1 to 2 feet high.

Leaves subulate or filiform, rather short, glabrous or slightly pubescent, the upper sheath scarcely dilated.

Ligula very short, more or less ciliate.

Panicle very loose, 6 inches to above 1 foot long, with long capillary, slightly spreading branches and pedicels.

Outer glumes at first almost hyaline, at length, especially in western specimens, often purplish or rigid, tapering into long points, the longest about ½ inch long.

Flowering glume about 2 lines long, silky-hairy, entire at the tip.

Awn fine, glabrous, 3 inches long or more.

Palea nearly as long as the glume.

Value as a fodder.—Believed to be nutritious ; perhaps one of the best of the genus from the point of view of the stockowner.

Habitat and range.—Found in all the Colonies except Tasmania. In New South Wales it is only recorded from the interior districts.

"It is worthy of note that some species of *Stipa* act upon cows, and more especially upon horses, as narcotics. The fact is established as regards *S. inebrians*, Hance ; *S. viridula*, Trin. ; and a species growing in Cashmere, probably *S. sibirica*, Lam." (Hackel.) The "Sleepy Grass" of New Mexico, U.S.A., is *S. viridula*, var. *robusta*.

Sub-tribe ii.—Agrostideæ.

51. Pentapogon.   54. Agrostis.
53. Dichelachne.   55. Deyeuxia.

51. PENTAPOGON.

Spikelets one-flowered, numerous in rather a dense much branched panicle ; the rhachis of the spikelet articulate above the two outer glumes, with a tuft of hairs surrounding the flowering glume and not continued above it.

Glumes three, two outer persistent, membranous, acute or shortly pointed.

Flowering glume narrow, rolled round the flower, divided at the end into five lobes or awns, the central one rigid, at length twisted, continuous with the keel and sometimes slightly dorsal, the lateral ones shorter and straight.

Palea narrow, enclosed in the flowering glume.

Lodicules two.

Styles short, distinct.

Grain enclosed in the glume, but free from it.

1. Pentapogon Billardieri, R. Br.

Botanical name.—*Pentapogon*—Greek, *penta*, five ; *pogon*, beard (awn), the flowering glume being divided at the end into five lobes or awns. *Billardieri* in honour of Jacques Julien Houton La Billardière, the celebrated botanist of the expedition despatched by the French Government in search of traces of La Perouse.

Where figured.—La Billardière, as *Agrostis quadrifida*; *Agricultural Gazette.*
Botanical description (B. Fl., vii, 572).—An erect annual, from under 1 foot to above 2 feet high.

Leaves narrow, hairy pubescent or rarely glabrous.
Panicle narrow, erect or somewhat nodding, 2 to 6 inches long.
Spikelets numerous, nearly sessile on the branches.
Outer glumes narrow, varying from 3 to 6 lines long, almost hyaline, with a prominent shortly ciliate keel often produced into a short point.
Flowering glume on a very short hairy stipes, the central awn terete, rigid, ½ to 1 inch long, the lateral lobes, two on each side, much shorter, erect, slightly flattened, and one-nerved.

Value as a fodder.—Unknown.
Habitat and range.—Found in all the Colonies except Western Australia and Queensland. In New South Wales found in the extreme south of the Colony.

53. DICHELACHNE.

Spikelets one-flowered, numerous in a narrow usually dense panicle, the rhachis of the spikelet articulate immediately above the two outer glumes and not continued beyond the flower.
Glumes three, narrow, the two outer ones persistent, membranous, acute, keeled. Flowering glume raised on a short hairy stipes (rhachis of the spikelet), membranous at the time of flowering, hyaline and entire or two-lobed at the end, with a fine scarcely twisted dorsal awn a little below the end, slightly hardened round the fruit.
Palea two-nerved.
Stamens three or fewer; anthers glabrous.
Styles distinct.
Grain enclosed in the glume and palea, free from them.

Panicle very dense, the awns above 1 inch long, very numerous and
concealing the spikelets ... ... 1. *D. crinita.*
Panicle rather loose, the awns 6 to 8 lines long... ... ... 2. *D. sciurea.*

1. Dichelachne crinita, Hook., f.

Botanical name.—*Dichelachne*—Greek, *dis*, double; *cheilos*, a lip; *achne*, chaff (glumes), the flowering glumes being two-lobed; *crinita*, Latin, having much or long hair, in allusion to the long hair-like awns.
Synonym.—*Stipa Dichelachne*, Steud. in F.v.M. *Census.*
Vernacular name.—"Long-hair Plume-grass."
Where figured.—Labillardière, as *Anthoxanthum crinitum*; Bailey, Buchanan, *Agricultural Gazette.*
Botanical description (B. Fl., vii, 574).—

Stems 2 to 3 feet high.
Leaves flat, glabrous or softly pubescent, the upper ones rather long with long sheaths.
Panicle very dense and spikelike, 4 to 8 inches long, the spikelets imbricate on the short erect branches, but concealed by the numerous long hair-like awns.
Outer glumes very narrow, hyaline with a slightly scabrous keel, nearly equal, about 2½ lines long.
Flowering glumes shorter, glabrous, the hyaline tip entire but readily splitting.
Awn dorsal, very slender, bent but scarcely twisted, above 1 inch long.

Value as a fodder.—A widely diffused, ornamental grass, affording a large bulk of fodder readily eaten by stock. " It is a valuable grass, and forms, when in flower, a prominent feature in pasture. As a pasture grass, when grown under favourable circumstances on rich valley bottoms with perennial moisture, it is very succulent, but when on dry clay hills, it is harsh and scanty ; its nutrient qualities may be admitted, forming, as it does, a large constituent of pastures famous for fattening stock. As a fodder grass it possesses considerable bulk, and would add much value to a mixed crop of hay." (Buchanan.) " In favourable—that is, rather dry—situations, this grass grows over 3 feet high, standing the heat well. It is an excellent pasture grass, thrives well with Kangaroo-grass, and flowers about the same time. The two make excellent hay, or if grazed, a very fattening mixture." (Bacchus.)

Other uses.—Dodge quotes Mueller as stating that this species yields a tenacious paper, especially fit for thin wrapping or packing paper. He adds that it is not unlikely to make fair printing paper and the less costly kinds of writing and tissue paper.

Habitat and range.—Found in all the Colonies, including New Zealand. In New South Wales it occurs from the coast to the table-land.

2. Dichelachne sciurea, Hook., f.

Botanical name.—*Sciurea*—Latin, *sciurus*, a squirrel, the panicle, with its long hair-like awns, being thought to resemble the tail of a squirrel in appearance.

Synonym.—*Stipa micrantha*, Cav., in the opinion of Mueller (*Census*), but not of Bentham.

Vernacular name.—" Short-hair Plume-grass."

Where figured.—Hooker, *Fl. Tasmania*; Buchanan; *Agricultural Gazette.*

Botanical description (B. Fl., vii, 574).—

Stems densely tufted, slender, 1 to 1½, rarely 2 feet, high, quite glabrous, the nodes usually dark-coloured.

Leaves short, chiefly at the base of the stem, scabrous-pubescent, or glabrous.

Panicle narrower and looser than in *D. crinita*, 3 to 6 inches long.

Rhachis and filiform branches scabrous.

Outer glumes very narrow, about 2½ lines long, the outermost rather shorter than the second.

Fruiting glume rather more rigid than in *D. crinita*, and minutely pitted-rugose.

Awns 6 to 8 lines long, not nearly so crowded as in that species.

Botanical notes.—Var. *setifolia*, Benth. Very slender, with almost filiform leaves, the sheaths scabrous. Parramatta.

Value as a fodder.—A useful grass, readily eaten by stock, though not of the highest merit.

Habitat and range.—Same range as the preceding species. Recorded from Norfolk Island.

54. AGROSTIS.

Spikelets small, one-flowered, pedicellate in a loose, spreading or narrow panicle, the rhachis of the spikelet articulate above the outer glumes, glabrous or nearly so, not produced beyond the flower.

Glumes three; two outer empty ones narrow, keeled, acute, unawned. Flowering glume shorter, broad, thin, enveloping the flower, unawned, or with a dorsal awn, attached below the middle, fine and twisted.

Palea not above half the length of the glume, very thin and hyaline, often very minute or none.

Styles very short, distinct.

Grain enclosed in the glume, free from it.

Palea none, or rudimentary, (section *Trichodium*).

    No awn. Outer glumes above 1 line long. Panicle narrow .... 2. *A. Muelleri*.
    No awn. Outer glumes about ⅔ line long. Panicle spreading...... 3. *A. scabra*.
    Awn nearly basal. Outer glumes about 1 line. Panicle spreading... 4. *A. venusta*.

2. Agrostis Muelleri, Benth.

Botanical name.—Agrostis, a Greek word signifying grasses in general, a derivative of *agros*, a field; hence the word "Agrostology," the science of grasses. *Muelleri*, after Baron von Mueller.

Synonyms.—A. canina, Linn.; var. *gelida. A. gelida*, F.v.M.

Vernacular name.—Mueller's Bent-grass.

Where figured.—Buchanan, as *A canina*, Linn.; var. *gelida.*

Botanical description (B. Fl., vii, 576).—A densely tufted grass, 2 to 6 inches high.

Leaves very narrow.

Panicle narrow, though rather loose, 1 to 1½ inches long, with short, erect, capillary branches.

Spikelets purplish.

Outer glumes very pointed, about 1¼ lines long, glabrous, or the keel minutely ciliate.

Flowering glume much shorter, thin and hyaline, obtuse, enveloping the flower and grain, without any (or a minute and rudimentary?) palea.

Stamens three.

Value as a fodder.—A valuable pasture grass.

Habitat and range.—An Alpine species, confined to the Alps of New South Wales and Victoria. We have it from 5,000 to 6,000 ft. on Mount Kosciusko. This grass is also found on high mountains in New Zealand.

3. Agrostis scabra, Willd.

Botanical name.—Scabra—Latin, rough, the grass being somewhat harsh.

Synonym.—A. parviflora, R. Br.

Vernacular names.—The "Slender Bent-grass" of Buchanan, the "Plain Grass" of the United States; other American names in "Rough Bent," "Fly-away Grass (because the delicate particles, when mature, break away from the stalk, and are blown away by the wind), "Tickle-grass," "Fool-hay," "Silk-grass."

Where figured.—Hooker, *Fl., Tasmania*; Buchanan, as *A. parviflora*
Gray's Manual of Botany (American) Pl. 7, fig. 3.
Botanical description (B. Fl., vii, 576).—

Stems slender, tufted, 6 inches to above 1 foot high.
Leaves very narrow, almost filiform in the typical form, chiefly at the base of the stem.
Panicle compound, very loose and slender, with spreading capillary branches.
Outer glumes narrow, keeled, rather acute, about ¾ line long.
Flowering glume shorter, hyaline, broad, and enveloping the flower, obtuse, truncate or slightly jagged, unawned.
Palea none (or very minute?).
Stamens three.

Var., *elatior*, Benth. ; taller, leaves flatter and flaccid, panicle very loose and spreading.
Southern Mountain Ranges and New England ; also in Victoria.
Value as a fodder.—Produces a neat turf, which has been reported by some writers to be valuable for fodder. The judicious Bacchus, whose writings on Australian grasses form the basis of much that has since been written on the subject, says of the normal species : "Perennial, about 18 inches high, vegetates rather late, making small patches of close turf." Of the variety *elatior* he says : "This grass is not so much eaten by stock as I had expected from its inviting appearance."
Buchanan also speaks of it as a valuable grass.
In the Colorado *Agricultural Bulletin*, No. 12 ("Some Colorado Grasses") this grass is alluded to as "this worthless species, abundant in wet meadows at all elevations." Lamson-Scribner states that "it possesses little or no agricultural value." These statements carry the greater weight, since the species is widely distributed in the United States.
I do not know to what extent these conflicting opinions are capable of reconciliation ; certain it is that there have always been differences of opinion as to the fodder value of some species of *Agrostis*, and it is hoped that the matter will be inquired into in regard to plants whose botanical origin is open to no doubt. The matter is discussed by Buchanan under *A. parviflora*.
Other uses.—"Before the panicle has expanded, the grass is sometimes gathered and sold, under the name of 'silk-grass', for dry bouquets." (Lamson-Scribner.)
Habitat and range.—Found in all the Colonies except Western Australia. In New South Wales found on the southern mountain ranges and high tablelands south and north. We have it from Pretty Point (Mt. Kosciusko), 5,500 feet, also from the Guy Fawkes country, New England. A grass of cold localities exclusively.

4. Agrostis venusta, Trin.

Botanical name.—*Venusta*—Latin for graceful, in allusion to the appearance of the grass when in flower.
Where figured.—Hooker, *Fl. Tasmania.*

Botanical description (B. Fl., vii, 576).—A slender, tufted grass, closely resembling the typical form of *A. scabra*, with still finer leaves.

Panicle loose, with long capillary branches or contracted in some of the smaller specimens.

Outer glumes very acute, about 1 line long.

Flowering glume shorter, broad, hyaline, and remarkably truncate, enveloping the flower, with a dorsal twisted awn, affixed very near the base and protruding beyond the outer glumes.

Palea none.

Value as a fodder.—Unknown.

Habitat and range.—Found in all the Colonies. In New South Wales found in southern mountainous (particularly Alpine) districts. We have it from Pretty Point (Mt. Kosciusko), 5,500 feet.

55. DEYEUXIA.

Spikelets one-flowered, pedicellate or rarely sessile in a panicle either loose and spreading or narrow and spikelike, the *rhachis* of the spikelet articulate above the outer glumes, usually bearing a tuft of hairs round the flowering glume and usually produced beyond it in a small ciliate or rarely glabrous bristle very rarely bearing an empty glume or imperfect flower, sometimes very minute, rarely deficient.

Glumes three; two outer ones persistent, keeled, unawned, flowering shorter and very thin, about as long or rarely longer and membranous, broad, enclosing the flower, five-nerved, with a fine dorsal awn usually bent and twisted, rarely short and straight or very rarely deficient.

Palea thin, more than half as long as the glume, faintly or prominently two-nerved.

Styles distinct, short.

Grain enclosed in the glume and palea and sometimes partially adhering to them.

Flowering glume very thin, almost hyaline, much shorter than the empty ones.
  Panicle loose and spreading or in smaller plants narrow. Rhachis of the spikelet produced into a hairy bristle.
    Spikelets 1½ to 2 lines long. Flowering glume usually hairy, truncate, or shortly-toothed, the awn about the middle.
      Panicle spreading ... ... 2. *D. Forsteri.*
    Spikelets about 3 lines. Flowering glume glabrous, with two long points, the awn almost basal. Panicle spreading ... 4. *D. Billardieri.*
    Spikelets about 1½ lines. Flowering glume hairy, with two long points, the awn almost basal. Panicle narrow ... 5. *D. plebeia.*
  Panicle dense and spikelike or shortly branched. Rhachis of the spikelet produced into a glabrous or minute bristle or not continued beyond the flower.
    Spikelets 2 to 2½ lines long. Awn almost basal. Bristles of the rhachis conspicuous ... ... 6. *D. montana.*
    Spikelets 1½ to 2 lines. Awn almost basal. Bristle of the rhachis minute or none ... ... 7. *D. quadriseta.*
Flowering glume nearly or quite as long as the outer ones, membranous, often minutely scabrous or pubescent.
  Panicle very loose and long. Awn dorsal about the middle of the flowering glume but very deciduous... ... ... 11. *D. frigida.*

123

Panicle very loose. Awn very small and straight above the middle
of the flowering glume or reduced to a small point near
the summit ... ... 12. *D. scabra.*
Panicle dense and spikelike. Leaves broad. Awn small and
straight near the summit of the flowering glume ... ... 13. *D. nivalis.*
Flowering glume twice as long as the truncate outer ones. Spikelets
very small in a loose panicle, awnless, or with a minute
point on the flowering glume. Outer glumes not keeled,
truncate. Stems 1 to 1½ feet... ... ... 15. *D. breviglumis.*

2. Deyeuxia Forsteri, Kunth.

Botanical name.—*Deyeuxia*, in honour of Deyeux; *Forsteri*, in honour
of the Forsters; Johan Reinhold and George, the latter of whom accompanied Captain Cook as botanist during his second voyage of circumnavigation.

Synonym.—*Agrostis Solandri*, F.v.M. in *Census*; *A. æmula*, R. Br.
Vernacular names.—"Toothed Bent-grass"; the "Winter-grass"
of Bacchus.
Where figured.—Buchanan (as *A. æmula*), *Agricultural Gazette.*
Botanical description (B.Fl., vii, 579).—A common grass, very
variable in habit, usually erect or decumbent; 1 to 2 feet high or rather
more, with flat, rather flaccid leaves, but sometimes smaller, with
convolute or fine, almost filiform, leaves.

Panicles usually very loose and spreading when fully out, 6 inches to 1 foot long,
with long capillary divided branches in distant whorls or clusters.
Spikelets very numerous.
Outer glumes narrow, very pointed, 1 to 1½ lines long, or in some varieties, nearly
2 lines.
Flowering glume about half as long, thin and almost hyaline, broad, enveloping the
flower, truncate, or very shortly and unequally two- or four-toothed, sprinkled
or densely covered with hairs on the back, rarely almost glabrous, surrounded
by the hairs of the *rhachis*, with a fine twisted awn attached about the middle
of the back.
Palea very narrow.
Rhachis produced into a bristle, usually very short and ciliate with a few long hairs.

Botanical notes.—Normally with a very hairy flowering glume. Var.
læviglumis with flowering glume nearly glabrous, except marginal cilia.
Lake George, N.S.W., and in Victoria.

Value as a fodder.—A very abundant grass in the cooler parts of
the year, disappearing during the hot summer months. It produces
large quantities of excellent pasture. As the seed ripens the panicles
break off the stalk and blow about, frequently accumulating in large
quantities against obstacles. Here follow a Victorian and a New
Zealand account of the grass:—

"It is the first grass to spring up after summer rains, and keeps
up a supply of nutritive herbage. During winter it seeds freely. I
consider it a useful winter grass. When summer comes it dries up,
making room for other sorts." (Bacchus.)

"Often forming a prominent part of the pasture on dry, stony, or
sandy soils. It is valuable as a sheep-grass in such places, probably
proving perennial when prevented by grazing from ripening its seed,
the permanence of such grasses often depending on their capability to
stole or form off-sets or branches at the roots before flowering and

seeding. This grass possesses a large adaptation of growth to varied soils, although most abundant on arid clay land, probably from the absence there of larger grasses; yet, on good soil, when sheltered by shrubs, it attains its greatest height, and is greedily eaten by horses and cattle." (Buchanan.)

Habitat and range.—Found in all the Colonies, including New Zealand, and occurring in most parts of New South Wales.

4. Deyeuxia Billardieri, Kunth.

Botanical name.—*Billardieri,* in honour of La Billardière, *ante,* p. 117.
Synonym.—Included under *Agrostis Solandri* by Mueller.
Vernacular names.—Same as preceding species.
Where figured.—Labillardière, as *Avena filiformis;* Buchanan; *Agricultural Gazette.*
Botanical description (B. Fl., vii, 580).—

Stems sometimes very short and tufted, usually about 1 foot high or more, leafy to the inflorescence, which is usually enclosed at the base in the broad sheath of the upper leaf.

Panicle, when fully out, often nearly 1 foot long, though sometimes much smaller, with long capillary divided branches in regular whorls.

Outer glumes very narrow and pointed, about 3 lines long.

Flowering glume not half so long, quite glabrous, with two narrow pointed teeth, the dorsal awn attached much below the middle, and rather longer than the outer glumes.

Palea shorter and narrow.

Rhachis produced into a hairy bristle.

Value as a fodder.—Annual on dry clay hills, and perennial on good moist land. Fodder value same as the preceding species.

Habitat and range.—Found in all the Colonies. In New South Wales extending from the coast north of Port Jackson west to the highest mountains of the New England district. Speaking of New Zealand, Buchanan states that it has a very extensive range of growth and adaptation to circumstances of soil, moisture and heat, growing with equal vigour in littoral swamps, on sand-hills, and good pasture land.

5. Deyeuxia plebeia, Benth.

Botanical name.—*Plebeia*—Latin, poor, mean; hence small and dwarf. This grass is small and slender.
Synonym.—Included under *Agrostis Solandri,* by Mueller.
Botanical description (B. Fl., vii, 580).—A slender, tufted, erect grass, of 6 to 10 inches; apparently annual.

Leaves very narrow, almost filiform.

Panicle narrow but loose, 2 to 4 inches long, the filiform branches scattered or in twos or threes, erect or slightly spreading.

Outer glumes very narrow, and pointed, under 1½ lines long.

Flowering glume thin and hairy, about half as long, but with two fine teeth or lobes, almost as long as the outer glumes.

Awn attached very near the base, exceeding the outer glumes.

Palea small and narrow.

Rhachis produced into a minute hairy bristle, almost concealed in the hairs surrounding the glume.

Value as a fodder.—Probably same as *D. Forsteri*, but a smaller grass. *Habitat and range.*—Recorded from Western and South Australia, besides our own Colony. Found in the coast district and mountain ranges.

6. Deyeuxia montana, Benth.

Botanical name.—*Montana*—Latin, growing on the mountains—in reference to the habitat of the grass.

Synonym.—*Agrostis montana*, R.Br. in F.v.M. *Census.*

Botanical description (B. Fl., vii, 581).—

Stems from under 1 foot to above 2 feet high.

Leaves in the smaller specimens very narrow almost subulate, in the larger ones flat and 2 to 3 lines broad.

Panicle dense and spikelike, or slightly branched and interrupted at the base, 2 to 4 inches long.

Spikelets crowded on the short erect branches.

Outer glumes narrow, very acute, rather rigid, 2 to 2½ lines long.

Flowering glume short, glabrous, shortly 2- or 4-toothed, the awn attached much below the middle and exserted.

Palea smaller.

Rhachis bearing but few short hairs, and produced into a glabrous or slightly hairy bristle, either very short or lengthened, and occasionally bearing an empty glume or imperfect flower.

Value as a fodder.—Unknown.

Habitat and range.—Found in Tasmania, Victoria, and South Australia, besides our own Colony. In New South Wales confined to the southern mountain ranges.

7. Deyeuxia quadriseta, Benth.

Botanical name.—*Quadriseta*—Latin, from *quatuor*, four ; *seta*, a bristle—in allusion to the four nerves (two on each side) of the flowering glume, more or less produced into acute teeth or points.

Synonym.—*Agrostis quadriseta*, R.Br., in F.v.M. *Census.*

Vernacular names.—The " Reed-grass" of Bacchus, and the "Spiked Bent or Reed-grass" of Buchanan.

Where figured.—Labillardière, as *Avena quadriseta ;* Trinius, as *Agrostis quadriseta ;* Buchanan ; *Agricultural Gazette.*

Botanical description (B. Fl., vii, 581).—A glabrous and smooth or scabrous erect perennial, very variable in stature, usually 1 to 3 feet high.

Leaves narrow, erect or spreading, flat or convolute when dry.

Panicle dense and spike-like, varying from 1½ or 2 inches to 8 or 10 inches long ; when small closely cylindrical, when large more branched ; but the spikelets always densely crowded from the base of the short erect branches.

Outer glumes narrow, very acute, with a scabrous or minutely ciliate keel, the sides smooth, 1½ to near 2 lines long.

Flowering glume shorter, broad, hyaline, and rolled round the flower, the two nerves on each side more or less produced into acute teeth or points.

Awn attached much below the middle or close to the base, usually not much longer than the outer glumes.

Palea narrow.

Rhachis of the spikelet hairy round the flower, produced sometimes into a minute bristle, which, however, appears to be generally deficient.

Value as a fodder.—"An excellent grass, which might be improved by cultivation. There is a dwarf variety with a more spreading habit of growth and a greater number of radical leaves. Both sorts do not wither up in summer and grow during winter." (Bacchus.) "An erect stiff grass, met with in Queensland on granite country; a fair cattle grass, at times making a good bottom, but the cane-like stem seldom touched by stock." (Bailey.) "Variable, the smaller forms being usually most succulent, especially in sub-Alpine districts, the larger again being harsh, and best adapted for cattle." (Buchanan.)

Habitat and range.—Found in all the Colonies, including New Zealand. In New South Wales found in many parts of the colony.

11. Deyeuxia frigida, F.v.M.

Botanical name.—*Frigida*—Latin, cold—in allusion to the situations in which it grows.

Synonym.—*Agrostis frigida*, F.v.M., in *Census*.

Botanical description (B. Fl., vii, 583).—

Stems weak, and general habit of *D. scabra*, but usually taller, attaining sometimes 4 to 5 feet.

Panicle as in that species, long and loose with scattered branches.

Spikelets rather larger.

Outer glumes very acute, 2 lines long or rather more.

Flowering glume not much shorter, five-nerved, nearly smooth or slightly scabrous in fruit, with a fine twisted awn attached a little above the middle and very deciduous, leaving usually on the fruiting glume a small dorsal notch.

Value as a fodder.—Unknown.

Habitat and range.—Found in Tasmania, and also in the Australian Alps, in both Victoria and New South Wales. We have it from Mount Kosciusko.

12. Deyeuxia scabra, Benth.

Botanical name.—*Scabra*—Latin, rough—in allusion to the flowering glume.

Synonym.—*Agrostis rudis*, Roem. et Schult., in F.v.M. *Census*. Must not be confused with *A. scabra*, Willd.

Where figured.—Buchanan; Hooker, *Fl. Tasmania.*

Botanical description (B. Fl., vii, 583).—

Stems usually weak and decumbent, 1 to 2 feet long.

Leaves flat, flaccid.

Panicle loose, varying from 2 to 8 inches, the capillary branches short, scattered, or in twos or threes, distant in the longer panicles, few in the short ones, not very spreading.

Outer glumes 1 to 1¼ lines long, acute, keeled or the second three-nerved.

Flowering glume scarcely shorter or at length rather longer, membranous, rather stiff in fruit and minutely scabrous-pubescent; the awn minute and straight, attached far above the middle and usually not exceeding the glume.

Palea almost as long, rather broad.

Rhachis with few hairs, and produced into a bristle, minute and glabrous or longer and hairy.

Value as a fodder.—Unknown.

Habitat and range.—Found in Tasmania, Victoria, New South Wales, and Queensland. As regards New South Wales, found on the Australian Alps, and other southern mountain ranges.

13. Deyeuxia nivalis, Benth.

Botanical name.—Nivalis—Latin, accompanying snow—in allusion to the localities in which it grows.
Synonym.—Agrostis nivalis, F.v.M., in *Census*.
Botanical description (B. Fl., vii, 583).—

> *Stems* rather stout, under 1 foot high, covered to the inflorescence by the leaf-sheaths.
> *Leaves* flat, short, and broad, rather stiff, crowded at the base of the stem.
> *Panicle* dense and spikelike, 1½ to 2 inches long, rather dark coloured, the short fine awns scarcely conspicuous.
> *Outer glumes* under 2 lines long, very acute, rather rigid and shining.
> *Flowering glume* rather shorter, glabrous but surrounded by the hairs of the very short rhachis or stipes, the hyaline apex obtuse and entire or scarcely notched.
> *Awn* slender, attached below the summit and projecting but little beyond it.
> *Palea* rather broad.
> *Rhachis* produced into a short glabrous bristle.

Value as a fodder.—While somewhat harsh, a good leafy grass, and doubtless valuable.
Habitat and range.—Found on the Australian Alps of both Victoria and New South Wales (near summit of Mt. Kosciusko).

15. Deyeuxia breviglumis, Benth.

Botanical name.—Breviglumis, Latin—*brevis*, short; *gluma*, chaff (glume), the outer glume being very small.
Synonym.—Agrostis breviglumis, F.v.M., in *Census*.
Botanical description (B. Fl., vii, 584).—A slender grass of 1 to 1½ feet.

> *Leaves* almost filiform.
> *Panicle* rather loose, pyramidal, 1½ to 2 inches long, with capillary but short and rather rigid divided branches, the very small spikelets pedicellate.
> *Outer glume* scarcely ¼ line long, very broad, obtuse and truncate.
> *Flowering glume* nearly twice as long, rather obtuse, the keel often produced into a very short point.
> *Palea* nearly as long as the glume.
> *Rhachis* glabrous, continued into a glabrous bristle nearly as long as the palea.

Value as a fodder.—Unknown.
Habitat and range.—Found in Victoria and New South Wales in the Clyde and Braidwood district, and also in New England. It is usually found growing on damp rocks at the edges of creeks in the mountain districts named.

Sub-tribe iii.—Avenaceæ.

56. Aira.
59. Deschampsia.
60. Trisetum.
62. Amphibromus.
63. Anisopogon.
64. Danthonia.

56. AIRA.

Spikelets two-flowered, small, in a loose or rarely contracted panicle with capillary branches, the rhachis of the spikelet articulate and minutely hairy between the flowering glumes, and not at all or scarcely produced beyond them.

Glumes thinly scarious, two outer empty ones nearly equal, acute; flowering glumes close above them, shorter, thin and hyaline, finely pointed or shortly bifid, with a fine awn dorsally attached below the middle, and twisted at the base.

Palea two-nerved.

Styles short, distinct.

Grain enclosed in, and more or less adnate to, the very thin glume and palea.

1. Aira caryophyllea, Linn.

Botanical name.—*Aira.* Dioscorides called a grass by this name, but the origin of the word is doubtful. Linnæus adopted this name, though the grass is not identical with that of Dioscorides. *Caryophyllea*—Latin, a clove gilly-flower, having foliage resembling that of a pink.

Botanical description (B. Fl., vii, 585).—A slender, elegant, tufted annual, rarely above 6 inches high.

Leaves short and fine.
Panicle loose and spreading, the capillary branches in pairs or threes.
Spikelets erect, silvery-shining.
Outer glumes 1 to 1½ lines long, almost scarious, very acute.
Flowering glumes shorter, the dorsal awn projecting about a line beyond the outer glume.

Value as a fodder.—Unknown.

Habitat and range.—Found in Tasmania, Victoria, and New South Wales. In the last named Colony it has been recorded from the Mudgee district. It is a native of most temperate countries.

59. DESCHAMPSIA.

Spikelets two-flowered, in a loose or rarely contracted panicle with slender branches, the rhachis of the spikelet articulate, hairy, more or less produced between the flowering glumes and beyond the upper one as a hairy bristle, or rarely bearing a terminal empty glume.

Glumes keeled, with thinly scarious sides, two outer empty ones rather acute; flowering glumes obtuse or truncate, and more or less four-toothed, with a fine dorsal awn attached below the middle, the lowest close above the empty glumes, the upper raised on a stipes (the rhachis of the spikelet).

Palea prominently two-nerved, often two-toothed.

Styles short, distinct.

Grain enclosed in the glume and palea, usually free from them. Perennial grasses with the shining spikelets of *Trisetum* and *Aira*, usually smaller than in the former, larger than in the latter genus.

1. Deschampsia cæspitosa, Beauv.

Botanical names.—*Deschampsia*, after M. H. Deschamps, a French chemist (? naturalist), who accompanied La Perouse's disastrous expedition. *Cæspitosa*, a Latin adjective derived from *cæspes*, a turf or sod.

Deschampsia cæspitosa, Beauv.

"Tufted Hair Grass."

Synonym.—Aira cæspitosa, Linn., the name under which it will be found in Mueller's *Census.*

Vernacular name.—" Tufted Hair Grass" is a name under which it is known in England and the United States, and as we have not fixed on a name we may perhaps follow the above designation.

Where figured.—Buchanan ; Agricultural Gazette ; Hackel (see. fig.) Trinius, as *Aira cæspitosa.*

Botanical description (B. Fl., vii, 587).—A tall perennial, forming large dense tufts.

> *Leaves* stiff, narrow, usually rough on the upper surface, flat or convolute when dry.
> *Stems* attaining 2 to 4 feet, although sometimes much shorter.
> *Panicle* 4 inches to near 1 foot long ; at first rather dense, spreading with capillary branches when fully out.
> *Outer glumes* 1½ to near 2 lines long, the *flowering* ones not exceeding them ; truncate and 4-toothed ; the *awns* very slender, scarcely or not at all twisted at the base, and usually shorter than the glumes themselves.

*Value as a fodder.—*This is one of the tussocky grasses, and is not of high forage value—in fact, in many English works on the subject careful directions are given to show how the grass may be got rid of. We may bear in mind that English meadows are of a different character to our own, and some even of our nutritious tussocky grasses would not be appreciated because of their appearance alone.

For instance, Sinclair, *Hortus Gramineus Woburnensis,* says : " The above details prove the innutritious nature of this grass ; but even if it had greater nutritive powers, the extreme coarseness of the foliage would render it unfit for cultivation. Cattle sometimes crop the ends of the young leaves, but in all the instances that have come under my observation it appeared to be from supreme necessity. The only point to be considered here, therefore, is how to overcome or destroy it on soils where it has got possession. It delights in the most clayey soils, where the water stagnates, but is found in almost every kind of soil, from the dry sandy heath to the bog."

Again, Sowerby, *English Botany :* "This grass, according to Parnell, has a most unsightly appearance in meadow-pastures and parks, as it grows into large tufts, and forms irregularities on the surface which are termed by farmers ' rough cups' or ' hossacks,' and are difficult to get rid of. From the extreme roughness and coarseness of the leaves, cattle seldom touch it ; and, as it contains little nutritious matter, it is not worth the attention of the agriculturist. It is a sure indication, wherever found on the farm, that the land wants under-draining, without which no cutting it out will destroy it ; but the efficiency of the drainage, where it occurs, is seen by its dying away and scattering the fields with its turned up rough branches of dried leaves."

Dr. George Vasey, however, speaking of it in the United States, says: " It is one of the common bunch grasses which afford pasturage to cattle and horses. It grows in bunches, which are firmly rooted. Its culms are too light for hay-making, but the abundant root-leaves may make it valuable for pasturage, especially in the arid districts."

" In several very wet places in the Rocky Mountains, U.S.A., we saw forms of this grass which produced a great bulk of hay of fair quality." (Rydberg and Shear.)

I

Baron von Mueller, quoting Stirling, remarks that it is a rough fodder-grass, best utilised for laying dry and moist meadows, and that it affords a fair pasturage if periodically burnt down. This opinion of its value, as far as Australia is concerned, is probably the correct one; but as so few observations have been recorded in regard to it in Australia, perhaps our pastoralists on and near the Australian Alps will send notes on the grass now that attention has been drawn to it. It is true the same species is found in Europe, but it is quite possible that our Australian plants differ in forage value from those of the Northern Hemisphere. Most of my specimens have been nipped by grazing animals.

Other uses.—Door-mats are sometimes made of the hay by cottagers in Scotland.

I wish to draw attention to the highly ornamental character of this grass when in flower. Its spikelets are of a beautiful silvery gray, and are almost of metallic lustre. They vary somewhat in size and tint, and the panicles are well worthy of being gathered for decorative purposes.

Habitat and range.—This grass is rather common on the Australian Alps at an elevation of 5,000 to 6,000 feet. It is found in damp, cold localities in the southern ranges, but as its precise northern limit in this colony is not ascertained, correspondence on the subject is invited. It is very common in Tasmania, and is also found in Victoria and South Australia. Outside Australia, it is found in Europe, Asia and America, also in New Zealand and Fuegia, but never in warm climates.

Reference to plate.—A. Spikelet showing fine dorsal awn attached below the middle of the flowering glumes, one flowering glume close above the empty glumes and the other raised on a stipes. Flowering glumes truncate and four-toothed.

60. TRISETUM.

Spikelets two- rarely three-flowered, in a narrow and dense or loose panicle, the rhachis of the spikelet articulate, hairy and more or less produced between the flowering glumes and beyond the upper one as a hairy bristle, or bearing a terminal empty glume or male flower.

Outer empty glumes unequal, acute, keeled, thinly scarious on the sides.

Flowering glumes more hyaline, keeled, acute or shortly two-fid, with a dorsal awn attached above the middle, usually twisted at the base and bent in the middle.

Palea prominently two-nerved, usually two-toothed.

Styles distinct, stigmatic from near the base.

Grain glabrous, enclosed in the glume and palea but free from them.

Seed not furrowed.

1. Trisetum subspicatum, Beauv.

Botanical name. Trisetum—Latin, *tres* three, *seta* a bristle, the "three bristles" being the two-fid flowering glume with two sharp teeth and a recurved awn inserted a short distance below the apex; *subspicatum*—Latin, *sub* nearly, *spicatus* eared like corn, equivalent to " somewhat spikelike."

Vernacular name.—" Spiked Oat-grass " (Buchanan).

Where figured.—Buchanan ; Vasey ; *Agricultural Gazette.*

Botanical description (B. Fl., vii, 588) :—

A tufted perennial varying from 6 inches to above 2 feet high.

Leaves flat, glabrous or rarely pubescent, the sheaths rather loose, the ligula large and scarious.

Panicle dense, almost spikelike, but much interrupted or shortly branched in the lower part, 2 to 4 inches long, silvery-shining as in *Deschampsia.*

Spikelets loose and flattened, the lowest outer glume nearly 2 lines long, the second rather longer, the keel minutely ciliate.

Lowest flowering glume sessile above the outer ones, 2½ to near 3 lines long, the *awn* sometimes scarcely exceeding it, sometimes twice as long.

Upper flowering glume smaller but inserted higher up so as to be raised to the same level and sometimes containing only a male flower, the rhachis produced beyond it into a slender bristle, rarely bearing a terminal empty glume.

Value as a fodder.—A perennial grass of the mountainous regions of Europe and North America ; undoubtedly furnishes a considerable portion of mountain pasturage. (Vasey.)

It seems improbable that a grass of such vitality and adaptation could be otherwise than valuable, and so, no doubt, it will prove to be when stockowners are enabled to distinguish it from other species. (Buchanan.)

Habitat and range.—Few grasses have such a range as this, nor am I acquainted with any other Arctic species which is equally an inhabitant of the opposite polar regions. (Hooker.)

It occurs in Tasmania, Victoria, and New South Wales, in our own Colony being confined to the southern mountain ranges. Abundant on Mount Kosciusko, even to the summit.

62. AMPHIBROMUS.

Spikelets several-flowered, in a loose panicle, the rhachis of the spikelet articulate, hairy and slender between the flowering glumes.

Outer empty glumes acute, keeled, with scarious margins, five-nerved near the base.

Flowering glumes more rigid, prominently five-nerved, with a dorsal twisted and bent awn attached about the middle.

Palea prominently two-toothed.

Styles short, distinct.

Grain glabrous, enclosed in the glume and palea, and, perhaps, adnate.

Seed deeply furrowed.

1. Amphibromus Neesii, Steud.

Botanical name.—*Amphibromus,* from two Greek words, *amphi,* " around " or " on both sides " ; *bromus,* a wild oat, in reference to the resemblance of the grass to a *bromus,* but the glumes are not distichous like those of that genus, but *all round* the axis; *Neesii*, in honour of Christian Gottfried Nees von Esenbeck, the celebrated German botanist, who specialised on grasses as well as other plants.

Synonym.—Danthonia nervosa, Hook., in Mueller's *Census.*

Where figured.—Hooker, *Fl. Tasmania* (as *D. Archeri*); *Agricultural Gazette.*

Botanical description (B. Fl., vii, 589).—A glabrous erect grass of 2 or 3 feet, or even taller in marshy situations.

> *Leaves* very narrow in the smaller specimens, broader in the larger ones, with rather broad loose sheaths.
> *Panicle* 6 to 10 inches long, loose and narrow.
> *Spikelets* all pedicellate on capillary branches, usually about ½ inch long without the awns, five- to ten-flowered.
> *Outer glumes* varying from 2 to 4 lines long.
> *Flowering glumes* rather longer, the five nerves reaching to the end, and when old often splitting at the apex between the nerves, rather rigid and scabrous-rugose when in fruit.

Value as a fodder.—A tall bulky grass, nutritious and palatable to stock, but not very abundant.

Habitat and range.—Such as margins of claypans, marshes, &c., with fresh water. It occurs in all the Colonies, except Queensland, in moist localities, and it is found over the greater part of New South Wales.

63. ANISOPOGON.

Spikelets one-flowered, large, in a loose but scarcely branched panicle, the rhachis of the spikelet articulate above the two outer glumes and produced into a slender bristle above the flower, occasionally bearing an imperfect spikelet.

Glumes three, the two outer herbaceous; flowering glume raised on a short stipes (the rhachis of the spikelet), narrow, convolute, hard, with three rigid awns between two small hyaline terminal lobes, the central awn long, twisted and bent.

Palea hard, ending in a long, rigid two-nerved point.

Styles distinct.

Ovary crowned by a tuft of hairs.

1. Anisopogon avenaceus, R.Br.

Botanical name.—Anisopogon—Greek, *anisos* unequal, *pogon* a beard, in allusion to the unequal size of the awns of this grass; *avenaceus*, Latin adjective, signifying oat-like.

Vernacular name.—Sometimes called "Oat-grass," from the general resemblance of its inflorescence to that of oats.

Where figured.—Trinius, as *Danthonia anisopogon; Agricultural Gazette.*

Botanical description (B. Fl., vii, 590).—An erect glabrous grass of 2 or 3 feet, branching at the base only.

> *Leaves* convolute, terminating in subulate points.
> *Ligula* very short, truncate, often ciliate.
> *Panicle* long, the large spikelets hanging from slender pedicels.

Anisopogon avenaceus, R. Br.

"An Oat Grass."

133

Outer glumes narrow, about nine-nerved, 1½ to 2 inches long.
Flowering glume about ½ inch long, the central awn 2½ to 3 inches long, the lateral
  ones finer and not half so long.
Palea longer than the entire part of the glume.
Lodicules long and lanceolate.
Terminal barren spikelet, when present, small and silky-villous.

It is an ornamental oat-like grass, its persistent, pale-coloured, very
long outer glumes making the plant very conspicuous.

Value as a fodder.—Very few observations have been made on this
point, so that there is some uncertainty in regard to it. I fancy it is
not generally known, perhaps being confused with other grasses. I
have been in places where cattle appeared scarcely to touch it, but it
must be borne in mind that it is chiefly found in poor sandstone
country, and that it is sparsely tussocky, so that stock could only feed
it down with difficulty. Against this I have the statement of a correspondent from Cape Hawke that it is a palatable and fattening grass
for cows.

Habitat and range.—Principally a New South Wales species, though
it extends to Queensland on the north, and Victoria on the south. It
is confined to the coast districts and coast mountain ranges, preferring,
as far as I have noticed, sterile, rocky country.

Reference to plate.—1. Spikelet opened out. 2. Flowering glume showing large central
awn and fine lateral awns.

64. DANTHONIA.

Spikelets several-flowered, pedicellate or rarely almost sessile, in a
panicle, either loose or reduced to a single raceme, the rhachis of the
spikelet articulate above the outer glumes, hairy round the flowering
ones.

Outer empty glumes two, narrow, keeled, acute, unawned, usually as
long as the spikelet.

Flowering glumes convex at the back, usually nine-nerved, with two
rigid or scarious terminal lobes more or less one- or three-nerved at
least at the base, and a twisted and bent awn between them (almost
reduced to a point in one species).

Palea broad, as long as, or usually longer, than the entire part of
the glume, obtuse or two-pointed.

Styles distinct.
Ovary glabrous.
Grain free.

[*Fungi found on Danthonias. Ustilago destruens*, Schlecht; and *U.
segetum*, Bull; have both been recorded on *Danthonia spp.*]

SECTION I.—MICRATHERA.

Panicle very loose. Spikelets nearly glabrous. Awn of the flowering glume not exceeding the very short lateral lobes.

Single species ... ... 1. *D. paradoxa.*

SECTION II.—MONACHATHERA.

Panicle almost reduced to a raceme or very short. Flowering glumes with a broad obliquely turbinate hard base and ciliate with long hairs, the awn shorter or scarcely longer than the lobes.

Spikelets distant, in an almost simple raceme. Lobes of the flowering glumes lanceolate, two or three times as long as the base ... ... 2. *D. bipartita*.
Spikelets few, in a very short panicle. Lobes of the flowering glumes not longer than the base ... ... 3. *D. carphoides*.

SECTION III.—EUDANTHONIA.

Flowering glume ovoid or oblong at the base, scarcely oblique, ciliate at least at the base. Awn longer than the lateral lobes.

Panicle loose. Spikelets numerous. Hairs of the flowering glume marginal and scattered, or in longitudinal series on the back ; lateral lobes acute or scarcely awned .. .. 4. *D. pallida*.
Panicle rather dense. Flowering glumes very small, with copious long hairs, lateral lobes very short, with long awns. Leaves long and filiform ... ... 5. *D. longifolia*.
Panicle narrow or dense. Flowering glumes oblong, with long marginal cilia, but very few hairs on the back.
Stems stout, 3 to 5 feet high. Leaves long, with long loose sheaths. Panicle branched ... ... 6. *D. robusta*.
Stems under 2 feet high. Leaves narrow. Panicle reduced to a single raceme, or the lower panicles with two spikelets... 7. *D. racemosa*.
Stems under 2 feet high. Leaves very narrow. Panicle dense 8. *D. pilosa*.
Panicle dense or rather loose. Flowering glumes oblong, with a ring of long hairs at or below the base of the lobes. Outer glumes not much exceeding the spikelet. Leaves narrow, but not setaceous ... ... 9. *D. semiannularis*.
Panicle small, few-flowered. Flowering glumes ciliate with long hairs, the lobes broad, not longer than the base. Small Alpine plant ... ...11. *D. pauciflora*.

1. Danthonia paradoxa, R.Br.

Botanical name.—Danthonia, in honour of M. Danthoine, a French botanist (none of his works are mentioned in Pritzel's *Thesaurus*). *Paradoxa*, Latin, something unexpected. This species is of unusual appearance for a *Danthonia*.

Botanical description (B. Fl., vii, 591).

Stems 2 to 3 feet high.

Leaves long and narrow, glabrous.

Panicle very loose, 3 to 4 inches long, with long capillary divided branches at length spreading.

Spikelets pedicellate, flat, three- or four-flowered, 3 to 4 lines long.

Outer empty glumes rather rigid, acute, 2 to 2½ lines long.

Flowering glumes shorter, very shortly hairy or pubescent below the middle, the two lobes shorter than the base, broad, shortly nerved, unawned.

Central awn not exceeding them, somewhat flattened and brown at the base as in other species, but rarely long enough to show any twist.

Botanical notes.—The almost glabrous spikelets have much the appearance of those of a *Poa*, but the structure is quite that of a short-awned *Danthonia* (Benth.)

Value as a fodder.—A wiry and rather rigid grass, cropped by stock only when young.
Habitat and range.—Confined to New South Wales, and to the Port Jackson district and the Blue Mountains.

2. Danthonia bipartita, F.v.M.

Botanical name.—*Bipartita*, Latin, divided into two parts, in allusion to the bipartite outer glume.
Where figured.—*Agricultural Gazette.*
Botanical description (B. Fl., vii, 592).

Stems from an almost bulbous often woolly base 1 to 2 feet high.

Leaves flat but narrow, glabrous or sprinkled with long hairs.

Panicle almost reduced to a simple raceme of 3 to 6 inches.

Spikelets few, on short erect distant pedicels, or the lower pedicels shortly branched, with two or three spikelets.

Outer glumes herbaceous, many-nerved, 5 to 8 lines long, tapering into fine points.

Flowering glumes four to eight, scarcely exceeding the outer ones, the oblique base a little more than 1 line long and broad, with a dense ring of long hairs under the lobes.

Lobes narrow-lanceolate, very acute, unawned, 3 to 4 lines long, the central awn scarcely longer.

Palea obtuse or truncate.

Value as a fodder.—Useful as a tender-leaved and productive perennial grass for arid country.
Habitat and range.—Found in all the colonies except Tasmania. It is confined to the arid districts.

3. Danthonia carphoides, F.v.M.

Botanical name.—*Carphoides*, *Carpha*, *oidos* (like), the inflorescence superficially resembling that of *Carpha*, a genus of Cyperaceous plants.
Vernacular name.—Has been sent under the name of "Wallaby-grass."
Where figured.—*Agricultural Gazette.*
Botanical description (B. Fl. vii, 592).

Stems from 3 or 4 inches to 1 foot high.

Leaves very narrow, not long, glabrous.

Panicle ovate, dense, 1 to 1½ inches long.

Spikelets few, very shortly pedicellate.

Outer glumes 4 to 5 lines long, rather broad, with scarious margins.

Flowering glumes three to six, with a broad oblique base as in *D. bipartita*, the ring of hairs almost broken into clusters.

Lateral lobes shorter than the base, the very fine awn scarcely exceeding them.

Value as a fodder.—A useful fodder-plant, not of the highest class.
Habitat and range.—Found in South Australia, Victoria, and New South Wales. In our colony it extends from the ranges and table-lands from New England south to the Macquarie and Murray Rivers.

136

4. Danthonia pallida, R. Br.

Botanical name.—Pallida, Latin, pale, in allusion to the colour of the inflorescence.
Synonym.—Danthonia penicillata, F.v.M. in Census.
Venacular names.—" Silver-grass " ; " White-topped grass."
*Where figured.—*Trinius ; *Agricultural Gazette.*
Botanical description (B. Fl., vii, 592).

Stems 2 feet high or more, often rigid, but not stout.
Leaves long, terete when dry, very narrow and sometimes as slender as in *D. longi-folia*, the sheaths more or less ciliate at the orifice.
Panicle usually loosely branched, pale-coloured, 3 to 6 inches long.
Spikelets rather numerous, the *outer glumes* under ½ inch long.
Flowering glumes three or four, not exceeding the outer ones, with long hairs on the back as well as on the margins, but scattered or in vertical lines, without the transverse ring of *D. semiannularis ;* lateral lobes lanceolate, three-nerved at the base, often scarious upwards, but the central nerve continued to the apex or produced into a point or short awn.

Var. *subracemosa*, Benth : Panicle narrow, very little branched. Marginal hairs of the flowering glumes copious, those on the back less so than in the typical form.
Northern rivers, New South Wales ; also in Queensland.
*Value as a fodder.—*A good grass yielding abundance of palatable fodder.
*Habitat and range.—*Found in all the colonies. In New South Wales from the coast districts to the table-lands.

5. Danthonia longifolia, R.Br.

Botanical name.—Longifolia, Latin, long-leaved.
Synonym.—Danthonia penicillata, F.v.M. in Census.
Vernacular name.—" White-topped Grass."
Botanical description (B. Fl., vii, 593).

Stems densely tufted, 1 to 2 feet high.
Leaves long and filiform, often rather rigid and curved, quite glabrous without any cilia at the orifice of the sheath.
Panicle dense, pale-coloured, ovate or narrow, 3 to 4 inches long.
Outer glumes exceeding the spikelet, 4 to 6 lines long.
Flowering glumes three to five, very short, almost covered with soft hairs, the upper ones very long, the two lobes broad and short, usually with long awns, very fine as well as the longer central one.

*Value as a fodder.—*A good pasture grass.
*Habitat and range.—*Found in Victoria, New South Wales, and Queensland. In New South Wales it extends from the coast west as far as New England and Wellington.

6. Danthonia robusta, F.v.M.

Botanical name.—Robusta, Latin, strong, sturdy ; this grass being large and coarse.
Vernacular name.—" Ribbony Grass " of Mount Kosciusko.
Where figured.—Agricultural Gazette.

Botanical description (B. Fl., vii, 593).

Stems from a thick horizontal rhizome, stout, 3 to 5 feet high.

Leaves long, narrow, convolute when dry, glabrous, the upper one w th a long loose sheath.

Panicle dense, rather secund, 3 to 6 inches long.

Spikelets pedicellate, about ½ inch long, five- to eight-flowered.

Outer glumes scarcely so long, the lowest rather obtuse, the second tapering to a sharp point.

Flowering glumes densely ciliate on the margins, with very few hairs scattered on the back, the lobes broad, tapering into short awns, the central awn long, flat, and much twisted below the bend.

Value as a fodder.—This Alpine grass is tall enough to hide sheep, and is a coarse, strong grass, but much liked in spite of its coarseness. (Helms.) It reminds one somewhat of Blady Grass *(Imperata)*, when not in flower. Horses feed on it greedily.

Habitat and range.—Forms large patches of rich foliage, up to nearly the very summits of the highest peaks in the Australian Alps of both New South Wales and Victoria.

7. Danthonia racemosa, R.Br.

Botanical name.—*Racemosa*, Latin, "very full of clusters;" in botanical language, racemose, having inflorescence in a raceme.

Synonym.—*Danthonia penicillata*, F.v.M. in Census.

Vernacular names.—A "Mulga Grass." It derives its vernacular name from being only found where the Mulga tree (*Acacia aneura* and other species) grows; see *Neurachne.* "Bunch Danthonia." (Bacchus.)

Botanical description (B. Fl. vii, 594).

Stems slender, 1 to 2 feet high.

Leaves very narrow, almost setaceous, glabrous, or sprinkled with spreading hairs.

Spikelets, in the typical form, singly and very shortly pedicellate, or almost sessile, or rather distant along the rhachis of a simple raceme, but sometimes more approximate, and the lower pedicels with two spikelets.

Spikelets narrow, erect, under ½ inch long, the outer glume nearly as long.

Flowering glumes 6 to 8, or more in some varieties, hairy at the base and margins, glabrous, or with very few hairs on the back, but the hairs variable, the marginal ones sometimes long in a dense tuft on each side of the lobes, sometimes in several distinct marginal tufts.

Lateral lobes in the typical form broad, with short fine points, but more awned in some varieties.

Var. *obtusata*, F.v.M. A smaller plant, leaves more hairy. Lateral lobes of the flowering glumes with scarcely any points. New England.

Var. *biaristata*, Benth. Lateral lobes of the flowering glumes broad, but with rather long points or awns. New South Wales, Victoria, South Australia and Tasmania.

Var. *multiflora*, Benth. Spikelets often two together, and all approximate. Flowers rather numerous in the spikelet. Hunter River and New England, also Queensland and South Australia.

Value as a fodder.—A grass widely distributed over Australia in one or other of its forms. It is one of the best of the *Danthonias* for the pastoralist, forming a good close turf of nutritious, palatable grass. "The principal grass of which a large portion of Victorian pastures is composed. It is very hardy, and bears over-stocking better than any other native grass known to me. If attended to it would make a close turf. Its nutritive properties are considerable. It appears to thrive with rye grass and clover, which many native grasses will not do." (Bacchus.)

Habitat and range.—Found in all the colonies, except Western Australia. In New South Wales it extends from the coast to the table-lands and the southern mountain ranges.

8. Danthonia pilosa, R.Br.

Botanical name.—*Pilosa*, Latin, hairy.

Synonym.—*Danthonia penicillata*, F.v.M. in Census.

Vernacular names.—"Purple-awned Oat-grass." (Buchanan.)

Where figured.—Buchanan; Bacchus, (Trinius, t. 51, is *D. setacea?).*

Botanical description (B. Fl., vii, 594).

Stems rather slender, 1 to 2 feet high.

Leaves chiefly in radical tufts, very narrow, but not so slender as in *D. setacea*; usually more or less hairy, the hairs sometimes long and spreading.

Panicle narrow and dense, not much branched, and sometimes almost as simple as in *D. racemosa.*

Spikelets shortly pedicellate, about ¼ inch long, the

Outer glumes about as long,

Flowering glumes six to eight, with lanceolate lobes tapering into fine awns almost as in *D. semiannularis*, but hairy on the margin only, without the transverse ring under the lobes of that species, and very few hairs (if any) on the back, except at the base.

Botanical note.—Some forms approach in habit *D. racemosa*, but the spikelets are those of *D. semiannularis*, except in the want of the ring of hairs on the back under the lobes. (Benth.)

Value as a fodder.—A useful fodder-grass. Bailey points out that as it is such a good seed-bearer, it is not so likely to be lost through overstocking as other grasses. Bacchus refers to it as a hardy and good pasture grass, which does not, however, stand the summer heat well.

Habitat and range.—Found in all the colonies except Tasmania and Western Australia. Extends from the coast to the table-land.

9. Danthonia semiannularis, R.Br.

Botanical name.—*Semiannularis;* Latin, *semi* half, *annulus* a little ring, in allusion to the half-ring of hairs at the back of the flowering glume.

Synonym.—*Danthonia penicillata*, F.v.M. in Census.

Where figured.—Labillardière, as *Arundo semiannularis;* Trinius; Buchanan; *Agricultural Gazette.*

Botanical description (B. Fl., vii, 595).

A variable plant, the

Stems usually 2 to 3 feet high, but sometimes much lower.

Leaves very narrow, flat or convolute, never so fine as in *D. setacea*, the sheaths glabrous or hairy, more or less ciliate at the orifice.

Panicle sometimes loose and spreading, more frequently narrow and compact.

139

Outer glumes acute, above ½ inch, and sometimes nearly 1 inch long.

Flowering glumes usually four to eight, not exceeding the outer ones, the lobes lanceolate, with a broad or narrow hyaline margin, acute or tapering into a point or rather a short fine awn, the long hairs of the cilia copious at the base and margins, and forming a ring round the back immediately under the lobes, the twisted awn varying from ½ to 1 inch.

Palea longer than the entire base of the glume, often two-pointed.

Botanical Notes.—The common form, apparently abundant in the Southern Colonies, has usually a compact narrow panicle and the pale or greenish outer glumes often smooth and shining. The loose-flowered form with the outer glumes dark-coloured appears to be chiefly about Port Jackson and the Blue Mountains, and occasionally in Tasmania.

Var. alpina.—Stems short and densely tufted. Leaves rather stout, convolute and very glabrous. Australian Alps.

Value as a fodder.—A valuable grass when young, but in arid country it becomes very harsh when old. A Wilcannia correspondent writes:— " Grows strong on country near the tank, but nothing will eat it, not even the rabbits, and there is no sign of any other feed. On Baden Park and Mount Manaro Stations with same results."

Habitat and Range.—Found in all the colonies, and in most parts of New South Wales, from the coast to the interior. Perhaps our most widely diffused *Danthonia.*

11. Danthonia pauciflora, R.Br.

Botanical name.—*Pauciflora*, Latin, *pauci* few, *flos-floris* flower; few-flowered, the panicle containing but few flowers.

Vernacular name.—" Few-flowered Oat-grass."

Where figured.—Buchanan ; Hooker, *Fl. Tasmania.*

Botanical description (B. Fl., vii, 596). A small plant forming low dense branching tufts of fine rigid leaves not above 1 inch long and the *stems* not above 6 inches, or when luxuriant both weaker and longer.

Panicle ovoid, of few shortly pedicellate spikelets, sometimes reduced to 2 or 3.

Outer glumes three lines long or rather more.

Flowering glumes 3 or 4, very short, with short broad lobes, acute or with short fine awns, the hairs chiefly at the base and margins not forming a transverse ring, the central awn rather longer than the lobes or lateral awns.

Palea obtuse.

Var. *? alpina*, F.v.M. Panicle small and narrow. Glumes small, the flowering ones with very few hairs and very short awns, but with the short broad lateral lobes of the typical form. Summits of the Australian Alps.

Value as a fodder.—A small Alpine pasture grass. Its small rigid leaves do not recommend it as a pasture grass, yet, from its evident perennial habit, it may prove valuable on those higher altitudes where few grasses can exist. (Buchanan.) It is cropped by sheep.

Habitat and Range.—Found in Tasmania, Victoria, and New South Wales, as well as in New Zealand. In Victoria and New South Wales on the Australian Alps.

Tribe vi.—ASTREPTÆ.

Sub-tribe i.—*Pappophoreæ*.

65. Amphipogon.   68. Astrebla.
66. Echinopogon.   69. Triraphis.
67. Pappophorum.   70. Triodia.

65. AMPHIPOGON.

Spikelets one-flowered, nearly sessile in a dense panicle contracted into a head or short spike, the rhachis of the spikelet articulate above the two outer glumes, and not continued beyond the flower.

Glumes three, two outer persistent, membranous, three-nerved, acute or tapering to an awnlike point, rarely three-fid.

Flowering glume raised on a short hairy stipes (the rhachis of the spikelet), closed round the flower, deeply divided into three narrow lobes tapering into straight points or awns.

Palea usually as long as the flowering glume, deeply divided into two narrow rigid lobes or awns.

Styles united at the base, free upwards.

Grain enclosed in the slightly hardened upper glume.

Perennial grasses with convolute terete or subulate leaves.

2. Amphipogon strictus, R.Br.

Botanical name.—*Amphipogon*, Greek *amphi*, around, *pogon*, a beard, in allusion to the short hairy stipes of the flowering glume ; *strictus*, Latin, rigid, which is the habit of the plant.

Where figured.—*Agricultural Gazette.*

Botanical description (B. Fl., vii, 597).

Stems from a horizontal rhizome or tufted branching base erect and slender, usually above 1 foot high.

Leaves rather short, erect, subulate, glabrous.

Spikelike panicle dense, oblong or cylindrical, ½ to 1½ inches long, but little branched.

Outer glumes broad, concave, faintly three-nerved, almost scarious, entire when perfect, the outer one about 2 lines, the inner rather longer and more acute.

Flowering glume on the short hairy stipes shorter than the outer glume, with two short rows of hairs on the back, divided into three rigid ciliate linear lobes or awns longer than the entire part.

Palea narrow, deeply divided into two rigid lobes similar to those of the flowering glume.

Seed separable from the membranous pericarp.

Value as a fodder.—A rather harsh grass not readily eaten by stock except when quite young.

Fungus recorded on this grass.—*Ustilago Tepperi*, Lud.

Habitat and range.—Found in all the Colonies except Tasmania, and pretty well all over the Colony of New South Wales.

66. ECHINOPOGON.

Spikelets one-flowered, nearly sessile in a dense panicle contracted into a head or short spike, the rhachis of the spikelet articulate above the two outer glumes and produced into a short bristle above the flower.

Glumes three, two outer persistent, acute, keeled; flowering glume thin, five-nerved, three-lobed, the lateral lobes unawned, the central one produced into a fine straight awn.

Palea narrow.

Styles distinct, the stigmas very shortly plumose.

Grain enclosed in the flowering glume, but free from it.

1. Echinopogon ovatus, Beauv.

Botanical name.—Echinopogon, Greek *echinos* a hedgehog, *pogon* a beard, in allusion to the very rough flower-head; *ovatus,* Latin egg-shaped, or of an oval figure, in allusion to the shape of the flower-head.

Vernacular name.— "Rough-bearded Grass."

*Where figured.—*Labillardière as *Agrostis ovata;* Buchanan; *Agricultural Gazette.*

Botanical description (B. Fl., vii, 599).—An erect glabrous grass, from under 1 foot to above 2 feet high.

Leaves flat, very scabrous, the asperites reversed on the sheath and back of the blade, erect on the upper surface.

Head or spikelike panicle on a long terminal peduncle, varying from ovoid-globular and ½ inch diameter to oblong-cylindrical and 2 inches long.

Spikelets numerous and densely crowded, about 1½ lines long without the awns.

Outer glumes lanceolate, boat-shaped, the keel prominent, green and ciliate.

Flowering glume rather broad, surrounded by a tuft of hairs, the lateral lobes very short, acute, rigid at the base, the central one shortly flat at the base, tapering to an awn of 2 to 4 lines.

Palea nearly as long as the glume.

Bristle continuing the axis at the back of the palea usually shorter than the glume, bearing a short tuft of hairs or rudimentary glume.

*Value as a fodder.—*A harsh grass of very little fodder value. It seeks the protection of shrubs and fences, and hence occasionally affords a bite to hungry stock when more palatable grasses have been eaten down.

*Habitat and range.—*Found in all the Colonies, including New Zealand. In New South Wales, extending from the coast to the table-land, and up to nearly 5,000 feet on Mount Kosciusko.

67. PAPPOPHORUM.

Spikelets with one hermaphrodite flower and 1 or more male or rudimentary flowers or empty glumes above it, in a short, dense and spikelike or narrow and loose panicle, the rhachis of the spikelet articulate above the outer glumes and hairy round the flowering glume.

Outer glumes membranous, many-nerved, awnless, as long as the spikelet.

Flowering glume broad, membranous, with 9, or in species not Australian, more nerves, produced into more or less plumose awns.

Palea two-nerved, as long as the glume or longer.

Styles distinct.

Grain enclosed in the glume and palea, free from them.

Outer glumes 1 to 2 lines long, 5- to 9-nerved............................ 1. *P. nigricans*

Outer glumes 3 lines long, 11- to 21-nerved................................ 2. *P. avenaceum*

1. Pappophorum nigricans, R.Br.

Botanical name.—Pappophorum, Latin (from the Greek) *pappus,* thistle-down, hence in botany the pappus of composites ; *phorum,* Greek *phoreo,* I bear, in allusion to the downiness or woolliness of the flowering glumes ; *nigricans,* Latin, blackish, the panicle being usually of a dark colour.

Synonym.—Included with *P. avenaceum* under *P. commune* F.v.M., by Mueller.

Vernacular name.—" Purple-topped Grass." (Bailey.)

Where figured.—Agricultural Gazette.

Botanical description.—(B. Fl. vii, 600).

Stems from under 1 foot to 1½ feet high.

Leaves flat or convolute, usually narrow, sometimes quite setaceous, glabrous, pubescent or villous, the nodes glabrous or bearded.

Panicle dense and spikelike, varying from ovoid-oblong and under ½ inch long, to narrow cylindrical and 3 inches long, or broader, more branched, and 2 to 3 inches long, but always dense, pale or dark-coloured.

Outer glumes varying from 1 to rather above 2 lines long, obtuse or acute, striate, with usually 7 or 9 nerves, but sometimes, especially on the lowest glume, reduced to 5 and 2 of those short.

Flowering glume not above 1 line long, more or less hairy outside, especially at the base, with 9 fine spreading plumose awns varying from the length of the glume to twice as long. Above the flowering glume and enclosed in it is usually a smaller one with a male or rudimentary flower, and 1 or 2 still smaller empty ones.

Value as a fodder.—A drought-resisting species, but not readily eaten by stock, so far as my experience goes.

" This is an erect grass, and, although wiry in appearance, furnishes a good quantity of feed and bears close cropping ; there are many forms of it, some of which would be worthy of cultivation as ornamental grasses." (Bailey.)

Habitat and range.—Found in all the Colonies except Tasmania ; also in New Guinea and the Pacific Islands. Found in most parts of the Colony of New South Wales. Ascends Mount Kosciusko to nearly 5,000 feet.

2. Pappophorum avenaceum, Lindl.

Botanical name.—Avenaceum, Latin, oat-like; the panicle somewhat resembling oats in appearance.

Synonym.—Included (with *P. nigricans*) under *P. commune,* F.v.M.

Where figured.—Agricultural Gazette.

Botanical description (B. Fl., vii, 601).—Very near the *P. nigricans,* with which F. Mueller unites it under the name of *P. commune,* and with the same habit but the spikelike panicle looser with fewer and larger spikelets.

Outer glumes fully 3 lines long with numerous nerves, usually more than eleven and sometimes as many as twenty-one.

Flowering glumes several, closely imbricate, the outer ones with a fertile flower enclosing one or two male (or sometimes a second fertile) flowers and one or two small empty glumes.

Value as a fodder.—See *P. nigricans.*

Habitat and range.—Found in the interior of New South Wales, Queensland, and South Australia.

68. ASTREBLA.

Spikelets few-flowered, sessile or nearly so in the alternate notches of the continuous rhachis of one or two simple secund spikes, the rhachis of the spikelet articulate above the two outer glumes.

Outer empty glumes two, glabrous, acute, many-nerved, unawned.

Flowering glumes silky-hairy, three-lobed, the central lobe with a broad base tapering into a straight or curved not twisted awn, the lateral lobes erect, rigid, two- or three-nerved.

Palea with two prominent ciliate nerves or keels.

Styles distinct, very short. In both species the spikes are usually single, very rarely two together at the end of the peduncle.

Spikelets closely imbricate on one side of a secund spike of 2 to 3 inches. Awn about as long as the lateral lobes .... 1. *A. pectinata.*

Spikelets at some distance, almost erect in a secund spike of 3 to 6 inches. Awn much longer than the lateral lobes, straight or hooked... 2. *A. triticoides.*

1. Astrebla pectinata, F.v.M.

Botanical name.—*Astrebla,* Greek *a* not, *strebla* twisted, referring to the awn, which is not twisted; *pectinata,* Latin, combed or comb-like, the spike reminding one of the appearance of a comb.

Vernacular names.—A "Mitchell Grass"; "Coarse Mitchell Grass." (Bailey.) Mr. Koch informs me that Mitchell grass is known as Taldra-auto by Cordillo blacks in South Australia.

Where figured.—Bailey; *Agricultural Gazette.*

Botanical description (B. Fl. vii, 602).—An erect glaucous grass of 1 to 2 feet, glabrous except sometimes a few hairs at the orifice of the sheaths.

Leaves flat, ending in long points, smooth or scarcely scabrous.

Spikelets sessile in the alternate notches of a secund spike of 2 to 3 inches, closely imbricate and turned to one side.

Outer glumes 4 to 5 lines long, glabrous, acute, 9- or 11-nerved, with scabrous margins.

Flowering glumes 3 or 4, the entire part scarcely 1 line long, densely villous outside as well as the broad base of the middle lobe; lateral lobes semi-lanceolate, glabrous, rigid, 4 to 5 lines long, acute, 2- or 3-nerved, with the outer margin broadly scarious; central lobe broad, ovate, concave, keeled, tapering into a slender straight awn about as long as, or rather longer than, the lateral lobes.

Rhachis of the spikelet articulate only above the outer glumes, very hairy between the flowering ones, continued and less hairy above the perfect flowers, with one or two glabrous glumes and paleæ empty or with rudimentary flowers.

Value as a fodder.—The Mitchell grasses rank amongst the most nutritious and drought enduring of the grasses of the interior of New South Wales. They are rather coarse grasses, but after the rains they yield an immense quantity of succulent, nutritious fodder.

Other uses.—The seeds of the genus are large and separate like wheat, free from chaff, and are in the interior largely used by the natives for food. (Bailey.)

When in seed this is a very handsome grass, and quite worthy to rank amongst the ornamental grasses for vases and decorative work.

Habitat and range.—Occurs in New South Wales, Queensland, and Northern Australia, also in Western and South Australia. In New South Wales more or less spread over the whole of the western country. Var. *elymoides*, Bail. (Syn. *A. elymoides*, F.v.M. et Bail.), is a Mitchell grass, hitherto supposed to be confined to Queensland. It has, however, been sent from Collarendabri, in the north-west of this colony, 500 miles from Sydney, and *via* Narrabri and Walgett towards the Queensland border.

It is figured by Bailey, who speaks of it as "a weak straggling grass, sprouting at the joints after every shower of rain, and affording a large amount of excellent fodder . . . . a great favourite with stockowners."

2. Astrebla triticoides, F.v.M.

Botanical name.—*Triticoides*, Latin, *Triticum*, wheat, Greek, *oidos*, like, indicating the similarity in appearance of the "head" to that of a "head" of wheat.

Vernacular name.—"Mitchell-grass."

Where figured.—*Agricultural Gazette.*

Botanical description (B. Fl., vii, 602).—Very near *A. pectinata*, apparently a taller plant, the

Leaves more or less scabrous or ciliate on the edges.

Spikes 3 to 6 inches long.

Spikelets alternate, not closely imbricate, and often almost erect and at some distance from each other.

Outer empty glumes usually very unequal, the lowest short, the second 4 or 5 lines long.

Flowering glumes shorter, the lateral lobes shorter and more rigid than in *A. pectinata*, and the awn much exceeding them, the dorsal hairs appressed and silky.

Var. *lappacea*, Benth. Spikelets usually thicker, the largest outer glume often ½ inch long. Awns of the flowering glumes usually longer than in the typical form, often bent about and some or nearly all with a rigid hook at the end, but exceedingly variable ; in some specimens the hook is very rare, and the length of the awns very irregular.

Localities.—Same as normal species.

Value as a fodder.—Much the same properties as the preceding species. It should be propagated as far as possible, for it is not as plentiful as could be wished. Patches of it should be fenced off, if necessary, for seed. The variety *lappacea* is coarser than the normal species, but its fodder-value is much the same.

Habitat and range.—Found in South Australia, also in New South Wales, Queensland, and Northern Australia. An interior species.

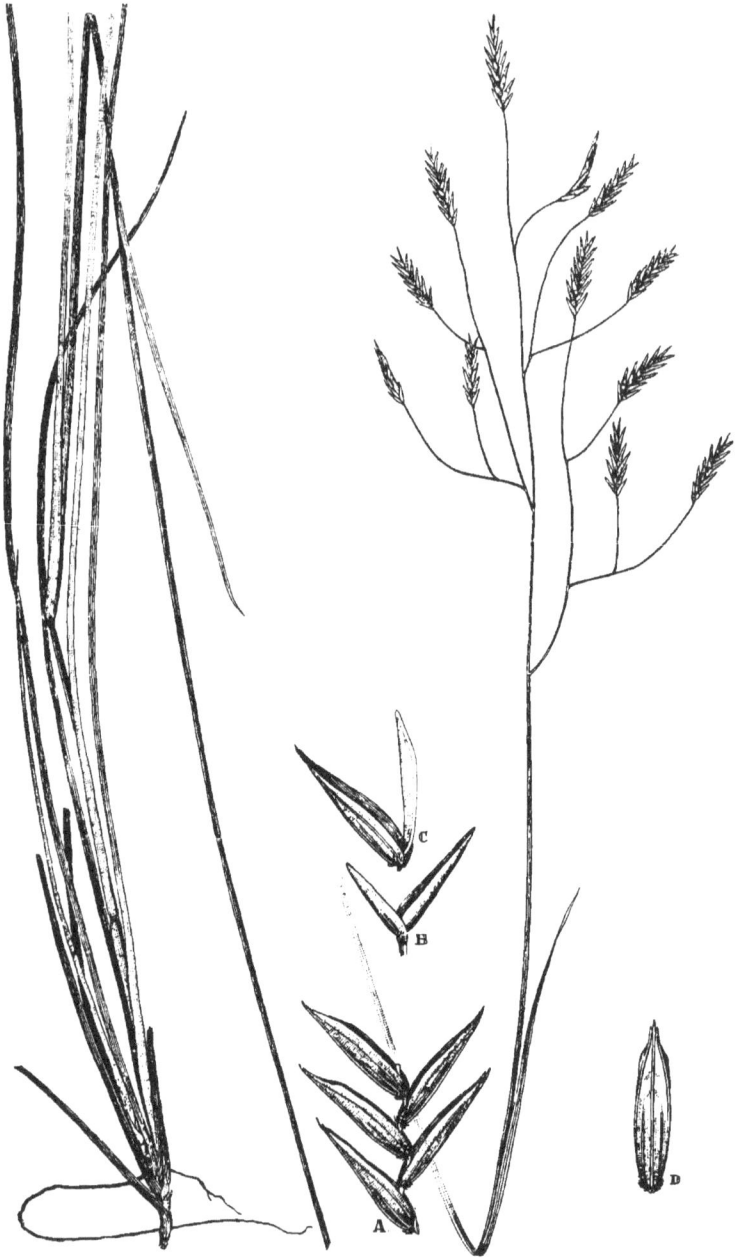

Triraphis microdon, Benth.

69. TRIRAPHIS.

Spikelets several-flowered, in a terminal panicle, the rhachis of the spikelet articulate above each glume, the terminal glume usually empty or with a male flower.

Outer empty glumes unawned, entire or the second occasionally notched with a short point in the notch.

Flowering glumes with three narrow lobes tapering into straight awns, the central occasionally with a short lobe or point on each side, or all three reduced to small teeth.

Palea narrow.

Styles distinct.

Grain enclosed in the thin or coriaceous glume and palea, free from them.

Panicle soft and dense ; flowering glumes hairy, with a pointed
lobe or short awn on each side of the central awn ... 1. *T. mollis.*

Panicle very loose ; flowering glumes coriaceous, with three
small teeth or points ... ... 5. *T. microdon.*

1. Triraphis mollis, R. Br.

Botanical name.—*Triraphis,* Greek *treis,* three, *raphis* a needle, in allusion to the three awns of the flowering glumes which are needle-like ; *mollis,* Latin, soft, in allusion to the soft, silky feel of the panicle.

Where figured.—*Agricultural Gazette.*

Botanical description (B. Fl. vii, 603).—A glabrous, rather slender, erect grass attaining 2 feet, but sometimes much smaller.

Leaves long and narrow ending in fine points.

Panicle narrow, dense, 6 to 10 inches long, with a soft look owing to the slender awns and hairs of the glumes.

Spikelets crowded on the short erect branches, narrow, about ½ inch long without the awns, with 8 to 10 or even more flowers.

Glumes narrow, membranous, about 1½ lines long, the two outer empty ones glabrous, entire or the second with a short tooth on each side of the point.

Flowering glumes sprinkled with a few long hairs, the central capillary awn three to four lines long, with a pointed lobe or short awn on each side, the lateral awns rather shorter.

Value as a fodder.—Inferior for this purpose, and only eaten when better grasses are scarce.

Other uses.—The long dense panicle possesses such a handsome appearance as to place this plant within the category of ornamental grasses.

Habitat and range.—Found in all the colonies except Tasmania. An interior species.

5. Triraphis microdon, Benth.

Botanical name.—*Microdon,* Greek, *micros,* small, *odous, odontos* a tooth, the three principal nerves of the flowering glume being produced into short terminal points or small teeth.

Synonym.—*Triodia microdon,* F. v. M., in *Census.* There seems little doubt that this species should be referred to *Triodia* rather than

K

to *Triraphis*, a view I should adopt in this Manual were it not for the convenience of as close adherence as possible to the nomenclature of the *Flora Australiensis*.

Botanical description (B. Fl. vii, 605). An erect glabrous grass of 2 or 3 feet.

Leaves narrow, flat, or convolute.
Panicle very loose, with long capillary branches, bearing each one to three large flat spikelets on capillary pedicels, at first erect, at length pendulous.
Spikelets ten- to fourteen-flowered, ¾ to 1 inch long, the rhachis with a tuft of short hairs under each flowering glume.
Outer empty glumes narrow, acute, keeled, with or without a faint nerve on each side.
Flowering glumes distant from each other, about four lines long, rigid with five very prominent nerves of which the three principal ones produced into short terminal points or teeth, the central one rather the largest.

Value as a fodder.—Unknown ; not likely to be important, on account of its rarity. It may also be mentioned that its affinities are with two genera not distinguished for yielding nutritious grasses.

Habitat and range.—Confined to New South Wales, and only recorded from the Blue Mountains. It is one of the rarest of our grasses.

Reference to Plate.— A. One of the flat spikelets enlarged and opened out. B.C. Two pairs of glumes, showing a tuft of short hairs under each flowering glume. D. End of a flowering glume, with its five prominent nerves, three of which are produced into short terminal points.

70. TRIODIA.

Spikelets several-flowered, paniculate, the rhachis articulate above the outer glumes and between the flowering ones, hairy round them or glabrous.

Glumes unawned, two outer empty ones acute, keeled, glabrous or the keel scabrous-ciliate.

Flowering glumes usually shorter, unawned, the lower part rounded on the back, more or less three-nerved at first, often hardened and nerveless in fruit, with three terminal one- or three-nerved lobes or teeth.

Palea about as long as the entire part of the glume, with two prominent nerves. Ovary glabrous.

Styles very short, distinct.

Grain somewhat dorsally compressed, enclosed in the glume and palea, free from them.

Leaves very pungent, the sheaths usually viscid ; flowering glumes silky-ciliate, divided nearly to the middle into three lobes. Panicle loose and spreading ; spikelets dark, ½ inch long, eight- to twelve-flowered...... .... 1. *T. Mitchelli*
Leaves very pungent, the sheaths not viscid ; flowering glumes silky-villous at the base, with three sets of nerves each, leading to three small obtuse teeth .... 4. *T. irritans*

1. Triodia Mitchelli, Benth.

Botanical name.—*Triodia*, Greek ; *treis*, three ; *odous odontos*, a tooth ; the flowering glumes having three terminal lobes or teeth ; *Mitchelli*, in honour of Sir Thomas Mitchell, *ante* p. 49.

Botanical description (B. Fl., vii, 606).

Leaves very nearly those of *T. pungens* but longer, nearly terete, pungent-pointed, with viscid sheaths.

Panicle very much looser, 3 to 4 inches long, with capillary branches more or less spreading ; the lower ones 1 to 1½ inches long, with three or four pedicellate spikelets ; the upper ones short with one or two spikelets.

Spikelets dark-coloured, ½ inch long when fully out, ovate or oblong, with eight to twelve flowers.

Outer glumes three-nerved, obtuse or minutely three-toothed, about 3 lines long.

Flowering glumes 2½ lines long, three-nerved, the entire part densely silky-villous and at length somewhat hardened, the three acute rigid glabrous lobes as long as the entire part or the central one rather longer.

Palea glabrous.

Value as a fodder.—A wiry, uninviting grass, utterly valueless for stock-feed except when quite young.

Habitat and range.—Found in all the Colonies except Tasmania and Victoria. An interior species.

4. Triodia irritans, R.Br.

Botanical name.—*Irritans*, Latin, provoking, which this harsh, prickly grass frequently is to travellers.

Botanical description (B. Fl., vii, 607).—A rigid, scrubby, glabrous grass with long rigid convolute pungent-pointed leaves, not viscid in any of the specimens seen.

Panicle narrow, almost spike-like, 3 to 6 inches long.

Spikelets solitary or few together, on short erect capillary pedicels or branches, mostly three- or four-flowered, 4 to 5 lines long.

Outer glumes glabrous, acute, five-nerved, 3 lines long.

Flowering glumes not quite so long, villous with silky hairs at the base but much less so than in *T. pungens*, truncate at the end, with three sets of three nerves, each leading to three very short obtuse or truncate lobes or teeth, the lateral ones rather broad, the central one smaller or minute.

Palea narrow.

Value as a fodder.—Of no value.

Habitat and range.—Found in all the colonies except Tasmania. Only found in the arid interior.

The occurrence of a resin in a *Triodia*, or in fact in any grass, is a very interesting circumstance, and I attach copies of two papers by myself on the subject. The matter is worthy of further inquiry.

Last year (1888) Sir William Macleay was kind enough to give me "a sample of gum used by the blacks for cementing the heads of spears,* and prepared from Spinifex roots," which had been collected by Mr. Walter Froggatt in the Napier Range (locally called Barrier Range), 100 miles inland from Derby, North-west Australia.

I was dubious as to it being the product of a " Spinifex," never having heard of a grass yielding a resin, but Mr. Froggatt is emphatic that he is not mistaken, nor is so experienced a collector likely to be. The Spinifex is probably *Triodia irritans*, R.Br., but further information on the subject, giving the mode of preparation of the resin

---

* "The heads of spears from Western Australia in my collection are coated with a hard gum, forming a ridge on one side, in which pieces of glass are impacted." Brough Smyth's *Aborigines of Victoria*, &c., i, 336. Mr. Froggatt informs me that Spinifex resin is put to such a purpose in the locality from which he obtained it.

would be very acceptable. Mr. Froggatt states that it is obtained from the roots, and local Europeans and aborigines all make similar statements as to its origin.

It is in a cake about 4 inches in diameter, and 1¼ inches in thickness. The smell is something like bees-wax, but at the same time it has an exceedingly disagreeable and persistent odour which is not easily described. It reminds one of the smell of the fabric known as corduroy. It is of especial interest because it is of aboriginal preparation. Its colour is that of a dirty dark bronze-green, or almost of a slaty colour with a little green in it. To the naked eye it looks very like finely chopped hay or grass-seed cemented into a compact mass. It is exceedingly tough, a sharp blow with a hammer on a cold chisel being necessary to fracture it.

Petroleum spirit extracts 3·2 per cent. of a colourless fixed oil or fat, which possesses a little of the disagreeable odour of the original substance. The solvent extracts no resin. As the substance has been made up into cakes by the blacks, and is to that extent not an absolutely natural product, it may be that the fat, or a portion of it has been introduced.

The substance was then digested in alcohol, which extracts a transparent, hard, golden-yellow resin, possessing some odour, and which appears to be an interesting substance. The amount of this resin is 67·3 per cent., and it darkens on keeping.

Water digested on the residue dissolves out 6·9 per cent. of colouring matter and salts. It contains no arabin. The remainder, 23·1 per cent., consists of dirt and particles of chopped grass. This also is quite free from gummy matter.

Summary—

Fat, soluble in petroleum spirit	...	...	3·1
Resin, soluble in alcohol	...	...	67·3
Extractive and salts, soluble in water	...	6·9
Accidental impurity ...	...	...	23·1

100·4

A second sample, treated with alcohol direct, yielded 70·8 per cent. to that solvent, *Proc. Linn. Society, N.S.W.* [2], iv, 639 (1889).

Following is my report on an allied substance recently collected by the Horn Expedition to Central Australia.

No. 1. "Portion of an ants' nest consisting of sand agglutinated by gum from *Triodia pungens*, formed around the base of the grass, and continued as cylinders around leaves and flower stalks. Tempe Downs." This substance has the appearance of a lump of reddish-brown clinker. When treated at a very low temperature the resin melts (even in the flame of a match), and in its crude state would make a useful cement. When the resin has burned away, the residue consists of sand, principally quartz with ferric oxide, the latter being removed by dilute hydrochloric acid. This ferric oxide assists to give the original mass its reddish-brown appearance. When the original substance is treated with alcohol (rectified spirit), the resin readily dissolves, leaving the sand, which differs in no way from that obtained by burning off the resin. Ether dissolves the greater portion of the resin, but instead of the residual resin being dark brown, as in the case when alcohol is used, it is of a golden yellowish colour, and when ignited burns away without residue, while that portion extracted by alcohol after the ethereal extract has been removed, leaves a small quantity of residue.

The bright yellow resin melts at 83° C. The original resin extracted by alcohol melts at 110° C., while the alcoholic residue left on removal of the resin soluable in ether does not melt at 140° C. It consists partly of inorganic material. As it was present in small quantities, its composition could not be determined in the small portion of material forwarded. The resin obtained from *Triodia irritans*, R.Br., by ether, in appearance and colour resembles that obtained from *Triodia pungens*, but it has a lower melting point, melting at 63° C. The brown resin obtained by alcohol, corresponding to that obtained by alcohol from *Triodia pungens* melts at 102° C. From the results of the examination of the bodies contained in the resinous material of *Triodia irritans*, it was suggested that the fat found was artificially introduced; its presence would lower the melting point of the resin. Judging from the appearance of the two resins, their colour, odour, melting points, &c., there appears to be but little difference in the resins obtained from *Triodia pungens* and *Triodia irritans*, and they may prove to be identical when prepared under similar conditions.

We have so few records of the finding of the Porcupine resin, that the following is of interest :—" Samples of resinous matter from roots of Spinifex, and tunnels made by ants, found here for the first time, lying on the surface of the sandy ground between bunches of Spinifex, apparently made of sand cemented with some agglutinuous secretion of the insect, or what is more probable, the resinous substance found at the roots of the Spinifex plants." (W. T. Tietkens' Exploration of West Central Australia, in *Trans. Roy. Geog. Soc. Vict.*, viii., 35). (*Report of Horn Expedition to Central Australia*, pp. 195 and 196).

Sub-tribe ii.—Chlorideæ.

72. Cynodon.   74. Eleusine.
73. Chloris.   75. Leptochloa.
          76. Diplachne.

72. CYNODON.

Spikelets one-flowered, awnless, singly sessile in two rows on one side of slender spikes, digitate at the end of the peduncle, the rhachis of the spikelet articulate immediately above the outer glumes, and either not produced beyond the flower or continued into a minute point behind the palea.

Outer empty glumes two, keeled, persistent or deciduous.

Flowering glume broader, boat-shaped, with a prominent keel.
Palea narrow or rather broad, the two nerves prominent, distant or closely contiguous.
Grain smooth, enclosed in the glume and palea, but free from them.

1. Cynodon dactylon, Pers.

Botanical name.—*Cynodon*—Greek, *Kuon, kunos* a dog, *odous, odontos* a tooth, dog's tooth. This grass is still known in some places as "Dog's Tooth Grass," but whether the vernacular name is a translation of the botanical one, or the reverse is the case, I do not know. *Dactylon*—Greek, *dactulos* a finger, in reference to the finger-like spikes.

Vernacular names.—"Couch Grass," the "Doub Grass" of India, and the "Bermuda Grass" of the United States; sometimes known as "Dog's Tooth Grass."

Where figured.—Hackel, Vasey, Kearney, *Agricultural Gazette*.

Botanical description (B. Fl., vii, 609).

Stems prostrate, often creeping and rooting to a great extent, the flowering branches shortly ascending.

Leaves short, of a glaucous green.

Spikes two to five, often purplish, 1 to 2 inches long.

Spikelets sessile, outer glumes narrow, acute, persistent, keeled, under 1 line long.

Flowering glume rather above 1 line long, broadly boat-shaped, the keel usually minutely ciliate.

Palea narrow.

Rhachis of the spikelet produced into a point or bristle shorter than the glume, and often very minute.

Var. *pulchellus*, F.v.M. Flowering glume ciliate on the keel with long hairs. Murray River.

Value as a fodder.—It is a useful pasture grass, stock eating it readily. It is the best all-round lawn grass we have, but it is a troublesome weed in gardens. It is so widely diffused and so largely cultivated that the fact that it is an Australian native is sometimes lost sight of. At the same time, in many of its situations it has been introduced by the hand of man. As O'Shanesy points out: "Its presence is one of the surest signs of settlement."

"It is by far the most useful of all fodder grasses in India, especially for horses. It is perennial, and flowers nearly all the year round. The foliage becomes scanty during the cold weather months, at which time it may be said to be at rest. It varies considerably in habit as well as in its nutritive qualities, according to the nature of the soil or climate. It makes excellent hay, and will keep good for many years in stack." (Duthie.) The Hindoos consider it sacred.

"This is undoubtedly, on the whole, the most valuable grass in the Southern United States. It is a native of Southern Europe, and of all tropical countries. It is a common pasture-grass in the West Indies, and the Sandwich Islands, and has long been known in the United States, but the difficulty of eradicating it when once established has retarded its introduction into cultivation. Its value, however, is becoming more appreciated now that more attention is being given to grass and relatively less to cotton, and better methods and implements of cultivation are being employed. Still, it seems probable, from the reports received, that at the present time a majority of farmers would prefer not to have it on their farms. It seeds very sparingly in the United States, and as the imported seed is not always to be had, and is expensive and often of poor quality, those who have desired to cultivate it on a large scale have seldom been able to do so. It is generally used as a lawn grass, and to hold levels or railroad embankments, and for small pastures." (Vasey.)

"Perhaps no one plant represents more value to the south than does 'Bermuda'; certainly no other forage plant is more precious to that section. Whether for hay or for pasturage, it is everywhere placed first, and is considered the most nutritious grass that can be successfully grown in the Southern United States. While it requires a fertile soil for its best development, it will grow on the thinnest soil, being a common plant of sea-beaches. In such situations the plants are very small, the erect flowering stems being quite short, and long sterile shoots (sometimes 6 feet long), rooting at every joint, are produced. In better land a light loamy soil seems to suit it best, the tendency to send out long creeping shoots is checked, the upward growth is much greater, and the amount of leafage increases correspondingly, the whole plant becoming much taller and succulent. Besides its great value as a forage plant, Bermuda is one of the most effective of soil holders. When growing on sandy river banks and ocean beaches it is, apparently, the most valuable sand-binding grass of the Southern States. It is sometimes planted by roadsides and upon embankments for this purpose, and is a favourite lawn grass in most towns and cities, forming a close, fine turf, and remaining green in the driest and most sun-exposed situations." (Kearney.)

Other uses.—Used largely in medicinal preparations by the natives of India, and also by them for some sacred and ceremonial purposes. It really does possess some medicinal properties, as certified to by properly qualified medical men in India. For further particulars, Watts' *Dictionary of the Economic Products of India* may be referred to.

Habitat and range.—Found in all the colonies except Tasmania; well diffused in New South Wales.

"This is a common and troublesome weed in all hot and some temperate countries, and although generally spread over the settled parts of extra-tropical Australia, it may have been introduced as suggested by R. Brown." (Benth.)

73. CHLORIS.

Spikelets one-flowered, awned, singly sessile in two rows on one side of simple spikes, either solitary or digitate at the end of the peduncle, the rhachis of the spikelet articulate immediately above the outer glumes.

Outer empty glumes two, keeled, persistent, awnless.

Flowering glume produced into a fine straight awn, entire or with a tooth, lobe or short awn on each side of the terminal awn.

Palea folded or with two prominent nerves.

Rhachis of the spikelet produced behind the palea and bearing one or more empty glumes, all awned, and usually with their ends on a level with that of the flowering glume.

Spikes digitate, slender. Spikelets acute. Flowering glume usually with a tooth, lobe or short awn on each side of the terminal one.

Spikes six to twelve or more, 3 to 6 inches long. Spikelets distant, 3 lines long. Flowering glumes tapering into the awn, or very minutely toothed... ... ... 5. *C. acicularis.*

Spikes digitate, slender, 3 to 6 inches long. Spikelets very obtuse or truncate.

Spikelets cuneate, truncate, 1 to 1½ lines long. Flowering glume, oblong, obtuse. Upper empty one broad, truncate 6. *C. truncata.*

Spikelets very obtuse, 1½ to 2 lines. Flowering glume very broad, embracing the narrower empty one ... ... 7. *C. ventricosa.*

Spikes digitate, dense, 1 to 2 inches long.

Flowering glume broad, rigidly scarious, ciliate. Upper empty glumes several. Broad, scarious, very spreading... ... 9. *C. scariosa.*

5. Chloris acicularis, Lindl.

Botanical name.—Chloris, the Greek word for pale green, in allusion to the colour of some of these grasses; *acicularis,* from the Latin needle-shaped or acicular, in allusion to the shape of the spikelets.

Vernacular name.— "Lesser Star Grass."

Where figured.—Agricultural Gazette.

Botanical description. (B. Fl. vii, 612).—A glabrous erect grass of 1 to 2 feet.

Leaves flat, the lower sheaths broad and flattened.

Spikes six to twelve or even more, at first erect, but at length horizontally spreading as in *C. divaricata,* 3 to 4 inches long, slender, and often purplish.

Spikelets rather distant.

Outer glumes narrow, keeled, tapering to fine points, the lowest 1½ to 2 lines, the second 3 lines long.

Flowering glume about 2 lines, narrow, three-nerved, tapering into an awn of about ½ inch, with sometimes, but not always, a short point on each side at the base.

Palea long, narrow, prominently two-nerved.

Terminal empty glume with an awn sometimes as long as that of the flowering glume, but usually shorter.

*Value as a fodder.—*The very closely allied *C. Roxburghiana,* Edgew., is not uncommon in Northern India, and often grows amongst bushes, where its stems attain a considerable height. It is stated to be a good fodder grass in Ajmere. (Duthie.)

*Habitat and range.—*Found in all the colonies except Tasmania. In New South Wales it extends from the table-land to the interior.

6. Chloris truncata, R.Br.

Botanical name.—Truncata, Latin, maimed or mangled, hence "cut off" (truncate), which the glumes appear to be.

Vernacular names.— "Windmill Grass" or "Star Grass."

Where figured.—Agricultural Gazette.

Botanical description (B. Fl., vii, 612).—A glabrous erect grass of 1 to 3 feet.

Leaves usually flat but narrow, with flattened sheaths.

Spikes six to ten, slender, 3 to 6 inches long, at length horizontally spreading.

Spikelets numerous but not crowded, cuneate, 1 to 1½ lines long without the awns.

Lowest outer glume very small, almost setaceous, the second narrow and fine-pointed, about as long as the spikelet.

Flowering glume oblong, obtuse, keeled, slightly ciliate, with a fine awn of 3 to 6 lines.

Terminal empty glume much shorter and broader, raised to the level of the flowering glume and flat-topped, giving the spikelet its cuneate truncate form.

Value as a fodder.—This is an elegant and at the same time useful fodder-grass. It is both palatable to stock and nutritious, and forms a compact turf. It is common in the coast districts, while at the same time it withstands prolonged droughts. Mr. T. Kidston, of Condobolin, who possesses great experience in such matters, reports it as one of the best summer grasses for the western country.

Habitat and range.—Found in South Australia, Victoria, New South Wales, and Queensland. In the western districts of New South Wales it frequents Yarran country, when ringbarked, growing freely all over the river flats and uplands. It is, however, wide diffused over the Colony.

7. Chloris ventricosa, R.Br.

Botanical name.—*Ventricosa*, Latin, big-bellied, in allusion to the inflated spikelet.

Vernacular names.—" Blue Star Grass "; " Tall Star Grass."

Botanical description (B. Fl., vii, 613).—Uusually rather taller than *C. truncata*, often above 2 feet high, with few flat leaves.

Spikes five to seven in the typical specimens, 3 to 4 inches long.

Spikelets cuneate and obtuse as in *C. truncata*, but larger, from 1½ to 2 lines long, and often, but not always, dark-coloured.

Flowering glume broad, very obtuse, embracing the much smaller terminal one, which is raised and truncate as in *C. truncata*, usually emarginate, the awns of both much shorter than the spikelet.

Another long-awned form has spikes of 3 to 4 inches. (Cabramatta and Ash Island, Hunter River.)

Value as a fodder.—An excellent grass, having much the same value as the preceding.

Habitat and range.—Found in New South Wales and Queensland. In New South Wales it occurs from the coast to the interior.

9. Chloris scariosa, F.v.M.

Botanical name.—*Scariosa*, Latin, thin, dry, membranous, in allusion to the glumes.

Vernacular names.—" Rockhampton Star Grass " or " Gracemere Star Grass," of Bailey.

Botanical description (B. Fl., vii, 614).—

Stems erect, slender but rigid, 1 to 2 feet high.

Leaves narrow with subulate points or almost entirely flat in the larger specimens, glabrous.

Spikes four to six, dense, 1 to 1½ inches long.

Spikelets sessile, 3 to 4 lines long.

Lowest glume narrow, hyaline, almost obtuse, scarcely keeled, about 2 lines long, the second rather longer, with a more prominent keel.

Flowering glume raised on a hairy rhachis of about 1 line, rather above 1 line long, very broad and concave, prominently three-nerved, ciliate with long hairs at the end, with a fine awn of 2 to 3 lines.

Terminal empty glumes several (four to seven), the lowest two broader than the flowering one, five- to seven-nerved at the base, hyaline and not ciliate, very spreading and at length rigidly scarious; the upper ones gradually smaller sessile and not exceeding the outer ones.

Value as a fodder.—A beautiful grass, but perhaps of little value for pasture; worthy of garden cultivation. It may, however, prove to be of more value to the pastoralist when we know more about it.

Habitat and range.—Found in Western and South Australia, also in New South Wales and Queensland. In our own Colony it has only been recorded from Hungerford, and may be looked for in other localities in the north-west of the Colony.

74. ELEUSINE.

Spikelets several-flowered, flat, imbricate in two rows along one side of the digitate or scattered branches of a simple panicle, the rhachis of the spikelet articulate above the outer glumes.

Glumes spreading, keeled and complicate, thin, but rigid, the two outer empty ones usually shorter, unequal, obtuse, acute or tapering to a short point.

Flowering glumes obtuse or less pointed, the terminal one usually empty or rudimentary.

Palea folded.

Styles short, distinct.

Seed rugose within a loose membranous pericarp, which either persists round the ripe seed or breaks up and falls away or otherwise disappears as the ovary enlarges.

Spikes digitate, short. Spikelets very closely packed, the glumes very pointed, the second outer one almost awned. Pericarp evanescent ... ... 1. *E. ægyptiaca.*

Spikes digitate, or with one lower down, 2 to 3 inches long. Glumes obtuse. Pericarp persistent ... ... 2. *E. indica.*

1. Eleusine ægyptiaca, Pers.

Botanical name.—*Eleusine,* Latin *eleusinius,* of or belonging to Ceres, the goddess of corn and tillage; *ægyptiaca,* Egyptian.

Synonym.—*E. cruciata,* Lam.; *Dactyloctenium ægyptiacum,* Willd.

Vernacular names.—"Small Crow-foot Grass"; "Egyptian Finger-grass."

Where figured.—Duthie, Kearney, *Agricultural Gazette.*

Botanical description (B. Fl., vii, 615).—

Stems tufted or creeping and rooting at the base and shortly ascending like the *Cynodon dactylon*, or rarely above 1 foot high.

Leaves flat, ciliate, flaccid, with long points.

Spikes usually three to five, digitate, and under half an inch in most of the Australian specimens, but sometimes 1 inch long, the angular rhachis prominent on the upper or inner side, the spikelets regularly and very closely packed at right angles to it on the opposite side.

Outer glume about 1 line long, acute, the second broader, obtuse, or emarginate, the keel produced into a short dorsal awn, the rhachis of the spikelet produced above the outer glumes, but glabrous.

Flowering glumes broad, complicate, tapering into short spreading points.

Pericarp loose over the enlarged ovary, disappearing from the ripe rugose seed.

Value as a fodder.—An excellent grass for the hotter, drier parts of the Colony, and worthy of every encouragement. In the Bourke district, for instance, it grows luxuriantly, and Mr. D. G. Macdougall reports it as a grass " possessing wonderful nutritious properties, stock of all descriptions fattening on it quickly."

Abundant in all cultivated fields in S. Carolina, and commonly used for hay. (Ravenel, quoted by Vasey.)

It is generally considered to be a very nutritious grass, both as forage and fodder. In the Lahore district it is said to be eaten by cattle, but not by horses. (Duthie.)

Other uses.—In India the grain is sometimes used for food by the natives in times of scarcity. The Mohave Indians of California also use the grain for food, grinding it and making the flour into cakes or mush. (Orcutt, quoted by Lamson-Scribner.)

A decoction is prepared from the seeds, which is used in Africa for inflammation of the kidneys. (Hackel.)

Habitat and range.—Found in all the colonies except Tasmania, also in New Guinea and the Pacific Islands. It is found in the interior of New South Wales.

It is a common weed of warm countries.

2. Eleusine indica, Gærtn.

Botanical name.—*Indica*, Latin, Indian.

Vernacular names.—Has been called "Gigantic Couch" near Casino ; "Crab Grass" is perhaps the most usual name ; "Crow-foot" ; "Yard Grass," "Goose Grass," "Crop Grass," "Wire Grass," "Buzzard Grass," "Dutch Grass" are names more or less in use in the United States.

Where figured.—Trinius, Duthie, Kearney, *Agricultural Gazette*.

Botanical description. (B. Fl., vii, 615).—A coarse, erect, tufted grass, 1 to 2 feet high.

Leaves narrow, the sheaths flattened and distichous, ciliate with a few long hairs.

Spikes five to seven, 2 to 3 inches long, digitate, with usually one inserted rather lower down, the rhachis prominent on the upper or inner side, the spikelets loosely imbricate on the opposite side. Each spikelet 1½ to 2 lines long, containing three to five flowers.

Glumes obtuse, the lowest small and one-nerved, the second empty one, and the lower flowering ones usually three-nerved.

Pericarp persistent, very loose and membranous, enclosing the rugose seed.

Value as a fodder.—This is a grass found on the northern rivers, but is spreading, and opinions in regard to its value in New South Wales appear to be divided. As a matter of fact, few people have experience of it at present. It is a common weed of warm countries, and I give notes on the experience of observers in other parts of the world. The late Mr. Thomas Bawden, of Grafton, wrote :—"The enclosed grass is spreading very much here, even overrunning the common Couch. Stock do not seem to care much for it."

A Casino correspondent, however, writes, " Eagerly eaten by cattle and horses."

Mr. Bailey speaks of it as a good summer grass in Queensland, but not liked by the farmer, as it spreads into cultivated places.

" An annual grass belonging to tropical countries, but now naturalised in most temperate climates. In the Southern States it is found in every door-yard and in all waste places."

Professor Phares, of Mississippi, says : " The clumps have many long leaves and stems rising 1 or 2 feet high, and many long, strong, deeply-penetrating, fibrous roots. It grows readily in door-yards, barn-yards, and rich, cultivated grounds, and produces an immense quantity of seeds. It is a very nutritious grass, and good for grazing, soiling, and hay. The succulent lower part of the stems, covered with the sheaths of the leaves, render it difficult to cure well, for which several days are required. It may be cut two or three times, and yields a large quantity of hay." (Vasey.)

" Confined to rich waste places and old yards and gardens, and is rarely or never seen in ordinary cultivated fields, and is never used for hay, as it is only found in tufts and sparsely." (Ravenel, quoted by Vasey.)

" It is eaten by horses and cattle, and in some districts of India is considered to be a good fodder-grass, though Roxburgh says that cattle are not fond of it ; this remark may, however, apply chiefly to the Bengal form, which the nature of the climate would render more rank and unpalatable." (Duthie.)

Other uses.—A decoction of this grass is said to be used in British Guiana in the convulsions of infants.

Habitat and range.—A native of Queensland and New South Wales, which is advancing down the coast and has arrived at least as far south as Port Jackson. It is found in most warm countries.

75. LEPTOCHLOA.

Spikelets several-flowered, or rarely one-flowered, sessile in two rows along one side of the slender usually numerous branches of a simple panicle, the rhachis of the spikelet articulate above the outer glumes and more or less produced above the flowering ones.

Glumes keeled, acute or obtuse, unawned, the two outer empty ones shorter or rarely as long as the flowering ones.

Palea prominently two-nerved or folded.

Grain smooth or nearly so, the pericarp very thin and adnate.

Spikelets five- or six-flowered. Flowering glumes rather obtuse.
Spikes dense, mostly crowded at the end of the rhachis ... 1. *L. subdigitata.*
Spikes slender, scattered along the long slender rhachis ... 2. *L. chinensis.*

1. Leptochloa subdigitata, Trin.

*Botanical name—Leptochloa—*Greek, *leptos,* slender, *chloe* grass; *subdigitata—*Latin, *sub* having the sense of almost; *digitata—*Latin, that which has fingers,—hence a slender grass with the panicle almost digitate, or spread out like the fingers of a hand.

Synonym.—Eleusine digitata, Spreng.

Vernacular name.—" Cane-grass."

Botanical description (B.Fl. vii, 617).—An erect, rigid, usually glaucous grass, attaining 4 or 5 ft.

Leaves short, with rigid rather loose sheaths.

Spikes or panicle branches 6 to 10, crowded at the end of the peduncle, with usually 1 or 2 lower down, 2 to 4 inches long.

Spikelets 1½ or rarely 2 lines long, five- or six-flowered, the rhachis bearing a few short hairs under each glume.

Glumes about ½ line long, obtuse, or almost acute, the outer empty ones usually rather smaller, especially the lowest.

Palea folded.

Grain oblong, perfectly smooth, the pericarp very thin and adnate.

*Value as a fodder.—*A tall tussock-grass, with numerous erect branching leafy stems ; usually met with around dams and river banks, and affording a large supply of coarse herbage (Bailey).

*Habitat and range.—*Found in all the colonies except Tasmania and Victoria. In New South Wales it is found in the interior (Lachlan River).

2. Leptochloa chinensis, Nees.

Botanical name—chinensis; a Latinised adjective meaning Chinese, or belonging to China (the country whence this grass was first described).

Synonym.—Eleusine chinensis, F.v.M.

*Where figured.—*Duthie.

Botanical description (B.Fl. vii, 617).—

Stems from a creeping and rooting base ascending to 2 or 3 feet, glabrous and usually slender.

Leaves narrow, flat, tapering to a point.

Panicle 6 inches to above 1 foot long, the numerous simple branches scattered or clustered along the rhachis, very slender, 2 to 4 inches long, or in the smaller weaker specimens under 2 inches.

Spikelets sessile or nearly so, distant or rather crowded, narrow, 1 to 2 lines long, usually four- to six-flowered.

Outer empty glumes rather unequal, acute, flowering ones broader, obtuse.

*Value as a fodder.—*Used more or less for fodder in Northern India, though nothing definite appears to be known regarding its real value. (Duthie.) The same remarks may be applied to this grass as far as New South Wales is concerned. Stock eat it.

*Habitat and range.—*Found in New South Wales and Queensland. In the former colony it is confined to localities between the northern rivers and the table-land, usually on the banks of streams. It is also found in Asia.

76. DIPLACHNE.

Spikelets several- often many-flowered, linear, sessile, or very shortly pedicellate, but distant along the rhachis of a simple spike or of the elongated branches of a simple panicle, the rhachis of the spikelet articulate and usually hairy under the flowering glumes.
Outer empty glumes keeled, acute, unawned.
Flowering glumes with a hyaline shortly two-lobed apex, the keel produced into a short point or awn between or shortly below the lobes.
Palea thin, prominently two-nerved.
Styles short, distinct.
Grain smooth, free.

Spike slender, simple ..   .. 1. *D. loliiformis.*
Spikes numerous in a simple panicle. Spikelets usually dark-coloured, 4 lines long or rather more, with more than six flowers, rhachis glabrous, or nearly so ...   . 3. *D. fusca.*

1. Diplachne loliiformis, F.v.M.

Botanical name.—*Diplachne* Greek, *diplous* two-fold or double, *achne,* chaff (glume), the flowering-glume being two-lobed; *loliiformis,* Latin, having the general appearance of the grasses belonging to the genus *Lolium.*
Botanical description (B. Fl., vii, 618).—A slender apparently annual erect grass, usually 6 to 8 inches, but a few specimens above 1 foot high.

Leaves chiefly at the base, short and narrow, usually sprinkled with a few long hairs, the sheaths ciliate at the orifice, with a short jagged ligula.
Spike slender and simple, 2 to 4 inches long, on a long peduncle.
Spikelets sessile, rather distant, erect and appressed, turned somewhat to one side, narrow, 3 to 4 lines long, six- to twelve-flowered, the rhachis hairy round the flowering glumes.
Flowering glumes about 1 line long, glabrous, three-nerved, the central nerve produced into a fine point or awn shortly exceeding the hyaline lobes.

Value as a fodder.—Quite a small grass, eaten by sheep, but not of much value for forage.
Habitat and range.—Found in all the colonies except Tasmania and Western Australia. An interior species. Found also in Asia.

3. Diplachne fusca, Beauv.

Botanical name.—*Fusca,* Latin, brownish or tawny, referring to the colour of the spikelets.
Where figured.—*Agricultural Gazette.*
Botanical description (B. Fl., vii, 619).—A glabrous erect grass of several feet.

Leaves narrow, convolute when dry, with long loose sheaths, the ligula jagged.
Panicle narrow, 6 inches to 1 foot long, with erect branches, the lower ones long.
Spikelets sessile or nearly so, rather distant, linear, erect, six- to ten-flowered, 4 lines long or rather more and straw-coloured, or longer and dark, the rhachis glabrous or slightly hairy under each glume.
Flowering glumes nearly 2 lines long, shortly ciliate on the margins in the lower part, prominently three-nerved, the keel produced into a short point between or just below the short hyaline terminal lobes.
Keels of the *palea* shortly ciliate.

Value as a fodder.—Readily eaten by stock and believed to be a very nutritious grass. " Buffaloes are said to be very fond of this grass," in India. (Duthie.)

Habitat and range.—Found in all the colonies except Tasmania, usually in damp, often brackish situations. It is an interior species. It also occurs in Africa and India, and " in the plains of Northern India where water is liable to lodge. I have observed it in great abundance in the more depressed portions of the saline usar tracts in the Aligarh district." (Duthie.)

Sub-tribe iii.—Milieæ.

77. Sporobolus.	79. Isachne.
81. Eriachne.	

77. SPOROBOLUS.

Spikelets small, one-flowered, nearly sessile or pedicellate in a narrow spikelike or loose and pyramidal panicle, the rhachis of the spikelet very short, glabrous, scarcely articulate, not continued beyond the flower.

Glumes three, persistent or separately deciduous, unawned, slightly keeled or convex and obscurely nerved, two outer empty ones usually unequal ; flowering glume as long or longer.

Palea about as long as the glume, with two nerves usually prominent, and readily splitting between them.

Styles very short.

Grain free, readily falling away from the glume, the pericarp loosely enclosing the seed or very thin and evanescent.

Panicle narrow, spikelike, continuous or interrupted, the short erect
    branches flowering from the base.
    Outer and flowering glumes nearly equal. Leaves usually
        short, rigid, and spreading ... ... 1. *S. virginicus.*
    Outer glumes unequal, shorter than the flowering ones. Leaves
        rather long ... ... 2. *S. indicus.*
Panicle narrow, loose, with short spreading scattered branches ... 3. *S. diander.*
Panicle loosely pyramidal, the branches spreading in regular distant
    whorls.
    Spikelets loosely pedicellate, minute.
        Leaves rigidly ciliate. Glumes obtuse .. .. 4. *S. pulchellus.*
        Leaves not at all or minutely ciliate. Glumes narrow,
          acute ... ... 5. *S. Lindleyi.*
    Spikelets nearly sessile, crowded along the branches ... ...6. *S. actinocladus.*

1. Sporobolus virginicus, Kunth.

Botanical name.—*Sporobolus,* Greek *sporos,* a seed, *bolos* a throw with a casting-net, in allusion to the grains, which are on the outside of the panicle, as if they had fallen, or been thrown out ; *virginicus,* a Latinised word, Virginian, from the American locality whence the grass was first described.

Where figured.—Labillardière, as *Agrostis virginica*, Trinius as *Vilfa virginica.*

Botanical description (B. Fl., vii, 621).—

> *Stems* much branched and leafy at the base, erect or decumbent, 6 to 10 inches, or rarely 1 foot high.
>
> *Leaves* short and narrow, often very spreading, convolute when dry, rather rigid, glabrous or ciliate at the base.
>
> *Panicle* rather dense, narrow and spikelike or rather more branched at the base, 1 to 1½ inches long, often rather dark-coloured.
>
> *Glumes* keeled, rather acute, about 1 line long, the two outer and flowering one similar, or the lowest rather smaller.
>
> *Palea* rather longer, the two nerves close together so as to represent a broad keel, but very readily splitting, showing an inflexed margin between the nerves.
>
> *Grain* broadly obovoid, the very thin pericarp separable when soaked, but undistinguishable in the dried state.

Var., (?) *pallida*, Benth. Taller, often above 1 foot high; leaves narrower, and often more erect; spike looser, 2 to 4 inches long, the spikelets often small and pale-coloured. Found on the Richmond and Darling Rivers in this Colony; also in Queensland and Northern Australia.

Value as a fodder.—This grass has something of the habit of Couch grass (*Cynodon*), and is particularly valuable for saline situations. Cattle become readily accustomed to it, and it is a nutritious grass.

In Jamaica horses become rapidly and astonishingly fat while feeding upon this grass. (Jenman.)

Habitat and range.—Found in all the colonies, usually in saline country near tidal rivers, or near the sea-shore. Occurs also in Asia, Africa, and America.

2. Sporobolus indicus, R. Br.

Botanical name.—*Indicus*, Latin, Indian.

Vernacular names.—" Parramatta Grass," " Rat-tail Grass," " Chilian Grass," " Jil-crow-a-berry " of the aborigines of the Cloncurry River, Northern Australia. " Smut Grass," " Carpet Grass," and " Drop-seed Grass " are American names. The Brazilian name is Capim maurâo.

Where figured.—Trinius as *Vilfa tenacissima*, Vasey, Buchanan (as *S. elongatus*), *Agricultural Gazette.*

Botanical description (B.Fl., vii, 622).—An erect tufted grass of 1 to 2 feet, glabrous except a few cilia at the base of the leaves.

> *Leaves* chiefly at the base of the stem, narrow, ending in fine points, the upper ones few with long sheaths.
>
> *Spikelike* panicle very narrow, 3 to 8 inches or even longer, continuous throughout or when long often much interrupted.
>
> *Spikelets* very numerous, crowded along the very short erect almost imbricate or distant branches.
>
> *Outer glumes* almost hyaline, obtuse, one-nerved, the lowest about ½ line, the second ¾ line long, flowering glume about 1 line, of a firmer consistence, broad but almost tapering to a point, one-nerved (the whole spikelet rather smaller in some specimens).

Palea nearly as long, faintly two-nerved.

Grain broadly obovoid, the very thin pericarp sometimes appearing loose, though often evanescent or undistinguishable in the dried state.

Var. *elongatus.* Very like the type, but with narrower leaves, longer and looser panicle, and not quite so tufty.

Value as a fodder.—This tough grass has been known to pull the teeth out of cattle and horses which feed on it as other grass becomes scarce. When young it is often eaten with other pasture, but it soon becomes fibrous. It is a coarse grass, seeds freely, and disfigures a paddock or lawn of finer grasses.

Mr. Thos. H. Kearney, jun., of the U.S. Department of Agriculture, obligingly gave me the following note on this grass in the United States :—

" *Sporobolus indicus* is not, to my knowledge, anywhere cultivated in the States, though a farmer in Florida told me he intended to sow it on his land. But it is held in high esteem in the South for pasturage, especially for horses. It has the merit of growing readily on sandy commons where few other grasses will thrive in that part of the country. Here, as with you, it becomes very hard when old, and is consequently unfit for hay. I should not think to recommend it for cultivation anywhere, as it grows in clumps and makes no turf.

" This grass is a native of India, but has spread over most tropical and warm climates. It occurs more or less abundantly in all the Southern States, and is called Smut-grass, from the fact that after the flowering the heads become affected with a black smut. It grows in tufts or loose patches, from 1½ to 3 feet high."

Professor Phares says : " It grows abundantly and luxuriantly on many uncultivated fields and commons, and furnishes grazing from April till frost. It thrives under much grazing and many mowings, and grows promptly after each if the soil is moist enough. Cattle and horses are fond of it, if it is frequently cut or grazed down, but if allowed to remain untouched long they will not eat it unless very hungry, as it becomes tough and unpalatable and probably difficult to digest." (Vasey.)

In the Gujranwala district (Punjab) it is considered to be a good fodder-grass, especially for horses. At Balaghat (Central Provinces) it is used as fodder when young. (Duthie.)

Other uses.—Used in the manufacture of hats in Madagascar. (*Kew Bulletin,* 1890, 212.) " While the plant is not used industrially in this country (United States), it is employed in southern Brazil as a straw-plait material. The stalks from the flower to the last knot serve for the manufacture of straw-plait used for hats and other articles made of straw, which are softened by means of sulphur." (Dodge.) The stalks are steeped several hours in water, when the seeds are easily rubbed out, and then ground between two stones and baked for bread by the Cloncurry, Queensland, natives. (E. Palmer.)

Habitat and range.—Found in all the colonies except Tasmania. In New South Wales it is found in the coast district, and rarely in the high table-land. It is not truly indigenous in many of its present localities. It is also found in Asia, Africa, America, and New Zealand.

L

3. Sporobolus diander, Beauv.

Botanical name.—Diander, Greek *dis,* two, *aner andros,* a man (stamen), this grass having but two stamens in the flower.

*Where figured.—*Duthie, *Agricultural Gazette.*

Botanical description (B. Fl., vii, 622).—An erect glabrous grass of 1 to 2 or even 3 feet.

Leaves chiefly at the base, narrow, the upper sheaths not covering the stem.

Panicle narrow but loosely pyramidal, 6 inches to about 1 foot long, the branches scattered, at length spreading.

Spikelets very shortly pedicellate or almost sessile, ¾ to 1 line long.

Outer empty glumes very obtuse; hyaline, the upper one about ½ line, the other shorter.

Flowering glume longer, slightly keeled, obtuse or almost acute.

Palea broad, obtuse, faintly two-nerved, and not so readily splitting as in the other species.

Grain broadly obovoid, the pericarp not readily separable.

*Value as a fodder.—*Like the preceding species, it has some value when young, but when it becomes mature it is fibrous, and stock eat it only when compelled to do so by hunger. It is said to be readily eaten by horses and cattle at Lahore; is also favourably mentioned at Gujranwala and Shahpur in India. (Duthie.)

*Habitat and range.—*Found in New South Wales and Queensland. In New South Wales it is found from the coast to the Dividing Range, from the Blue Mountains north. As regards Queensland, Bailey says it is always met with on good land, especially on river flats. It also occurs in Asia.

4. Sporobolus pulchellus, R.Br.

Botanical name.—Pulchellus, Latin, pretty, the grass being ornamental when in flower.

Botanical description (B. Fl., vii, 623).—

Stems tufted, 6 inches to 1 foot high.

Leaves chiefly at the base, flat or keeled, broad or narrow, rather rigid, bordered by rigid cilia, tuberculate at the base.

Panicle loosely pyramidal, 2 to 5 inches long, with numerous capillary spreading branches verticillate at regular intervals.

Spikelets pedicellate, not ½ line long, shining.

Glumes almost hyaline, rather obtuse, slightly keeled, the second outer empty one and the flowering one nearly equal and similar, the lowest empty one about ½ as long, narrow but obtuse.

Palea very readily splitting in two.

Grain globular, enclosed in a loose hyaline pericarp.

*Value as a fodder.—*Similar to *S. actinocladus,* but not abundant.

*Habitat and range.—*It extends from New South Wales to Northern Australia. As regards New South Wales, it is found in the dry north west.

5. Sporobolus Lindleyi, Benth.

Botanical name.—Lindleyi, in honour of J. Lindley, the celebrated British botanist who described a number of Australian plants.

Vernacular name.—" Yak-ka Berry," of the aborigines of the Cloncurry River, North Queensland.

Where figured.—Agricultural Gazette.

Botanical description (B. Fl., vii, 623).—Nearly allied to *S. pulchellus.*

Leaves narrow, not at all or only very shortly ciliate.

Panicle very loose, broadly pyramidal, 3 to 5 inches long and broad when fully out, the branches capillary, the lower ones elongated in a dense verticil, the upper ones more scattered.

Spikelets ½ to ¾ line long.

Glumes very acute, the lowest outer one very small and narrow, the second also empty, and the flowering glume nearly equal, usually dark-coloured.

Palea usually divided to the base into two, even at the time of flowering.

Seeds enclosed in a loose pericarp, as in *S. pulchellus.*

Value as a fodder.—This is one of the prettiest of our native grasses. It is at the same time nutritious and readily eaten by stock.

Other uses.—The fine seeds are gathered and ground up with water into a paste and baked in the ashes by some Queensland aborigines. (E. Palmer.)

Habitat and range.—It is found in all the colonies except Tasmania. In New South Wales it extends from the table-land to the interior.

6. Sporobolus actinocladus, F.v.M.

Botanical name.—Actinocladus, Greek, *actis, actinos*, a ray (of the sun), a spoke of a wheel, &c.; *clados*, a young branch or shoot, the panicle branches being verticillate (rayed).

Botanical description (B. Fl., vii, 623).—

Stems 1 to 2 feet high.

Leaves flat, tapering to fine points, glabrous.

Panicle pyramidal, 3 to 5 inches long, the branches numerous, spreading, the lower ones or nearly all verticillate at regular intervals, the upper ones scattered, all capillary and shortly bare at the base, but bearing narrow dense spikelike partial panicles of ½ to 1 inch.

Spikelets sessile and crowded, nearly 1 line long.

Outer glume very small, hyaline, almost obtuse ; second very acute, keeled, ½ to ¾ line long.

Flowering glume similar, but longer.

Palea divided into two from the base, even at the time of flowering.

Seed enclosed in a loose pericarp.

Value as a fodder.—A useful grass for the dry, hot districts of the colony.

Habitat and range.—Found in all the colonies except Western Australia, Tasmania, and Victoria. It occurs in the dry western districts of New South Wales.

79. ISACHNE.

Spikelets two-flowered, both flowers hermaphrodite or the upper female or the lower male, small in loose panicles, the *rhachis* of the spikelet articulate above the empty glumes, glabrous and not produced above the flowering ones.

Glumes unawned, convex, faintly nerved, two outer empty ones nearly equal; flowering ones of a firmer consistence, closely sessile or the upper one slightly raised.

Palea as long as the glume.

Styles distinct.

Grain enclosed in the hardened glume and palea, free from them.

1. Isachne australis, R. Br.

Botanical name.—Isachne—Greek, *isos*, equal; *achne*, chaff (glume), the two outer glumes being equal; *australis*, Latin, southern (Australian).

Synonym.—Panicum atrovirens, Trin.

Vernacular name.—" Swamp Millet."

*Where figured.—*Buchanan; *Agricultural Gazette.*

Botanical description (B. Fl., vii, 625).—

Stems rather slender, decumbent, creeping, and rooting at the lower nodes, ascending to 1 foot or more.

Leaves lanceolate, rough, with a minute pubescence.

Panicle loose, spreading, ovoid in circumscription, 1½ to 3 inches long, with numerous filiform branches.

Spikelets all pedicellate, nearly 1 line long.

Outer glume quite glabrous.

Lower flower usually male, with a glabrous glume, the upper female, shortly stipitate, with the glume usually minutely and slightly pubescent, the *rhachis* slightly dilated, and articulate immediately under the upper glume.

*Value as a fodder.—*A swamp-loving grass, nutritious, and readily eaten by stock. It is a tender, green grass, of rapid growth, and bears abundance of seed. Symonds, "Indian Grasses," p. 33, says that horses and cattle are very fond of it. (Duthie).

*Habitat and range.—*Found in Victoria, New South Wales, and Queensland. In New South Wales it extends from the coast to the tableland. Its favourite habitat is swampy land, or by the sides of streams. It also occurs in New Zealand, and in tropical Asia from Ceylon and the Peninsula to the Malayan Archipelago and South China.

81. ERIACHNE.

Spikelets two-flowered, usually not very numerous, in a loose or dense panicle, the flowers both hemaphrodite and similar, the *rhachis* of the spikelet articulate above the outer glumes and hairy round the flowering ones.

Empty glumes two, persistent, acute or tapering into a point or short awn, many- (usually nine- to eleven-) nerved.

Flowering glumes with fewer nerves, with long spreading hairs on the back or margins, awnless or tapering into a fine straight or curved awn not twisted.

Palea very flat, often hairy on the back, with two prominent almost marginal nerves.

Styles distinct, short.

Grain more or less flattened, enclosed in the glume and palea, free from them.

Fungi found on Eriachne.—Sorosporium eriachnes, Thun., and *Ustilago australis,* Cooke, have both been recorded from *Eriachne sp.*

Awns not longer than the glumes. Panicle loose. Spikelets pedicellate,
 usually few.
Leaves glabrous, flat. Outer glumes hairy, about 4 lines long.
 Flowering glume hairy all over ... ... 10. *E. aristidea.*
Awn none or reduced to a very small point.
Panicle narrow. Spikelets pedicellate. Outer glumes about 3 lines
 long. Tall plant, with glabrous flat leaves ... ... 15. *E. pallida.*
Panicle loose or reduced to two or three spikelets. Outer glumes
 not above 2 lines long. Leaves not pungent, the upper ones
 distant. Spikelets about 2 lines long.
Flowering glumes mucronate ... ... 17. *E. mucronata.*
Flowering glumes obtuse or scarcely acute ... ... 18. *E. obtusa.*

10. Eriachne aristidea, F.v.M.

Botanical Names.—Eriachne—Greek, *erios,* wool ; *achne,* chaff (Glume), the glumes being woolly or hairy ; *aristidea,* resembling a grass of the genus *Aristida* in habit.

Botanical description (B. Fl., vii, 629).—

> *Stems* branching and often decumbent at the base, ascending to from $\frac{1}{2}$ to $1\frac{1}{2}$ feet, the nodes usually bearded.
> *Leaves* flat, glabrous, the sheaths often broad.
> *Panicle* loose, with few spreading branches.
> *Spikelets* shortly pedicellate.
> *Outer glumes* usually purplish, about 4 lines long, acute, sprinkled with spreading hairs arising from tubercles.
> *Flowering glumes* densely silky-hairy except at the top, tapering into an awn scarcely so long as the glume itself.
> *Palea* hairy, tapering into a deeply bifid awnlike point.

Value as a fodder.—Not known.

Habitat and range.—Found in all the Colonies except Tasmania and Victoria. An interior species.

15. Eriachne pallida, F.v.M.

Botanical Names.—Pallida—Latin, pale, referring to the inflorescence.

Botanical description (B. Fl., vii, 631).—

> *Stems* apparently about 2 feet high, slender, and branching.
> *Leaves* flat but narrow, with subulate points, glabrous.
> *Panicle* loose but narrow, 2 to 4 inches long, the spikelets all pedicellate.
> *Outer glumes* glabrous, about 3 lines long, tapering into fine points.
> *Flowering glumes* longer, with fine points, scarcely awned, glabrous on the back except near the base, the margins ciliate with long hairs.
> *Palea* hairy, tapering to a fine bifid point.

Value as a fodder.—Not known.

Habitat and range.—Found in New South Wales ; also from New South Wales to Northern Australia. An interior species.

17. Eriachne mucronata, R. Br.

Botanical names.—*Mucronata*—Latin, sharp-pointed (mucronate), the flowering glumes being tipped with short points.

Botanical description (B. Fl., vii, 632).—

Stems very slender, but rigid ; about 1 foot high.
Leaves short, spreading, subulate, with fine points, but not so pungent as in *E. scleranthoides*, the lower sheaths sprinkled with rigid hairs, or glabrous, the upper ones distant.
Panicle rather loose, 1 to 1½ inches long, of few spikelets, closely resembling those of *E. obtusa*, but rather larger ; and the
Flowering glumes tipped with short points exceeding the outer glumes.

Value as a fodder.—Not known.

Habitat and range.—Found in South Australia, New South Wales, and Queensland. An interior species.

18. Eriachne obtusa, R. Br.

Botanical names.—*Obtusa*—Latin, blunt, or obtuse, referring to the appearance of the spikelets when in fruit.

Where figured.—*Agricultural Gazette.*

Botanical description (B. Fl., vii, 632).—A variable grass, usually 1 to 2 feet high, often branched in the lower part.

Leaves narrow, flat, or subulate, glabrous, or the lower sheaths sprinkled with rigid hairs.
Panicle loose, sometimes much-branched and 4 inches long, sometimes almost reduced to a raceme of half a dozen spikelets.
Spikelets ovoid, about 2 lines long, appearing acute when young, assuming the obtuse aspect when in fruit.
Outer glumes membranous, acute, with fewer nerves than in most species (usually five), sprinkled on the back and ciliate with a few long hairs, rarely quite glabrous.
Flowering glumes about as long, more obtuse, rarely with a minute point, densely ciliate to the top, and sprinkled on the back with spreading hairs.
Palea entire, slightly hairy.
Grain much flattened.

Value as a fodder.—" A fairly good pasture-grass, suitable for sheep ; it is variable as to height, but generally branches much from the base, and before seeding makes a good leafy bottom." (Bailey.)

Habitat and range.—Found in all the Colonies, except Tasmania and Victoria. Believed to be exclusively an interior species until recently discovered in the Port Jackson district.

Sub-tribe iv.—*Festucaceæ.*

82. Ectrosia.	92. Poa.
85. Phragmites.	93. Schedonorus.
86. Distichlis.	94. Glyceria.
87. Elytrophorus.	96. Bromus.
91. Eragrostis.	98. Festuca.

82. ECTROSIA.

Spikelets with one or rarely two fertile flowers, and two or more male flowers or empty glumes above them, in a terminal panicle ; the *rhachis* of the spikelet articulate above the two outer glumes.

Outer empty glumes unawned, the second rarely with a short point; glume of the perfect flower with a prominent point or short awn, the upper glumes tapering into fine straight awns.

Styles distinct.

Grain enclosed in the thin or scarcely hardened glume and palea.

2. Ectrosia leporina, R.Br.

Botanical name.—Ectrosia—Greek, *ectrope*, a turning off or aside; *leporina*—Latin, pertaining to a hare, referring to the softness of the panicle.

Vernacular name.—" Hare's-tail Grass."

Botanical description (B. Fl., vii, 633).—A glabrous, slender grass, attaining 2 feet or more, but sometimes smaller.

Leaves very narrow, ending in subulate points.

Panicle narrow, dense, 3 to 6 inches long, the fine awns giving it much of the aspect of *Triraphis mollis*.

Spikelets crowded along the short erect branches, often purplish, the very short pedicels often bearing a few long hairs.

Outer glumes narrow, very acute, about 1 line long.

Flowering glume nearly as long, narrow, hyaline, one-nerved, slightly notched, with a fine awn nearly as long as the glume.

Terminal empty glumes, usually two or three, smaller than the flowering one, but with longer fine awns.

Value as a fodder.—"A rather slender, dry, tufty grass; often attains a height of 2 feet." (Bailey.) It is ornamental, and is reputed to be a useful fodder grass.

*Habitat and range.—*Found in New South Wales and throughout Queensland and North Australia. An interior species in New South Wales.

85. PHRAGMITES.

Spikelets three- or more-flowered, flat when open, all pedicellate in a large, much-branched panicle, the *rhachis* of the spikelet elongated between the flowering glumes, and covered with very long silky hairs, enveloping the flowers.

Glumes thin, keeled, the two outer ones empty, acute, or shortly pointed; the third like them, but with a longer point, and enclosing a male or rudimentary flower; the others more distant, with long, almost awnlike points, the *rhachis* terminating in a rudimentary glume or bristle-like point.

Palea two-ribbed.

Stigmas nearly sessile.

Fungi found on this genus.—Coniosporium inquinas, Dk. and Mont., W.A., has been recorded on a species of *Arundo (Phragmites). Puccinia phragmites,* Schum., has been recorded from *Phragmites sp.*

168

1. Phragmites communis, Trin.

Botanical name.—Phragmites—Greek, *phragma*, a fence or palisade, the stems of this grass being used for such a purpose ; *communis*— Latin, common.

Synonym.—Arundo Phragmites, Linn.

Vernacular name.—" Reed-grass."

*Where figured.—*Sowerby, Vasey.

Botanical description (B. Fl., vii, 636).—A stout perennial, usually 5 or 6 feet high, but sometimes twice as much, with a long creeping root-stock, and numerous long leaves often an inch broad, the sheaths covering the stems to the inflorescence.

Panicle 6 inches to 1½ feet long, with numerous branches, more or less one-sided and drooping, often of a purplish-brown tinge.

Spikelets numerous, at first very narrow, 4 to 6 lines long, flat and spreading when in seed, the long silky hairs proceeding from the *rhachis*, and as long as, or longer, than the glumes, giving the panicle a beautiful silvery aspect; the glumes themselves and the short part of the *rhachis* below the third glume quite glabrous.

Value as a fodder.—" A tall, coarse, perennial grass, growing on the borders of ponds and streams, almost rivalling Sorghum in luxuriance. It is resorted to by cattle only when finer and more nutritious grasses fail." (Vasey.) " Used as fodder when quite young." (Duthie.)

This well-known plant, growing sometimes to over 15 feet high, is the tallest of our grasses, and at times a very useful one, too, for grazing purposes, as those who have known the reed-beds in Riverina and elsewhere can testify.

" In situations where the reed grows here, some of the most valuable pasture grasses, native and exotic, will grow also." (Bacchus.)

*Other uses.—*This grass was formerly much utilised by the aborigines of Victoria for making bags or baskets, and a figure of one made of this material will be found in Brough Smyth's "Aboriginals of Victoria," i, 343. It is not valuable for agricultural purposes, but it is of great importance for binding the earth on river banks with its extensively creeping root-stocks. The dry plant yields 4·7 per cent. of ash, and an analysis by Schulz-Fleeth will be found in "Watt's Dict.," i, 413. The reed is turned to account in so many ways, or rather used to be, that I copy some of them from "Withering's British Plants " :—" In Sweden by it the country people used to dye woollen cloth green. For thatching, reeds are more durable than straw. Garden screens are made of them, and they make a good foundation for plaster floors. They are also in demand by brickmakers. Till the introduction (in the seventh century) of pens made from quills of birds, they were in general use for writing. They also occasionally serve for arrows. The young shoots, cut from the roots, when not exposed to the light, make an excellent pickle. The nest of the Sedge-warbler is generally found suspended between the stems at a small height from the ground. Entomologists may sometimes find a considerable variety of insects on the panicles, where they resort for food or shelter."

Distichlis maritima, Rafin.

"Salt-grass"

169

"The largest panicles form very ornamental plumes, almost equal to those of *Arundo donax*, so much cultivated for ornamental purposes." (Vasey.)

"Sandals are made from the stems in Lodak, India." (Duthie.)

In addition to the above uses, Hackel observes that the culms are used for the mouthpieces of musical instruments, weavers' spools, &c., and an infusion of the root is used as a diuretic.

"In Mexico where the plant grows 20 to 25 feet high (near the water), the stems are used for various purposes by the natives according to Dr. E. Palmer, who says they cut it into certain lengths, and, having split it, beat it flat and then weave it in and out, making a large square mat, with which they form the ends of their houses. They place it over the rafters before the tule thatch is put on. It is also used to cover verandahs and as screens for doors." (Dodge.)

Habitat and range.—In swampy localities, all over the Colony. Found in all the other Colonies, and in many countries of the Old and New World.

86. DISTICHLIS.

Spikelets several-flowered, dioecious, shortly pedicellate in a narrow panicle often reduced to two or three spikelets, the *rhachis* glabrous, articulate between the flowering glumes—at least in the females.

Outer empty glumes narrow, keeled.

Flowering glumes broader, keeled, many-nerved, all acute, unawned.

Palea folded, the keels very prominent or narrowly winged.

Stamens in the males three, without any or with a small rudimentary ovary.

Staminodia in the females very rare.

Lodicules broad.

Ovary glabrous, tapering into two rather long styles with exserted stigmas.

Grain obovoid or elliptical, free, with a thick spongy pericarp.

1. Distichlis maritima, Rafin.

Botanical name.—*Distichlis*—Greek, *distichos*, of two rows, referring to the leaves which are so placed; *maritima*—Latin, belonging to the sea, this being a coast grass.

Synonym.—*Festuca distichophylla*, Hook. f.

Vernacular names.—"Salt-grass" and "Alkaline-grass" of the United States; "Spike-grass" and "Quack-grass" are also American names. The first two names are in allusion to the saline land in which this grass will flourish. I do not know any name which has been adopted in these colonies, and suggest that "Salt-grass" is as good as any.

Where figured.—Vasey; Labillardière, as *Uniola distichophylla*.

Botanical description (B. Fl., vii, 637).—A rigid, glabrous, much-branched grass, forming broad low leafy tufts, the branches sometimes growing out to 1 foot covered to the inflorescence with the leaf-sheaths.

Leaves narrow, rigid, very acute or pungent-pointed, usually distichously spreading.

Spikelets few, two or three in the females, rather more in the males, 6 to 9 lines long in the Australian specimens, rather smaller and more numerous in some American ones, flat but rather thick, eight- to twelve-flowered.

Glumes closely imbricate, about 3 lines long, rather rigid and straw-coloured.

Anthers in the males long.

Stigmas in the females protruding from the end of the glumes.

Value as a fodder.—"Although this cannot be considered a first-rate grass for agricultural purposes, it is freely cut with other marsh grasses, and on the alkaline plains of the Rocky Mountains of the United States it affords an inferior pasturage." (Vasey.)

"This dwarf creeping grass is of great value for binding soil, forming rough lawns; is useful for edging garden plots in arid places, and covering coast sand." (Mueller.)

In our own colony it has no recognised pastoral value, but it is undoubtedly useful as a sand-binder, consolidating land close to the edge of the sea, and affording a bite for stock in such localities. Of its comparative nutritive value we know nothing, but judging from its harsh nature it does not promise much.

Habitat and range.—A sea-coast grass, found in all the Colonies except Western Australia and Queensland.

"Grows in marshes near the sea-coast on both sides of the American Continent, and also abundantly in alkaline soil throughout the arid districts of the Rocky Mountains." (Vasey.)

"Prospectors and miners in California consider its presence a sure sign of water near the surface, and when crossing the desert select spots where it grows to dig for water." (Orcutt.)

Reference to Plate.—A. The spike-like inflorescence, showing the closely-imbricate glumes. B. C. Two pairs of the lowest glumes from an immature female plant.

87. ELYTROPHORUS.

Spikelets small and flat, few-flowered, sessile, in dense compound globular clusters crowded in a cylindrical spike or the lower ones distant, the *rhachis* of the spikelet glabrous, articulate under the flowering glumes.

Outer empty glumes narrow, membranous, keeled with short points.

Flowering glumes three-nerved, tapering into long points or short awns, one or two upper glumes empty or with male flowers.

Palea folded, with two dorsal wings.

Stamen one.

Styles free, distinct.

Grain smooth, free.

1. Elytrophorus articulatus, Beauv.

Botanical name.—*Elytrophorus*—Greek, *eleutron*, a covering ; *phoreo*, I bear, in allusion to the large outer glume; *articulatus*—Latin, jointed, referring to the interrupted (jointed) spike-like panicle.

Where figured.—Duthie.

Botanical description (B. Fl., vii, 638).—An erect glabrous annual, from under 6 inches to rather above 1 foot high, including the inflorescence.

Leaves flat, often longer than the stem, with loose sheaths.

Spikelets small and very numerous, the globular clusters sessile in a cylindrical spike 3 to 4 lines diameter, and often occupying the greater part of the plant, either continuous throughout or interrupted and shortly branched at the base.

Glumes rarely 1 line long without the points, the awns of the flowering ones about as long as or rarely longer than the glume.

Dorsal wings of the palea entire or denticulate, either both or one only rather broad.

Value as a fodder.—A handsome grass of little importance to the grazier.

Habitat and range.—Found in all the Colonies except Western Australia and Tasmania. It is an interior species with us. It is found on the plains of Northern India on damp clay soils; also in other countries of tropical Asia and in Africa.

91. ERAGROSTIS.

Spikelets several- usually many-flowered, pedicellate or sessile, in a loose and spreading or narrow and clustered panicle, the *rhachis* of the spikelet usually glabrous and articulate under the flowering glumes, but often very tardily so, and sometimes inarticulate.

Outer empty glumes unequal and rather shorter than the flowering ones, keeled, without any or only faint lateral nerves.

Flowering glumes obtuse or acute, unawned, three-nerved, the keel prominent, the lateral nerves in a few species very faint.

Palea shorter than the glume, with two prominent nerves or keels, often persisting after the glume and grain have fallen away.

Grain free, ovoid or oblong, not furrowed.

Section I.—Chaunostachya.

Spikelets somewhat flattened, the glumes rather distant, loosely imbricate, overlapping the *rhachis* at the base, so as not to leave a longitudinal furrow, usually very thin, with the lateral nerve on each side faint or marginal.

172

SECTION II.—MEGASTACHYA.

Spikelets when mature very flat. Glumes closely imbricate in two distinct rows, leaving a longitudinal furrow or depression between them on each side of the spikelet, the lateral nerve usually prominent in the middle of each side of the glume.

Base of the stems glabrous, not at all or scarcely thickened.

Spikelets under 3 lines, sessile in small dense globular or oblong clusters sessile along a simple *rhachis*. Stamens usually two ... 10. *E. diandra.*

Spikelets 3 to 6 lines, rather narrow, usually sessile and erect, scattered or clustered, rarely shortly pedicellate and spreading in a simple or branched panicle. Stamens usually three 11. *E. Brownii.*

Base of the stem and short sheath of radical leaves thickened into an almost bulbous woolly-hairy base.

Spikelets shortly pedicellate, nearly 2 lines broad, the base of the flowering glumes woolly-hairy ... .• ... ... 14. *E. laniflora.*

Spikelets sessile, scattered, glabrous, above 1 line broad ... 15. *E. eriopoda.*

Spikelets shortly pedicellate, glabrous, about ¾ line broad ... 16. *E. chœtophylla.*

SECTION III.—CYLINDROSTACHYA.

Spikelets very narrow, terete or nearly so ; glumes closely appressed.

Spikelets ten- to thirty-flowered, rather obtuse, shortly pedicellate in a small panicle ... ... 17. *E. lacunaria.*

Spikelets twelve- to fifty-flowered, obtuse, sessile, usually clustered, often incurved ... ... 18. *E. falcata.*

1. Eragrostis tenella, Beauv.

Botanical name.—*Eragrostis*, from two Greek words—*eros*, love, and *agrostis*, grass ; hence the name, " Love-grass," an allusion, Paxton says, " to the beautiful dancing spikelets " ; *tenella*—Latin, somewhat tender and dainty, referring to the graceful inflorescence.

Vernacular names.—I know of none. Grasses of the genus *Eragrostis* are sometimes (one can scarcely say popularly) called " Love-grasses."

Where figured.—Duthie.

Botanical description (B. Fl., vii, 643).—An erect, tufted annual, from 6 inches to near 2 feet high.

Leaves flat, usually narrow, glabrous.

Panicle usually occupying the greater part of the plant, with very numerous capillary much-divided branches, the lower ones in distant whorls or clusters.

Spikelets pedicellate, minute, rarely ¾ line long, with three or four, or rarely six flowers.

Glumes thin, almost hyaline, obtuse, about ¼ line long, the lateral nerve on each side almost marginal, very loosely imbricate, the *rhachis* articulate.

Palea glabrous, as long as the glume.

Stamens varying one to three.

Grain very small, ovoid.

Value as a fodder.—A small, tufted grass, excellent for pasture. Duthie says it is eaten by cattle both fresh and dry, and he also states that the seeds are said to be nutritious.

Habitat and range.—Found in all the Colonies, except Tasmania. In New South Wales it extends from the tableland to the interior. It is common on the inland plains of Northern Queensland, also in Central and North Australia, and widely spread through eastern and tropical Asia.

2. Eragrostis nigra, Nees. ; *var.* trachycarpa, Benth.

Botanical name.—Nigra—Latin, black, in allusion to the colour of the inflorescence; *trachycarpa*—Greek, *trachus*, rough; *carpos*, a fruit,— the grain being rough on the surface (rugose-tuberculate).

Botanical description (B. Fl., vii, 643).—

Leaves only seen in one specimen, narrow, rather short, glabrous.

Panicle 1 foot long or more, very loose, with very long capillary divided branches, bearing few small dark-coloured spikelets on long capillary pedicels, the spikelets ovate, 1 to 2 lines long, loosely two- to four-flowered, quite glabrous.

Flowering glumes broad, obtuse or scarcely acute, hyaline, the lateral nerves scarcely conspicuous.

Palea as long, usually broad.

Stamens three, with small anthers.

Grain large in proportion, globular, prominently rugose-tuberculate.

*Value as fodder.—*Not known.

*Habitat and range.—*Found in New South Wales and Queensland, also in Asia. In New South Wales it is found in northern New England.

6. Eragrostis megalosperma, F.v.M.

Botanical name.—Megalosperma, from two Greek words signifying large-seeded (*megalo-sperma*).

Botanical description (B. Fl., vii, 644).—

Stems 2 to 3 feet high, the branches almost filiform, but often rigid and clustered.

Leaves long and narrow, flat or convolute, glabrous.

Panicle narrow and compact, 3 to 8 inches long, with erect branches.

Spikelets sessile or shortly pedicellate, erect, crowded, linear, about 3 lines long when fully out, rather silvery-shining, loosely six- to eight-flowered, the *rhachis* glabrous, scarcely articulate.

Flowering glumes about 1 line long, acute, the lateral nerves often scarcely conspicuous except at the base.

Palea nearly as long, scarcely curved.

Stamens usually two, oblong.

Grain broadly ovoid, often three-fourths as long as the glume, readily falling away, leaving the glume and palea more persistent.

*Value as a fodder.—*Not known.

*Habitat and range.—*Found in New South Wales and Queensland. In the former Colony it is found on the north coast to New England.

7. Eragrostis pilosa, Beauv.

Botanical name.—Pilosa—Latin, hairy, the plant being hirsute.

Where figured.—Agricultural Gazette.

Botanical description (B. Fl., vii, 645).—A tufted erect or ascending annual, 1 to near 2 feet high.

Leaves narrow, usually flat.

Panicle 6 inches to 1 foot long, narrow at first, spreading when in fruit, with numerous long capillary divided branches.

Spikelets 2 to 4 lines long, narrow-linear, usually of a dark leaden colour, but pale when old, loosely six- to twenty-flowered, the *rhachis* scarcely articulate.

Glumes thin, distinctly keeled, the lateral nerves faint and short.

Palea nearly as long, slightly ciliate on the keels, often persistent after the glumes have fallen away.

Grain ovoid-oblong, smooth.

Value as a fodder.—A very abundant annual grass, nearly always in growth, and readily eaten by stock of all kinds. Mr. A. R. Crawford, in the following note, draws attention to the perfume of this grass. I have not observed it myself, but Mr. Crawford is a careful observer :—" Citron-like perfume. In the morning, when the dew begins to dry off, the scent is very noticeable; in the heat of the day there is a strong perfume, but quite different from that of the morning. The scent is given forth like that from a flower. Rubbing between the fingers makes no difference, as with *Chrysopogon parviflorus.* It is unfortunate that the scent of the *Eragrostis,* strong when the plant is growing, fades at once when it is cut." We have so few records of odours emitted by grasses, and particularly by *Eragrostis,* that the following is interesting :—" E. multiflora, Forsk, or 'Stink Grass,' is coarse and weedy, and has such a disagreeable odour when fresh that animals do not relish it. This odour disappears on drying." (*South Dakota Bulletin,* No. 40).

" *E. pilosa* is relished by buffaloes. Mr. Symonds says that cattle eat it readily, and that it would make good hay. Mr. Lowrie tells me that at Ajmere it is considered to be a good fodder grass." (Duthie.)

Other uses.—It is really a beautiful grass, and well worthy of cultivation for ornamental purposes. The Seeds are used for food in Ajmere, India, according to Duthie. " *E. abyssinica,* Link., is an important food-plant in Abyssinia. The various-coloured seeds have the appearance of grits, and the flour made from these is baked into bread. This grass is probably a cultivated form of *E. pilosa.*" (Hackel.)

Habitat and range.—Found in all the Colonies except Tasmania. Widely diffused in New South Wales. In India, usually in damp or swampy ground, according to Duthie.

A common weed in the warmer and some temperate regions of the northern hemisphere, chiefly in the Old World.

8. Eragrostis leptostachya, Steud.

Botanical name.—*Leptostachya*—Greek, *leptos,* slender ; *stachys,* an ear of corn, the inflorescence being slender.

Vernacular name.—" Slender Spiked-grass."

Where figured.—*Agricultural Gazette.*

Botanical description (B. Fl., vii, 645).—

Stems slender, usually about 1 ft. high.

Leaves at the base narrow, convolute or setaceous, glabrous.

Panicle loosely pyramidal, 3 to 5 inches long, with slender divided spreading branches.

Spikelets on capillary pedicels of 1 to 3 lines, loosely spreading, about 2 lines long, narrow, but much broader than in E. pilosa, much smaller than in E. Brownii, loosely six-to ten-flowered, usually dark-coloured.

Glumes acute, more spreading than in E. pilosa, the lateral nerves faint and almost marginal.

Palea nearly as long, glabrous.

Grain ovoid, smooth.

Value as a fodder.—A grass much of the same character as the preceding, and yielding tender feed for stock.

Habitat and range.—Found in New South Wales and Queensland. As regards New South Wales, occurring from the coast district and the tableland from the Illawarra northward ; as regards Queensland, abundant on the high land about Brisbane, reaching almost to the Darling Downs.

10. Eragrostis diandra, Steud.

Botanical name.—*Diandra-diander, ante*, p. 162.
Botanical description (B. Fl., vii, 646).—

Stems 1 to 2 feet high.
Leaves very narrow, often convolute, glabrous.
Panicle usually contracted into an interrupted spike of 3 to 6 inches.
Spikelets very numerous, rarely above 2 lines long, flat, scarcely 1 line broad, six-to twelve-flowered, sessile in dense sessile clusters, the upper ones forming a cylindrical spike 3 or 4 lines diameter, the lower clusters usually distant, the lowest oblong or forming a cylindrical sessile spike of ½ inch or more.
Flowering glumes closely distichous, thin, rather obtuse, the lateral nerve in the centre of each side or near the margin.
Rhachis tardily or not at all articulate.
Palea nearly as long as the glume, incurved.
Stamens two, with small anthers in the flowers examined, but perhaps sometimes three.
Grain ovoid.

" An erect grass, very like *E. Brownii*—perhaps only one of its many forms—the panicle never spreading, but remaining always spike-like." (Bentham.)
Value as a fodder.—" Excellent for pasture and hay." (Bailey.)
Habitat and range.—Found in all the Colonies except Tasmania. In New South Wales, occurring from the coast district to the tableland.

11. Eragrostis Brownii, Nees.

Botanical name.—*Brownii*, in honor of Robert Brown, author of the *Prodromus* and other works, perhaps the most eminent botanist who has ever specialised on Australian plants.
Botanical description (B. Fl., vii, 646).—A very variable plant in stature and aspect, usually above 1 foot high, with very narrow flat or convolute leaves, glabrous except a few cilia at the orifice of the sheaths, not by any means constant.

Panicle sometimes simple and dense, a few inches long, almost spikelike with numerous small densely clustered spikelets, always however, longer and more acute than in *E. diandra*, sometimes with short spreading branches and few spikelets, sometimes a foot long with few distant branches and long spikelets singly scattered or in distinct clusters, and a great variety of intermediate forms.
Spikelets always sessile or very nearly so, flat, varying from ¼ to ½ inch long, with ten to forty flowers, the *rhachis* very tardily articulate.
Flowering glumes closely distichous, the lateral nerve nearly central on each side and prominent.
Palea shorter than the glume, incurved, the keels usually minutely ciliate.
Stamens usually three, but sometimes only two even in the larger spikelets.
Grain ovoid-oblong, smooth.

Botanical notes.—" Easily recognised by its closely packed florets arranged in dark-coloured and flattened spikelets." (Duthie.)

Var. *interrupta*, Benth. A larger plant, often 3 or 4 feet high, with long flat leaves and large spikelets in dense distinct clusters. From the central coast districts to the mountain ranges and tablelands and northward into Queensland.

Var. *patens*, Benth. Panicle loose, often spreading. Spikelets rather small, most of them shortly pedicellate. Port Jackson to Blue Mountains ; also Victoria.

Value as a fodder.—A valuable grass, producing for many months of the year abundance of palatable and nutritious fodder. It shoots and seeds well.

" Perennial ; stems 1 to 2 feet high, common on both rich and poor soil, producing abundance of foliage. This grass has the great merit of keeping its verdure during the driest summers. A good fattening grass. Bears hard feeding. Produces plenty of seed." (Bacchus.)

" Keeps beautifully green in the driest Australian summer, even on poor soil. Pastor Kempe pronounces it to be the best of all grasses in Central Australian pastures. Eaten down by sheep, but readily springs up again from the root. No drought seems to subdue it." (Mueller.)

Var. *interrupta*. A stronger grower than the normal species, but its qualities are much the same.

" This variety and var. *patens* have sprung up at Mudgee, New South Wales, and are increasing. At present large patches of the river flats are covered with it, but neither sheep nor cattle seem to like it." (Hamilton, *Proc. Linn. Soc., N.S.W.* [2] ii, 302.)

Mudgee is over the Dividing Range, but the opinion of Mr. Bailey in regard to the coastal Queensland form is much the same :—" This is a very tall, or long, straggling, often hoary form, met with along the coast. Very harsh, and of little value as a fodder, but useful for binding coast sands, and affording a bite for stock in such localities."

Habitat and range.—Found in all the Colonies except Tasmania ; also in Asia. Widely diffused over New South Wales.

" *E. Brownii* is abundantly naturalised about the Bay of Islands, and is proving itself a valuable grass." (Sec., Auckland Acclim. Soc., quoted by Bacchus.)

14. Eragrostis laniflora, Benth.

Botanical name.—*Laniflora*—Latin, *lana*, wool; *flos, floris*, flower, the glumes being enveloped at the base with woolly hairs.

Botanical description (B. Fl., vii, 648).—

Rhizome and somewhat bulbous bases of the stems woolly-hairy.

Stems 1 to 1½ feet high, slightly cottony at the nodes.

Leaves narrow, flat, with scabrous sheaths.

Panicle loose, 4 to 6 inches long, with few divaricate or reflexed scabrous branches.

Spikelets very shortly pedicellate, and not numerous, divaricate, or reflexed, very flat, 4 to 8 inches long, nearly 2 lines broad, with twenty to fifty flowers, the *rhachis* tardily articulate.

Glumes rather broad, very thin, closely distichous, enveloped at the base in woolly hairs.

Palea nearly as long, the keels ciliate with soft hairs near the base.

Stamens three, with rather long anthers.

Grain globular.

Value as a fodder.—Not known.

Habitat and range.—Found in South Australia, Victoria, and New South Wales. An interior species.

15. Eragrostis eriopoda, Benth.

Botanical name.—*Eriopoda*—Greek, *erios*, wool ; *pous, podos,* a foot, the stems being densely woolly at the base.

Botanical description (B. Fl., vii, 648).—

Stems 1 to 1½ feet high, somewhat bulbous and densely woolly at the base.

Leaves very narrow, short, the lower sheaths pubescent or hirsute.

Panicle in some specimens reduced to an interrupted spike, in others divided into spreading branches.

Spikelets nearly sessile, scattered or in pairs, very flat, 3 to 9 lines long, above 1 line broad, with ten to thirty or more flowers.

Glumes closely distichous but rather spreading, obtuse, almost hyaline, with a dark green nerve on each side, glabrous.

Palea as long.

Stamens two only in all the flowers examined, with rather large anthers.

Value as a fodder.—Not known.

Habitat and range.—Found in all the Colonies except Tasmania and Victoria. An interior species.

16. Eragrostis chætophylla, Steud.

Botanical name.—*Chætophylla*—Greek, *chæte,* a bristle ; *phylla,* leaves, the leaves being bristle-like.

Synonym.—*E. setifolia,* Nees.

Botanical description (B. Fl., vii, 648).—

Stems from a shortly-thickened, almost bulbous, slightly woolly-hairy base densely tufted, slender but rigid, 6 inches to 1 foot high, often leafy to the inflorescence.

Leaves very narrow, convolute or setaceous, glabrous.

Panicle narrow, 1½ to 3 inches long, shortly branched.

Spikelets usually rather numerous, shortly pedicellate, scattered or crowded, flat and thin, 2 to 4 or rarely 6 lines long, 1 to 1¼ lines broad, six- to thirty-flowered.

Glumes closely distichous or rather loose, ¾ line long, obtuse or almost acute, hyaline or purplish, the lateral nerve prominent on each side at the base.

Palea nearly as long, glabrous.

Stamens three.

Grain small, ovoid-oblong.

Value as a fodder.—Inferior, because of its wiry nature. At the same time, it provides useful feed when quite young.

Habitat and range.—Found in all the Colonies except Tasmania. An interior species.

17. Eragrostis lacunaria, F.v.M.

Botanical name.—*Lacunaria*—Latin, *lacuna,* any little hole or hollow place, perhaps in reference to the localities in which the grass was originally found.

M

Where figured.—Agricultural Gazette.

Botanical description (B. Fl., vii, 649).—

Stems slender, almost filiform, but rigid, 6 inches to 1 foot, or rarely 1½ feet high, the base sometimes almost bulbous, but glabrous.

Leaves very narrow, almost setaceous, usually short.

Panicle loose, 2 to 4 inches long, with short, spreading, rather rigid branches.

Spikelets few on the branches, shortly pedicellate, very narrow, 3 to 6 lines long, ten-to twenty-four-flowered, terete or very slightly flattened.

Flowering glumes closely appressed, broad, obtuse, scarcely ¾ line long, usually purple, keeled, but the lateral nerves very faint or obsolete, the *rhachis* scarcely articulate.

Palea nearly as long.

" With the habit and inflorescence nearly of *E. chætophylla,* this has the spikelets rather of *E. falcata.*" (Benth.)

Value as a fodder.—A wiry grass of little value.

Habitat and range.—Found in all the Colonies except Tasmania and Western Australia. An interior species.

18. Eragrostis falcata, Gaud.

Botanical name.—*Falcata,* adjective, from the Latin *falx, falcis,* a sickle; used in botany to denote anything curved, in allusion to the curving of the spikelets.

Where figured.—Agricultural Gazette.

Botanical description (B. Fl., vii, 649).—A slender, tufted, glabrous grass, varying from a few inches to about 1 foot high.

Leaves narrow, convolute, erect.

Panicle narrow, usually secund, slightly compound, 2 to 4 inches long.

Spikelets sessile or nearly so, crowded or clustered along the short branches, very narrow, nearly terete, often curved, from 4 to 5 lines to 1 inch long and about ½ line broad, with twelve to fifty or even more flowers, the *rhachis* scarcely articulate.

Flowering glumes closely appressed, scarcely 1 line long, obtuse, hyaline at the end, the keel and a lateral nerve on each side very prominent.

Palea rather shorter, curved, persistent.

Styles slender.

Grain ovate, flattened.

Value as a fodder.—Isaac Tyson, quoted by Mueller, states that it is one of the best pasture-grasses in arid tracts in sub-tropical Western Australia. Such a statement is, of course, only comparative, for the grass is by no means of the highest merit. It is a small grass, wiry in appearance, with small leaves ; nevertheless, it affords useful feed until it is burnt up by the summer droughts. Much of the plant consists of inflorescence, and it produces seed readily.

Habitat and range.—This grass is found in all the Colonies except Tasmania. It is an interior species in most of the Colonies, although it comes near the coast in the south-western part of the Continent. It is common both on the far inland plains and also on the sand-ridges that skirt them.

Reference to Plate.—A. A typically falcate spikelet. B. Flowering glume, showing three prominent nerves.

92. POA.

Spikelets several usually few-flowered, in a panicle usually loose and spreading, rarely narrow and spikelike, the *rhachis* of the spikelet articulate between the flowering glumes.

Glumes keeled, unawned, the outer empty ones rather short, one- or three-nerved, sometimes acute, the flowering ones usually obtuse, five-nerved, often surrounded by a few loose woolly hairs, rarely with seven or more nerves.

Palea nearly as long, prominently two-nerved or two-keeled.

Grain enclosed in the glume and palea and falling off with them, but free or rarely adnate to the palea.

Perennials.—Grain enclosed in the glume and palea, but free from them.

Leaves setaceous or rigid and convolute or flat ending in long points. Panicle dense and contracted, or spreading. Spikelets usually four- to six-flowered. Glumes and palea glabrous or with woolly hairs at the base ... ... 3. *P. cæspitosa.*

Leaves flat, narrow, acuminate. Panicle rather dense. Spikelets five- to eight-flowered, the keels of the glumes ciliate-pubescent. Stems knotty at the base ... ... 5. *P. nodosa.*

Annuals.—Leaves flat, flaccid.

Panicle narrow. Spikelets clustered, 3 lines long. Flowering glumes seven-to eleven-nerved, the keel ciliate at the base with long hairs ... ... 8. *P. lepida.*

3. Poa cæspitosa, Forst.

Botanical name.—Poa, the Greek word for grass; *cæspitosa*—Latin, pertaining to a turf or sod.

Vernacular names.—" Wiry-grass," called " Bowat " by the Yarra (Victoria) aborigines.

Where figured.—Buchanan ; *Agricultural Gazette.*

Botanical description (B. Fl., vii, 651).—An exceedingly variable species from under 1 to 3 feet high, usually densely tufted and glabrous.

Leaves narrow, flat, convolute, or setaceous, chiefly at the base, sometimes longer than the inflorescence, sometimes very short, the ligula always very short or obsolete.

Panicle branched, compact, or spreading.

Spikelets usually four- to six-flowered.

Flowering glumes usually surrounded by a few fine woolly hairs, but sometimes the whole spikelet glabrous, the cilia of the palea-keels when present very minute.

Grain oblong, usually narrow, enclosed in the glume and palea, but free from them.

This is one of the most variable of the Australian grasses, and I give an account of its principal varieties chiefly from Bentham (*Flora Australiensis*) and from Bacchus (*Rept., Department Agriculture, Victoria*, 1874).

1. Var. *plebeia*, Benth.—Tall and leafy, leaves narrow, flat or more or less convolute. Panicle exceeding the leaves, rather large and loose. Glumes 2 to 2½ lines long, usually surrounded by a few woolly hairs. Port Jackson (also Western Australia).

Var. *latifolia*, Benth.—Very tall and luxuriant, with flat leaves, often 2 to 4 lines broad. Illawarra and Australian Alps; also in a mountain range in Southern Queensland.

" The only Queensland habitat of this variety at present known is on the rich land upon the top of Mount Mistake. There it grows 3 to 4 feet high, very leafy and succulent, and would probably under cultivation be profitable for cutting as green food for stock." (Bailey.)

The following grass may very probably be referred to var. *latifolia:—*
" *Poa australis.* Broad-leaved meadow grass; perennial; flowers in December; average height at time of flowering 3 feet, growing sometimes to 6 feet; leaves smooth, flat, and very long. Thrives on rich soil, in high, cold, and dry situations. A nice tender grass when young, but it soon grows into larger tussocks than any other grass we have. The herbage is of little value when suffered to grow old. If grazed or cut down close every year it would afford a good supply of valuable winter food." (Bacchus.)

2. Var. *lævis*, Benth.—Leaves, when most characteristic, rigid, erect, terete, smooth and shining, and the panicle contracted; but in many specimens the leaves more slender and sometimes filiform as in the var. *australis*, but always quite smooth, the stem then taller, and the panicle more diffuse; glumes usually about 1½ lines long. From all the Colonies except Queensland, and perhaps that Colony also.

" *Poa australis*; var. *lævis.*—An extremely variable grass, which has received different names by authors. It is not surprising, therefore, under such circumstances, that various estimates have been made of its value as food for stock, according to which variety prevailed in any district, some of the varieties being much more valuable than others. There is no doubt but that the true value of the larger tussock grasses, among which the present occupies a prominent place, has been much under-estimated, as they have never been treated fairly on their merits, and conclusions based on the readiness with which stock eat or refuse them cannot be accepted as a criterion of their value, unless they are cut down when in flower and treated as fodder. It is well known that even the most favourite grasses of cultivation, such as *Lolium perenne*, the common rye grass, if left uncut till the seed is shed will be refused by all kinds of stock; and so it is with the present species, which should always be treated as a fodder plant." (Buchanan.)

3. Var. *affinis*, Benth.—Leaves very narrow, but often flat, as in the var. *plebeia*, but the panicle more diffuse, with more numerous smaller spikelets; the glumes usually under 1½ lines long.

One of the commonest forms in the eastern Colonies, but passing much into the smooth *P. australis* and into *P. lævis*.

This grass is perhaps referred to by Bacchus in his notes on *Poa australis*.

4. Var. *australis*, Benth.—Leaves mostly radical, setaceous, much shorter than the stem, erect, and exceedingly scabrous. Stems under 1 foot high, with a very loose spreading, rather small panicle. Glumes 1 to 1½ lines long.

In Tasmania very abundant as above described. In Victoria and New South Wales the radical leaves are generally longer, and the

Eragrostis falcata, Gaud.

"The Falcate Love Grass."

stem taller. In the northern districts it is a common form, with very long scabrous, filiform leaves, and in New South Wales, Victoria, and South Australia it passes frequently into var. *affinis*.

Following are Bacchus' notes on two forms which may belong to this variety :—" *Poa australis*—(Wiry-grass)—Perennial ; in flower during November and December. A rather low-growing species, from 9 inches to 2 feet high ; common on the plains and elsewhere. Except when quite young, disliked by all kinds of stock. This grass seems to have no fattening qualities, but plenty of nutriment for stock to subsist on when forced by hunger to eat it. In this way it forms frequently their principal food during periods of drought." (Bacchus.)

" *Poa australis tenax*—Narrow-leaved Poa. Perennial. Found on the sides of watercourses and swamps. About 3 feet high ; flowering in December. Of little value for grazing ; but it may become of use as a fibre plant, and is probably the variety referred to by Baron von Mueller as the rough, tufty kind of meadow grass growing along river banks, used by the natives for making fishing lines and nets. About a year ago I noticed what I believed to be a distinct variety of this grass, remarkable for the toughness of its leaves." (Bacchus.)

5. Var. *tenera*, Benth.—A slender, weak variety, with very narrow or filiform but flaccid leaves, and a loose spreading, rather small panicle, with small spikelets, the glumes scarcely 1 line long.

Woods and shady places in New South Wales, Victoria, and Tasmania.

The following forms are, with diffidence, referred to var. *tenera*. The names of some of Bacchus' so-called varieties do not always have a holding in science :—

" *Poa australis decumbens.*—Perennial; flowering late in December. A small, delicate grass, with weak, slender stems, and thread-like leaves. I first noticed it here growing in some tussocks of dead rushes. It grows best in light moist soil, forming a kind of turf or cushion. Sheep graze upon it ; but I cannot speak with any certainty of its merits as a pasture grass." (Bacchus.)

" *Poa australis humilis.*—Perennial ; grows 1 or 2 feet high ; leaves narrow and succulent ; flowering in December. It thrives on light, dry soil, and appears to be a favourite with stock, and may possess superior merits for pasture." (Bacchus.)

Value as a fodder.—A tussocky, rather wiry grass. It is often eaten by stock ; but when it becomes old it is very fibrous, and contains but little nutriment. That stock are not partial to it may be noted from the frequently luxurious appearance of the tufts in places where stock have been running. A fuller account of the fodder value of this grass has already been given when dealing with its varieties.

Other uses.—The different varieties of this grass afford excellent paper material. It was formerly used by the Yarra (Victoria) blacks for making their net bags (Ballang-cowat). For a figure of such a basket, see Brough Smyth's *Aboriginals of Victoria*, i, 345.

Habitat and range.—Found in all the Colonies, also in New Zealand. Widely diffused throughout New South Wales.

182

5. Poa nodosa, Nees.

Botanical name.—*Nodosa*—Latin, full of knots or bumps, referring to the nodules at the base of the stem.

Botanical description (B. Fl., vii, 653).—

Stems usually about 2 feet high, forming at the base one, two, or three superposed globular or ovoid nodules, 3 or 4 lines diameter.

Leaves long, narrow, flat, usually scabrous.

Panicle loose, narrow or spreading.

Spikelets 3 to 4 lines long, five- to eight-flowered, rather narrow at first with closely appressed glumes, at length broad and flat, the glumes spreading out.

Flowering glumes about 2 lines long, five-nerved, without the woolly hairs at the base of most Poæ, but shortly ciliate-pubescent on the keel and margins below the middle.

Palea nearly as long, the keels minutely ciliate-pubescent or glabrous.

Grain free.

Value as a fodder.—" Perennial; grows in almost pure sand, and produces tuberous enlargements at the roots. It is tender and nutritious, but neither tall nor bulky." (Bailey.)

Habitat and range.—Found in all the Colonies except Tasmania. In New South Wales, found in the extreme southern districts.

8. Poa lepida, F.v.M.

Botanical name.—*Lepida*—Latin, pretty or pleasant, the grass being a desirable one.

Botanical description (B. Fl., vii, 654).—An erect annual, varying from 2 or 3 inches to nearly 1 foot high, more slender and less spreading than *P. annua.*

Leaves flat, flaccid, the ligula rather long, jagged.

Panicle very narrow, almost spike-like, 1 to 2 inches long.

Spikelets not numerous, nearly sessile, clustered on the very short branches, very flat, about 3 lines long, five- to seven- or more- flowered, the *rhachis* more or less silky-hairy.

Flowering glumes narrow, obtuse, nearly 1½ lines long, seven- to eleven-nerved, the keel prominent, ciliate with long hairs below the middle, outer glumes three-nerved.

Grain apparently broader than in most Poæ and broadly furrowed, but not seen ripe.

Value as a fodder.—Not known, but probably a useful grass.

Habitat and range.—Found in all the Colonies except Tasmania and Queensland. Found in the extreme southern part of New South Wales.

93. SCHEDONORUS.

Spikelets several-flowered, flattened in a narrow and spikelike or loose and spreading panicle, the *rhachis* of the spikelet glabrous or slightly hairy, articulate under the flowering glumes.

Outer empty glumes narrow, acute, keeled or three-nerved.

Flowering glumes usually five-nerved, rounded on the back at the base, obtuse or shortly notched at the apex, the keel prominent, at least in the upper part, and usually produced into a minute point in or just below the notch.

Schedonorus Hookerianus, F. v. M.

"Hooker's Fescue Grass."

Palea nearly as long, usually rather broad, prominently two-nerved. *Styles* distinct, slightly eccentrical. *Grain* very obtuse, usually broadly-furrowed, free from the palea.

Panicle narrow, dense and spike-like, or interrupted. Leaves
    long, erect, and rigid ... . 2. *S. littoralis.*
Panicle loose and spreading ... ... 3. *S. Hookerianus.*

2. Schedonorus littoralis, Beauv.

Botanical name.—Schedonorus—from two Greek words, *schedon* close to, and *oros* a mountain, in allusion to the mountainous localities frequented by grasses of this genus; *littoralis (litoralis)*—Latin, belonging to the sea-shore, this being a coast grass.

Synonym.—Festuca littoralis, Labill.

*Where figured.—*Buchanan ; Labillardière, as *Festuca littoralis,* and by Trinius as *Arundo triodoides.*

Botanical description (B. Fl., vii, 655).—

Stems 1 to 3 feet high, forming dense hard tufts of a pale yellow colour.
Leaves nearly cylindrical, erect, rigid, pungent-pointed, glabrous, often as long as the stems.
Panicle narrow, dense and spike-like, 2 to 4 inches long.
Spikelets few, flat, erect, 7 to 9 lines long, six- to eight-flowered.
Glumes about 4 lines long, rigid, straw-coloured, the flowering ones with two nerves on each side of the keel, acute or dilated and notched at the tip, the keel usually slightly protruding, the two outer empty ones narrower, three-nerved, acute.
Rhachis of the spikelet shortly hairy.

*Value as a fodder.—*Nil.

*Other uses.—*An important grass for binding drift-sands on sea-shores. It has been recommended as a paper-making material.

*Habitat and range.—*Found on the coast of all the Colonies, including New Zealand.

3. Schedonorus Hookerianus, Benth.

Botanical Name.—Hookerianus, in honor of Dr. (now Sir) J. D. Hooker, for many years Director of the Botanic Gardens at Kew.

Synonym.—Festuca Hookeriana, F.v.M., the name adopted by Baron von Mueller in his *Census.* It has also been placed under *Poa.*

*Vernacular names.—*I know of none in common use. This is readily accounted for, as this valuable grass is known to comparatively few persons, because of its usual occurrence in localities so little trodden by human beings. The name suggested is perhaps as good as any. Bacchus calls it " Georgie's Fescue."

Where figured.—Agricultural Gazette ; Hooker, *Fl. Tasmania.*

Botanical description (B. Fl., vii, 656).—A stout perennial of 2 to 4 feet, glabrous or slightly scabrous-pubescent.

Leaves flat, rather long.
Panicle very loose, 6 inches to 1 foot long, with rather short and erect or long and spreading branches.
Spikelets numerous, 4 to 5 lines long, four- to six-flowered.
Flowering glumes rigidly membranous, about 3 lines long, keeled only in the upper part, the tip hyaline, entire or notched, the keel produced into a short point.
Outer glumes shorter, unequal, prominently keeled, the second often three-nerved.

*Reference to Plate :—*A, spikelet ; B, outer empty glumes ; C, back and front views of grain (seed) ; D, fragment of inner side of leaf, showing the ribbed and scabrous appearance (much magnified.)

Value as a fodder.—This is a bulky grass, and is highly spoken of by holders of the "snow leases," and others competent to speak in regard to it. It can stand the severest cold we ever experience in New South Wales, and it might be desirable to introduce it into the coldest parts of New England. It might also be desirable to introduce it into cold districts outside Australia. It not only yields a large amount of fodder, but it is very nutritious, and it also has a handsome appearance when in bloom. Stock are fond of it.

Some specimens in my possession from the Bredbo River are badly ergotted ; all my other specimens are free from this undesirable fungus. It should be looked for now that attention has been drawn to the matter.

Habitat and range.—Most collectors who have visited Mount Kosciusko bring specimens of it, and it is fairly abundant in the Australian Alps. It extends into both New South Wales and Victoria, never descending to low elevations. Its most northerly locality would appear to be the Mittagong Ranges. It also occurs in a few localities in Tasmania.

Reference to Plate :—A, spikelet ; B, outer empty glumes ; c, back and front views of grain (seed) ; D, fragment of inner side of leaf, showing the ribbed and scabrous appearance (much magnified).

94. GLYCERIA.

Spikelets several-flowered, pedicellate in a narrow or spreading panicle, the *rhachis* of the spikelet articulate under the flowering glumes, glabrous or rarely hairy.

Outer empty glumes obtuse or acute, unawned.

Flowering glumes convex on the back, three- to nine-nerved, the nerves not reaching to the hyaline, obtuse, sometimes slightly denticulate apex.

Palea nearly as long as the glume.

Ovary glabrous.

Styles distinct, very short, the plumose stigmas frequently more branched than in other genera.

Grain glabrous, enclosed in the glume and palea, but free from them.

Flowering glumes with a tuft of hairs round the base or on the
    back below the middle. Panicle loose ... ... 1. *G. Fordeana.*

Rhachis and base of the flowering glumes glabrous or minutely
    pubescent.

Stems rarely 3 feet high. Panicle narrow. Panicle long and loose.
    Spikelets ½ to 1 inch. Flowering glumes distant, narrow,
    3 lines long; outer glumes much shorter ... ... 2. *G. fluitans.*

Panicle dense. Spikelets few, broad, ½ to ¾ inch. Flowering
    glumes paleaceous, 3 to 4 lines long ; outer glumes as long ... 3. *G. latispicea.*

Stems very rigid, tall, with few short leaves and often clusters of
    short branches. Flowering glumes hyaline, three-nerved at
    the base. Panicle very spreading. Spikelets six- to twelve-
    flowered ... ... 6. *G. ramigera.*

1. Glyceria Fordeana, F.v.M.

Botanical name.—*Glyceria*—Greek, *gluceros*, sweet, in allusion to the herbage of these grasses ; *Fordeana*, in honor of Mrs. Helena Forde, who first sent this grass to Baron von Muller.

Synonym.—Poa Fordeana, F.v.M.
Where figured.—Agricultural Gazette.
Botanical description (B. Fl., vii, 657).—An erect glabrous grass attaining 2 or 3 feet.

Leaves flat, very scabrous.
Panicle very loose, compound, 4 to 8 inches long, with very spreading capillary branches, mostly in pairs or threes.
Spikelets lanceolate, mostly 4 to 5 lines long, eight- to twelve-flowered.
Outer glumes acute, three-nerved.
Flowering glumes five- or seven-nerved, 1½ lines long, surrounded by a tuft of hairs and shortly hairy or pubescent in the lower part, the midrib prominent but not reaching the obtuse hyaline apex, the lateral nerves shorter.
Palea-keels scarcely ciliate.

Value as a fodder.—A useful fodder grass, succulent and palatable to stock.
Habitat and range.—Found in all the Colonies except Tasmania and Western Australia, in moist situations in the interior.

2. Glyceria fluitans, R. Br.

*Botanical name.—Fluitans—*Latin, floating, in allusion to the habitat of the plant, often floating in water.
Synonym.—Poa fluitans, Scop.
Vernacular names.—" Manna Grass," " Floating Manna Grass," " Water Grass " (Tasmania).
*Where figured.—*Hackel ; *Agricultural Gazette.*
Botanical description (B. Fl., vii, 657).—

Stems creeping in mud or floating at the base, ascending to 2 or 3 feet.
Leaves narrow, flat, glabrous, the ligula jagged.
Panicle loose, long and narrow.
Spikelets solitary in the distant notches, or two or three on a short branch from the same notch, erect, narrow, ½ to 1 inch long, six- to twenty-flowered, the *rhachis* glabrous as well as the glumes.
Outer glumes broad, obtuse, hyaline, faintly nerved at the base, the lowest about 1½ lines, the second longer.
Flowering glumes more rigid, about 3 lines long, with about seven nerves not reaching to the hyaline, obtuse, entire, or slightly denticulate apex.
Lodicules usually connate.

Value as a fodder.—One of the best fodder grasses for very damp localities.
" Grows from 2 to 4 feet high. It flourishes in rich soil and swampy ground, often extending far into the water, floating in luxuriant growth on the surface. Cattle and horses are fond of it, even when partially dry." (Bacchus.)
The statement was made in the *New Zealand Farmer* that this grass grows on land even if covered with a foot of water, and that stock neglect other pasture for it. It is much relished by cattle, horses, and pigs.
" There is a great difference of opinion amongst agricultural writers with respect to the fondness of animals for the leaves and culms of this grass. We have often seen the ends of the leaves cropped by

cattle but have never seen the culms or root-leaves touched by them. On the other hand, reliable writers have asserted that cattle, horses, and swine are alike fond of it." (Gould, quoted by Vasey.)

Other uses.—The seeds are sweet and palatable, and in many countries used for porridge.

" This grass yields a very nutritious and highly palatable grain, which is collected by Russian peasants. The peasant takes an old felt hat, and, wading in the water, skims the hat amongst the patches of *Glyceria* when the grain is ripe, and the seeds fall into the hat. Their collection is an important branch of industry." (*Pharm. Journ.*, xv, 548.)

" It is cultivated in many parts of Germany for the sake of its seeds, which are esteemed a delicacy in soup and gruel. When ground into meal they make bread very little inferior to that from wheat." (Schreber.)

Fish and all graminivorous birds are exceedingly fond of these seeds. "Trout, and, indeed, most fish, are very fond of them. Wherever it grows over the banks of streams the trout are always found in great numbers waiting to catch every seed that falls." (Gould, quoted by Vasey.)

Habitat and range.—Found in all the Colonies except Queensland. Coast district, and tableland from New England south. Always found in or near water. A cosmopolitan species.

" Grows in shallow water on the margins of lakes, ponds, and sluggish streams." (Vasey.)

"This grass is found growing in shallow water, overflowed meadows, and wet woods, but will bear cultivation on moderately dry grounds." (Gould, quoted by Vasey.)

3. Glyceria latispicea, F.v.M.

Botanical name.—*Latispicea*—Latin, *latus*, broad; *spicea*, belong to ears of corn, the spikelets being broad.

Synonym.—*Poa latispicea*, F.v.M.

Botanical description (B. Fl., vii, 658.)—

Stems erect, attaining 2 or 3 feet.

Leaves flat, glabrous, the ligula long and jagged.

Panicle narrow, the branches very short, erect, each bearing one to three spikelets, the lower ones distant.

Spikelets rather broad and loose, ½ inch long or rather more, pale-coloured, six- to twelve-flowered, the *rhachis* as well as the glumes glabrous or very minutely hairy.

Outer glumes obtuse, five-nerved; flowering ones 3 to 4 lines long, seven- or nine-nerved, rounded on the back as in the rest of the genus, but the midrib reaching the obtuse hyaline apex, the lateral nerves faint and shorter.

Grain oblong, flattened but concave on the inner face.

Value as a fodder.—Not definitely known, but probably a valuable grass.

Habitat and range.—Found in New South Wales and Queensland. In New South Wales, from New England to the interior, in moist situations.

187

6. Glyceria ramigera, F.v.M.

Botanical names.—Ramigera—Latin, *ramus*, a branch; *gero*, I bear, referring to the branching habit of the grass.

Synonym.—Poa ramigera, F.v.M.

Vernacular names.—" Cane Grass," " Bamboo Grass."

Where figured.—Agricultural Gazette.

Botanical description (B. Fl., vii, 659).—A tall glabrous rigid, almost bamboo-like grass, branched at the base, and often bearing clusters of branches higher up.

Leaves convolute and flat, few and short on the flowering stems.

Panicle 4 to 8 inches long, loosely ovate or at length spreading.

Spikelets rather numerous, usually 3 to 5 lines long with six to twelve flowers, but sometimes longer, the *rhachis* glabrous.

Outer glumes narrow, hyaline, acute, faintly one-nerved.

Flowering glumes distant, about 1½ lines long, broad and concave, hyaline, three-nerved, the nerves all short, the central one not reaching much above the middle.

Grain not seen ripe, but apparently that of *Glyceria.*

Value as a fodder.—Stock only eat the young shoots of this grass.

Other uses.—A tall cane-like species, growing plentifully in large detached tussocks in " clay pans," or as they are locally termed "cane swamps." It is largely used for thatching purposes, for which it is admirably adapted. Roofs twenty years old, made of this grass, are standing, and are waterproof still.

Habitat and range.—Found in all the Colonies except Tasmania. An interior species, found in clay soil liable to inundation.

96. BROMUS.

Spikelets several-flowered, oblong or lanceolate, pedicellate, erect or drooping in a more or less branched panicle, the *rhachis* of the spikelet articulate between the flowering glumes, glabrous or scabrous-pubescent.

Outer empty glumes acute or fine-pointed, unawned.

Flowering glumes convex on the back, five- or seven-nerved, the hyaline apex usually shortly bifid, the midrib produced into a straight or curved awn free from a little below the apex.

Palea nearly as long as the glume, the two prominent nerves usually scabrous-ciliate.

Ovary obovate, crowned by a hairy membranous appendage, the very short distinct styles more or less lateral.

Grain flattened, adhering to the palea, and often more or less to the base of the glume.

2. Bromus arenarius, Labill.

Botanical name.—Bromus, from the Greek word for a wild oat, *arenarius,* Latin for sandy, in allusion to the situations in which some of these grasses grow.

Vernacular names.—" Oat Grass," " Wild Oats," " Sea-side Brome Grass." It has even been called " Barley Grass "—not at all an appropriate name.

Where figured.—Buchanan ; Labillardière ; *Agricultural Gazette.*
Botanical description (B. Fl., vii, 661).—Apparently annual, from 1 to about 1½ feet high.

Leaves flat, flaccid, softly hairy or pubescent.
Panicle at first erect, at length drooping, the capillary branches clustered, the longer ones 2 to 3 inches long, with one to four spikelets on capillary pedicels.
Spikelets lanceolate, ½ to ¾ inch long without the awns, flat, five- to nine- flowered.
Glumes all pubescent or glabrous, the lowest about 3 lines long and five-nerved, the second longer and seven-nerved, both empty and acute.
Flowering glumes rather longer, about seven-nerved, convex on the back, the awn free from a little below the scarious tip, ½ to ¾ inch long.

Var. *macrostachya*, Benth. Spikelets 1 inch long, each with fifteen to twenty flowers. Yass, Darling River, &c.

Value as a fodder.—An ornamental grass, which, while not of the first-class, is a useful fodder plant. It cannot stand drought, withering off as the hot weather approaches. Buchanan speaks of it as a common sea-side weed, which, from its dry woolly nature, is very unpalatable to all kinds of stock. Others, *e.g.*, Woolls, speak of it as "a fine grass for cattle." Mr. A. R. Crawford writes to me concerning it :—" I received a few seeds of this grass from the Castlereagh, and cultivated it on the eastern slopes for many years. It is much liked by stock, is fattening, makes a good hay, and is quite an ornamental grass."

Fungus found on this grass.—*Ustilago bromivora*, Waldh., on this species, and also *B. mollis*. *Septoria bromi*, Sacc., has also been recorded from the leaves of *Bromus sp.*

Habitat and range.—Found in all the colonies except Tasmania ; also occurring in New Zealand. Found in most districts of New South Wales.

98. FESTUCA.

Spikelets several-flowered, pedicellate, in loose and spreading or compact and erect more or less one-sided panicles, the *rhachis* of the spikelet articulate under the flowering glumes, glabrous or nearly so.
Outer empty glumes narrow, acute, keeled, usually unequal.
Flowering glumes narrow, acute, or tapering into an untwisted awn or rarely obtuse, rounded on the back, faintly nerved.
Palea narrow, with prominent nerves or keels.
Ovary glabrous.
Styles very short, distinct.
Grain enclosed in the glume and palea and more or less adnate.

2. Festuca duriuscula, Linn.

Botanical name.—*Festuca*—Latin, the shoot or stalk of a tree or herb (the appellation not being specially appropriate) ; *duriuscula*—Latin, somewhat rough or harsh, the texture of the grass being thus described.

Vernacular name.—"Hard Fescue."

Where figured.—Buchanan.

Botanical description (B. Fl., vii, 663).—An erect perennial of 1 to 2 feet.

Leaves chiefly at the base, very narrow, almost setaceous.

Panicle loose but narrow, 2 to 4 inches long, with few erect branches.

Spikelets not numerous, erect, usually about ½ inch long, four- to six-flowered.

Glumes rather rigid, the outer ones pointed, the lowest very narrow, keeled, scarcely 2 lines long, the second rather longer, three-nerved.

Flowering glumes 3 lines long or rather more, faintly nerved, glabrous or pubescent, with a fine point or awn, usually about 1 line long.

Palea with a fine bifid point.

Stamens three.

Value as a fodder.—A useful pasture grass for the colder regions of the Colony. It grows well in hilly places, and is one of the best of the smaller fescues. It forms a close turf. All kinds of stock eat it readily, although it is somewhat harsh. Seed may be procured of most seedsmen.

Habitat and range.—Found in all the Colonies except Western Australia and Queensland. In New South Wales, apparently confined to the mountainous districts of the south-east. " One of the most widely dispersed forms of the sheep's fescue or *F. ovina*, Linn. Very abundant on downs and hilly pastures of the temperate regions of the New and Old World." (Bentham.)

Sub-tribe v.—Hordeaceæ.

99. Agropyrum. | 101. Lepturus.

99. AGROPYRUM.

Spikelets several-flowered, more or less flattened, distichous, and alternately sessile on the continuous or slightly notched *rhachis* of a simple spike, one face of the spikelet next the general *rhachis*, the *rhachis* of the spikelet more or less articulate under the flowering glumes.

Glumes rounded on the back or scarcely keeled, tapering into points or awns, the flowering ones three- to seven-nerved, the two outer empty ones usually shorter, narrower, three- or rarely one-nerved.

Palea nearly as long as the glume, the two prominent nerves almost marginal, scabrous-ciliate.

Ovary pubescent at the top.

Styles short, distinct.

Grain free or slightly adhering to the palea.

Spikelets narrow with long awns, erect and distant along the *rhachis*...   1. *A. scabrum.*

Spikelets broad, with short points or awns, erect and close together along the *rhachis*   ...   .   2. *A. velutinum.*

Spikelets very flat, with short points or awns, spreading or at length reflexed and not distant along the *rhachis*   ...   .3. *A. pectinatum.*

1. Agropyrum scabrum, Beauv.

Botanical name.—Agropyrum (more properly *Agropyron*)—Greek, *agros,* a field ; *puros,* wheat, owing to the resemblance of these grasess to wheat ; *scabrum*—Latin for rough, in allusion to the foliage.

Synonym.—Triticum scabrum, R. Br.

Vernacular names.—Mr. Bailey remarks that in New Zealand it often has a bluish tinge, and hence has received from the settlers the names of " Blue Tussac-grass " and " Blue Oat-grass," and adds that neither of which is suitable to the grass as seen in Australia. It would, however, appear to have a bluer appearance when growing in New South Wales than in Queensland. I have never seen a bluer and more glaucous looking grass than this species often presents in New England.

The name " Wheat-grass " is sometimes given to it in this Colony. It is closely related to the wheats, although it does not closely resemble, in appearance, those useful grasses.

Where figured.—Buchanan (as *Triticum scabrum*); Bacchus (as *Festuca Billardieri*) ; Labillardière as *Festuca scabra ; Agricultural Gazette.*

Botanical Description (B. Fl., vii., 665).—Very variable as to stature, sometimes under 1 foot high, slender with short filiform leaves, and from that to 3 or 4 feet with narrow spreading flat or convolute leaves.

Spike usually 6 inches to 1 foot long, the *rhachis* scarcely notched.

Spikelets distant, sessile, erect, ¾ to 1 inch long without the awns, narrow, six- to twenty-flowered ; in the small specimens, sometimes only one or two spikelets.

Glumes narrow, rigid, straw-coloured, mostly about five-nerved, not distinctly keeled, the two outer empty ones rather shorter, tapering into short points, the flowering ones 4 to 6 lines long without the awns, tapering into fine straight or at length spreading awns mostly longer than the glumes and sometimes above 1 inch long ; those of the upper and of the lower glumes often not so long as the intermediate ones.

Palea obtuse.

Botanical notes.—A large tufted, often straggling, grass, often of a bluish-green colour, rather harsh, commonly 1 or 2 feet long ; but on the Lachlan River, found by the late K. H. Bennett, up to 6 feet long, according to Baron von Mueller.

Buchanan figures a weak, elongated form, often 3 or 4 feet long, and trailing on the ground, under the name of variety *tenue.*

Value as a fodder.—" A rather harsh grass when in seed, but during winter and early spring it supplies a large quantity of feed. On poor land its height would be about a foot, but on good land it attains 3 or 4 feet. Cut when in flower it makes good hay ; the seeds are not injurious." (Bailey.)

When young there is no question not only as to its palatableness, but also as to its nutritious character.

The early settlers of New Zealand looked upon it as a good horse and cattle grass, and Buchanan calls it an excellent fodder, if cut in flower.

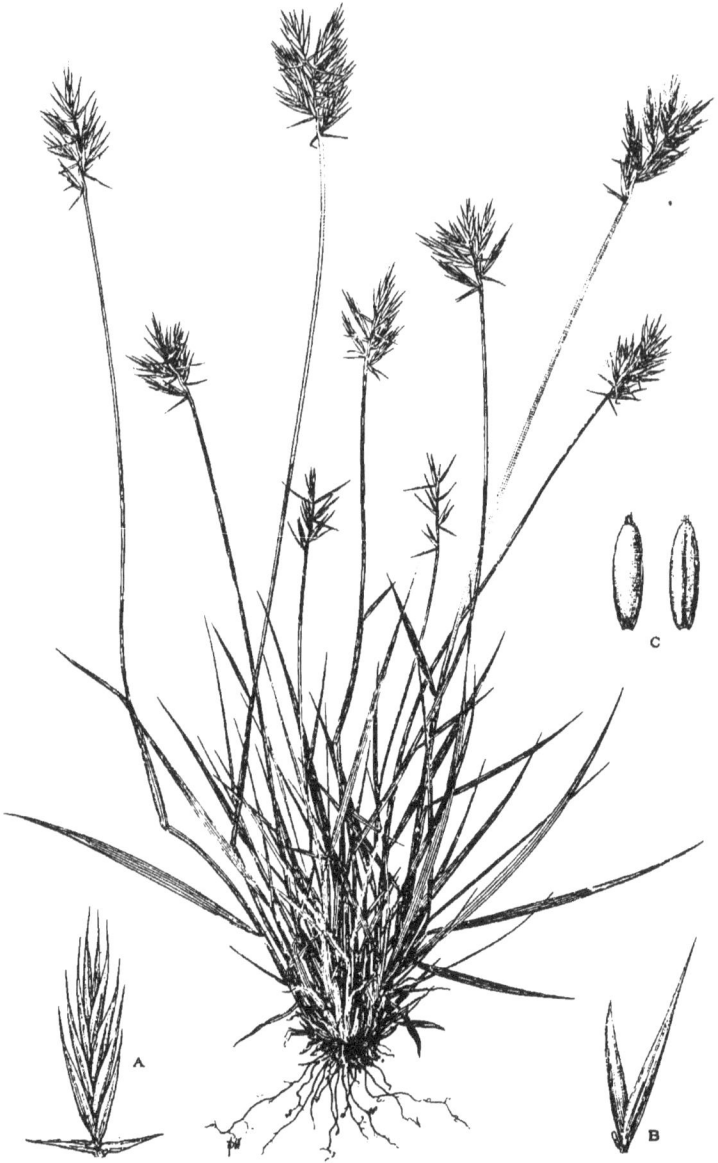

Agropyrum pectinatum.

"The Comb-like Wheat Fern."

Some other notes in regard to *Agropyrum* as a grass and fodder grasses will be found under *A. pectinatum.*

Habitat and range.—Found in all the Australian Colonies, also in Lord Howe Island and New Zealand. In the Australian Colonies it extends from the coast and coast ranges to the dry interior—in fact, it is one of the species with the widest range. I have collected it up to 5,500 feet on Mt. Kosciusko.

2. Agropyrum velutinum, Nees.

Botanical name.—*Velutinum*—Latin, velvety, in reference to the pubescent leaves.

Synonym.—*Triticum velutinum,* Hook.

Botanical description (B. Fl., vii, 665).—

Stems 6 inches to above 1 foot high.

Leaves chiefly at the base of the stem, flat or convolute when dry, not rigid, softly pubescent or nearly glabrous.

Spike raised on a long peduncle, 1 to 2 inches long, the *rhachis* pubescent and notched.

Spikelets almost erect, imbricate, or the lower ones distant, ovate or oblong, about ½ inch long, usually six- to eight-flowered.

Glumes 3 to 5 lines long, rigid, with short almost pungent points, the outer empty ones usually three-nerved, the flowering ones broader and five- or rarely seven-nerved.

Value as a fodder.—Not important. It is less harsh than the other species, but it does not appear to be very abundant.

Habitat and range.—Found in Tasmania ; also on the Victorian and New South Wales Alps, and other districts in the south-eastern parts of this Colony.

35. Agropyrum pectinatum, Beauv.

Botanical name.—*Pectinatum*—Latin, like a comb, in allusion to the appearance of the inflorescence.

Synonym.— *Triticum pectinatum,* R. Br.

Vernacular name.—I do not know any vernacular name actually in use for this grass. The rather clumsy name of the Comb-like Wheatgrass suggested for it may serve provisionally.

Where figured.—Labillardière, as *Festuca pectinata ; Agricultural Gazette.*

Botanical description (B. Fl., vii, 666).—

Stems from under 1 to 1½ feet high.

Leaves chiefly at the base of the stem, narrow, flat, usually hairy.

Spike raised on a long peduncle, 1 to 3 inches long, the *rhachis* pubescent, not notched.

Spikelets not very distant, spreading, or at length reflexed, mostly about ½ inch long, including the short points, three- to six-flowered.

Glumes spreading, the two outer empty ones shorter, with only the midrib or three-nerved.

Flowering glumes 4 to 5 lines long, rigid, three- or five-nerved, tapering into a rather long pungent point.

Value as a Fodder.—We know very little about its value in this respect, and I would ask residents of the districts in which it grows to give it more attention. It produces a fairly leafy bottom, and is probably eaten by stock with the other grasses when young, but while still perfectly green and only in inflorescence. I have seen acres of pasture in which it preponderates with scarcely a spike bitten off. Nevertheless, arguing from analogy, it is probably a nutritious grass.

We have three species of *Agropyrum*, and they are peculiar to Australia, with the exception that *A. scabrum* extends to New Zealand. We know so little about the genus from Australian experience, that perhaps a few notes of the experience of other countries in regard to other species of *Agropyrum* may be of some use. I quote from Vasey's "Agricultural Grasses and Forage Plants of the United States" (1889).

A. tenerum occurs mostly in low, moist ground, grows in clumps, and is one of the best grasses for hay.

A. repens* (Couch-grass of the United States; Quack-grass). "The farmers of the United States unite in one continuous howl of execration against this grass, and it seems strange, when every man's hand is against it, that it is not exterminated. Yet we could never really satisfy ourselves that its presence in meadows and pastures was such an unmitigated curse. In lands where alternate husbandry is practised it must be admitted to be an evil of great magnitude. Its hardiness is such, and its rapidity of growth so great, that it springs up much more rapidly than any crop that can be planted, and chokes it; still, this grass has many virtues. It is perfectly cosmopolitan in its habits. It is found in all sorts of soil and climates. Its creeping roots are succulent and very nutritive, and are greedily devoured by horses and cows."

Of *A. glaucum* (Blue stem or Blue joint), considered by some to be a variety of the preceding, Professor Scribner writes: "It is the most highly praised of the native grasses for hay. Wherever it occupies exclusively any large area of ground, as it does frequently in the lower districts, especially near Fort Benton, it is cut for hay. Naturally it does not yield a great bulk, but its quality is unsurpassed. After two or three cuttings the yield of hay diminishes so much that it is scarcely worth the harvesting. It is then customary to drag a short-toothed harrow over the sod, which breaks up the creeping roots or underground stems, and each fragment then makes a new plant."

Speaking of the genus in general in the United States, Mr. T. A. Williams says: "These grasses mature early, and are the chief forage plants in the Western (U.S.A.) cattle districts, on which thrive the choice beeves which command fancy prices in the eastern markets. They have few equals among the grasses of the western prairies in the quantity or quality of forage produced, and should be cultivated and improved as much as possible.'"

---

* Or rather *A. pseudo-repens*, Scribner and Smith, p. 34, Bulletin No. 4, "Studies in American Grasses" (1897).

Habitat and range.—It is confined to New South Wales, Victoria, and Tasmania. In New South Wales it is common in many parts of the Monaro, chiefly on black soil flats, often in swampy land. It ascends to high altitudes (I have it from 5,000 to 6,000 feet on Mount Kosciusko). In Victoria it is confined to Northern Gippsland, in situations similar to those it frequents over the border of the northern colony. In Tasmania it is found in the Hampshire Hills, Thomas Plains, and Recherche Bay.

Reference to Plate:—A, spikelet; B, empty glume; C, back and front views of seed; all enlarged.

101. LEPTURUS.

Spikelets one-flowered, or in a species not Australian two-flowered, sessile, and half embedded in the alternate notches of a more or less articulate simple spike.

Outer empty glumes two, one slightly overlapping the other on one side, or one only, appressed and covering the cavity, rigid and nerved.

Flowering glume and palea shorter, thin, and hyaline, embedded in the cavity, the axis of the spikelet produced behind the palea into a minute point, or bearing a small terminal empty glume.

Styles short.

Grain free from the glume.

Annuals.—Outer glumes with about five prominent nerves. Axis of
the spikelet produced into a minute point or bristle.
Outer glumes of the lateral spikelets two ... ... 1. *L. incurvatus.*
Outer glume of the lateral spikelets only one ... ... 2. *L. cylindricus.*

1. Lepturus incurvatus, Trin.

Botanical name.—*Lepturus*—Greek, *leptos,* slender; *oura,* a tail, in allusion to the pointed *rhachis; incurvatus*—Latin, crooked or bowed, in allusion to the spikes.

Botanical description (B. Fl., vii, 668).—A tufted or branching annual of 3 inches to 1 foot, or rarely more, slender in the Australian specimens with very narrow leaves.

Spikes nearly cylindrical, slender, 2 to 6 inches long, straight or curved.
Outer glumes two, rigid, acute, usually five-nerved, about 3 lines long, placed in the lateral spikelets apparently side by side outside the rest of the spikelet, but one slightly overlapping the other at the base.
Flowering glume and flower embedded in the cavity of the *rhachis* of the spike, the *rhachis* of the spikelet slightly produced behind the palea into a minute point sometimes almost obsolete. In the terminal spikelet the two outer glumes are normally exposed to each other.

Value as a fodder.—Not known, but probably small.

Habitat and range.—Found in South Australia, Victoria, and New South Wales. In the last Colony, in salt-marshes in the coast districts south from Parramatta to Victoria. Found also in the Mediterranean region; also in India and New Zealand.

N

2. Lepturus cylindricus, Trin.

Botanical name.—Cylindricus—Latin, cylindrical, in allusion to the spike.

Botanical description (B. Fl., vii, 668).—

> Habit and foliage of *L. incurvatus*, in the Australian specimens usually shorter, more tufted, the *leaves* not quite so narrow and the spikes rather thicker and more frequently curved ; but these differences are generally reversed in Mediterranean specimens.
>
> The *terminal spikelet* and the internal structure of the others the same in the two species, but the *L. cylindricus* has always only one rigid five-nerved very pointed outer empty glume instead of the two of *L. incurvatus*.

Value as a fodder.—Not known, but probably small.

Habitat and range.—Found in all the Colonies except Tasmania and Queensland. In New South Wales, from the coast district to the tableland, chiefly in salt-marshes, southwards from Liverpool Plains to Victoria, and westward to the Riverina. Found also in the Mediterranean region, South Africa, and Asia.

INDEX.

NOTE.—The botanical names of exotic grasses and the synonyms of the New South Wales species, also the names of fungi, are all in *italics*.

199

www.ingramcontent.com/pod-product-compliance
Lightning Source LLC
Chambersburg PA
CBHW020849270326

41928CB00006B/622